The Police Family

The Police Family

From Station House to Ranch House

Arthur Niederhoffer
John Jay College of Criminal Justice

Elaine Niederhoffer

Lexington Books
D.C. Heath and Company
Lexington, Massachusetts
Toronto

Library of Congress Cataloging in Publication Data

Niederhoffer, Arthur
    The police family.

    Includes bibliographical references and index.
    1. Police—Family relationships. 2. Police wives. 3. Police psychology.
I. Niederhoffer, Elaine, joint author. II. Title.
HV7921.N53   301.42   73-11678
ISBN 0-669-90498-8

Published simultaneously in Canada.

Printed in the United States of America.

International Standard Book Number: 0-669-90498-8

Library of Congress Catalog Card Number: 73-11678

Dedication

We dedicate this book with love to our family: First, to our older children, Victor and Diane, who lived their childhood as part of a police family. Their perceptions and remembrances of things past have enriched the content of this book. And their achievements have demonstrated that the passage from station house to ranch house can be successful.

Second, to our youngest child, Roy, born after Arthur's retirement from the police force, who learned about the police family from anecdotes and reminiscences. He has contributed his versatile talents to this manuscript as calculator, duplicator, and thesaurus-investigator extraordinary.

Third, to our daughter-in-law, Gail, and our son-in-law, Francis, who have extended the dimensions of our family with strands of warmth and affection.

And finally, to the little ones, Galt and Kate, for grandchildren are the blue-chips in any family.

Contents

List of Tables

Acknowledgments

We are grateful to the following organizations and publishers who have granted us permission to include material from their publications. The specific citations appear in the footnotes.

Coward, McCann and Geoghegan

The Forest Hospital Foundation

International Association of Chiefs of Police

LE Publishers

The New York Times Company

Northwestern University School of Law

Spring 3100

Naturally, a book of this kind required the contributions of innumerable police officers and their families. We wish to express our gratitude to all those who so patiently and thoughtfully responded to our questionnaires and cooperated in interviews and discussions.

We also appreciate the assistance of colleagues and students at John Jay College of Criminal Justice who helped in various phases of our study.

The Police Family

1

The Police Occupation: A Jealous Mistress

To become a police officer is to become a citizen of a different world that exists in another dimension from our own, but in the same time and place. And like the dominant plot in science fiction, a journey between the two involves some distortion and requires a period of reorientation after crossing the threshold. Values and behavior often clash when the two cultures interact. The point of intersection is the family.

Tolstoy could not have known about the police family when he wrote in his celebrated opening of *Anna Karenina,* "All happy families are like one another; each unhappy family is unhappy in its own way." We contend that all police families—happy or unhappy—are like one another, patterned by the lathe of the police occupation. They dwell in the shadow of the job. The rhythm of their life is metered by the ringing of the telephone and the implacable schedule of the duty chart. Police department imperatives supersede the most cherished family occasions; fundamental family relations take second place.

Why focus on the police family at a time when the traditional nuclear family is under attack and reeling? Social scientists trace the etiology of crime, delinquency, drug addiction, homosexuality, and mental illness to some flaw or weakness in the family constellation. The feminist movement condemns the family as the instrument of female degradation. The sociological anatomies of eight million families headed by women are being dissected and scrutinized. And experts pronounce the ultimate sentence of doom for the family: the doubling of the divorce rate in the last decade.

New forms of familial living arrangements—group, homosexual, communal, open, single parent, and swinging—are challenging hallowed customs. Is the family collapsing? And what is the prognosis when a police officer is a member of the family?

At the turn of the century, the police were permitted a degree of flexibility in courtship and companionate marriage that was not so different from other contemporary living styles. The great journalist H.L. Mencken nostalgically recalled his police friends on the Baltimore force who entered into informal conjugal relations with the ladies of the night on their post.

The girls in the red-light districts liked to crochet neckties, socks and pulse-warmers for them. It was not unheard of for a cop to get mashed on such a girl,

1

rescue her from her life of shame, and set her up as a more or less honest woman. I know of several cases in which holy matrimony followed.[1]

Mencken underscored the low status of policemen in those days when he reported that the more ambitious prostitutes were not satisfied to marry policemen because they wanted husbands who ranked higher in the social scale. In a way, the lack of interest of the executives of that department in the off-duty life of its members tacitly acknowledged the low social status of police officers and implied, "What can you expect from men of that type?"

By the 1940s, a complete reversal had occurred. The law enforcement occupation conceived a new self-image: the police officer as a middle-class professional worthy of respect for his important service to the community, his special expertise, and his admirable personal qualities.[2] Police departments extended their supervision into the private lives of their personnel. The plank of police protocol that decreed that a good police officer should be married to the job became a statement of fact rather than an aspiration. Inevitably, the force of biology displaced the ideology of the force, and weddings occurred. Every police marriage became a ménage à trois with the police occupation a jealous mistress.

This merger is not a temporary liaison, for a dedicated police officer becomes infatuated by the sensual, irresistible, appeal of the beat, which demands passionate devotion. Moreover, law enforcement is a "greedy institution," competing on every level with the obligations of family life.[3] The better the policeman, the more serious the problem of divided loyalty—that tug-of-war between job and family.

Because the job is such a powerful rival to the family, some behavioral scientists have conceptualized the police occupation as a symbolic family itself. Los Angeles Police Department psychologist Martin Reiser has clarified the dynamics of this second family.

The police department represents a family to the individuals working within it. The chief of police is the father figure, with all the consonant feelings related to power, dependency and independence. . . . Traditionally, the chief is all-powerful and rules with an iron, if not despotic, hand. The "brass" are usually older, more powerful "siblings" who behave in a paternal and patronizing way toward the young street policemen who occupy the role of younger siblings striving and competing for recognition, acceptance and adulthood.[4]

Like possessive parents, police departments tightened their surveillance and monitored the behavior of their off-duty members to make certain that it

[1] H.L. Mencken, "Recollections of Notable Cops," in Alistair Cooke, ed., *The Vintage Mencken* (New York: Vintage Books, 1955), p. 33.

[2] Ibid.

[3] Lewis A. Coser, *Greedy Institutions: Patterns of Individed Commitment* (New York: Free Press, 1974).

[4] Martin Reiser, "Some Organizational Stresses on Policemen," *Journal of Police Science and Administration* 2 (June 1974):156.

conformed to an ever stricter code, which outlined how to dress, how to style their hair, and even what type of woman to court. Rigidly conservative in their view of the family, police administrators conducted themselves in an embarrassingly puritanical fashion in protecting the hallowed marriage forms, which were to them the only permissible ones. To this day, the pressures of departmental expectations, spurred on by the movement for professionalization, are manipulating the strings to constrict the private lives of policemen. A perceptive officer commented, "The department and the rest of us don't expect police officers to be 'like anybody else.' We expect them to be better. As you talk to officers who are off-duty, you realize how much of a burden on them these high expectations can be."[5]

A while before our current era of sexual permissiveness, a young unmarried officer was dismissed from one of the largest police departments because the reputation of the young woman he was courting did not measure up to the high standards the department recommended for future wives of its police officers.[6] Soon after, a police rookie was brought up on charges and threatened with dismissal because he had an affair with a woman during his probationary period.[7] And more recently, a Florida department suspended an unmarried patrolman for thirty days without pay because he shared an apartment with his girl friend.[8]

But how can administration conquer love? If anything, the movement of the law enforcement occupation toward professionalism and middle-class status has enhanced the magic of the uniform and the charisma of the police, for the range of potential mates for policemen has increased tremendously to include teachers, nurses, and other female professionals.

However, there is no escape from the omnipresent grip of the occupation. Even off duty in the intimate environment of courtship or within the sanctuary of the family, the policeman is vulnerable. The signal for police action triggers the approach-avoidance conflict. Which role should prevail: policeman, lover, husband, or father? Whatever the decision, a residue of guilt remains.

Top honors for an exciting adventure of a policeman out on a date with a girl friend would uncontestedly be awarded to Frank Serpico, the iconoclastic hero cop. (During the Knapp investigation into police department corruption in New York City, he was instrumental in exposing the illegal activities of his co-workers. His life story later became a popular movie.) One night, while riding on his motorcycle with his female companion on the back seat clutching him closely, Serpico suddenly heard shots coming from a bar and grill. He pushed his friend off the bike, told her to wait, and raced after the gunman who had sped off in a gold-colored Oldsmobile. After a desperate chase, he managed to capture

[5] Georgette Bennett-Sandler and Earl Ubell, "Time Bombs in Blue," *New York*, March 21, 1977, p. 48.

[6] *New York Times*, August 8, 1964, p. 8.

[7] *New York Post*, May 10, 1965, p. 3.

[8] *New York Times*, July 16, 1974, p. 22.

one of the armed criminals. He called the precinct for assistance, radio cars responded, and everyone returned to the scene of the crime. When Serpico finally completed all the paperwork, he looked for his girl friend and found her deeply engrossed in a conversation with a stranger. Possessively, Serpico complained about her inconstancy. Then she let him have it:

"Well what did you expect?" the girl said irritably as she got back on the motorcycle. "You leave me in the middle of the street and go tearing off like that. Why can't you get a regular job like other men? Besides, you aren't even on duty."[9]

In our survey of police families (see the Appendix) most police officers indicated that they had met their wives-to-be in typical fashion: through friends, at work, or from introductions by members of the family. One sergeant dourly commented in a laconic but revealing statement, "I met my wife through a friend; he's not my friend anymore." Another officer vividly captured the moment of meeting, "Standing on a subway I pinched her rear end. She slapped me. I apologized. And from then on it was true love." After ten years of marriage to a patrolman, a romantic wife still recalls the glamour of her first impression:

He had a tour of duty at Coney Island. I spotted him standing at attention for the National Anthem and fell in love with him at first sight. He asked me for my phone number and called me a week later. We dated for two and one-half years and then married on October 31, 1964 (Halloween).

Even before we were married, we learned how traumatically the police occupation could disrupt a marriage. Significant dates stand out. Arthur joined the New York City Police Department in June 1940. We set our wedding day for the first Sunday in March 1943. Three weeks before, Arthur approached the commanding officer of the precinct and requested a day off for that Sunday, to get married. Dispassionately the captain told him that he would have to choose another day because he could not spare him on the weekend. Why so indispensable? At that time, Arthur was assigned to the Central Park precinct guarding half-frozen lakes and half-thawed lawns from the incursions of pedestrians. But having been a police officer for almost three years, Arthur had fatalistically expected the negative response. In those days, captains automatically refused any request from young patrolmen. Perhaps this was because the department believed implicitly that until a patrolman had five years of experience and abrasion, he was not a real cop and, therefore, not entitled to respect.

Daily, Arthur pleaded with him. Finally, the captain relented to the extent

[9] Peter Maas, *Serpico: The Cop Who Defied the System* (New York: Viking, 1973), p. 117.

that he switched Art's scheduled day off, which was Monday, to Sunday. And thankfully, we were permitted to marry on the prearranged date and to enjoy a honeymoon from 2 A.M. when the celebration ended until 6 A.M., when Arthur had to leave bed and bride to rush to work at lake and lawn.

A few years later, a close friend, a police officer attached to a Brooklyn detective office as a probationary detective, had an equally unnerving encounter with police authority. When he requested a four-day leave of absence to get married and take a brief honeymoon, his crusty commanding officer almost literally divorced him from the police department. Not only did he turn down the request, but also he drafted a written report to the chief inspector recommending that the officer be dropped from the detective division and sent back to pounding a beat. In support of his recommendation for transfer, the arbitrary captain argued that the supplicant would never make a good detective since he was obviously more interested in time off than in working the demanding hours expected of a man with a gold shield.

Strained by unusual stresses in adjusting to the police world and learning to live with the omnipresent sense of danger, the new police officer as well as his spouse are enveloped by a network of anxiety, and the roots often spread back into the parental generation. If the mate of a police officer worries about his personal safety on the job, it rather glorifies the marital relation through its implied depth of feeling. However, when a parent expresses concern, it reflects darkly on the police officer's independence and manliness.

The Jewish mother's notorious inclination to overprotect her children has been accepted good-humoredly as part of our folklore. But if her son should happen to be a police officer, the avowed protector of the public, this overpowering maternal solicitude can be demoralizing, as this embarrassed detective relates:

It could only happen to a Jewish rookie. The first day that I was walking my beat in Bedford-Stuyvesant, I looked behind and saw a familiar car—my father's purple and white Packard. . . . My father was at the wheel, my mother and sister seated beside him, and to add insult to injury, the baby on my sister's lap. As I walked along they followed slowly, they were protecting me. . . .
Once I caught them pursuing me in the car and begged, "Go home! They'll think I'm a baby. You'll cost me my job . . ."[10]

If a comparable incident, experienced by an Italian rookie, is any indication, the Jewish mother may have to share equal billing with the Italian father. On foot patrol in Harlem during a rainy late tour about 4 A.M., the novice police officer noticed a suspicious figure lurking in a doorway, shrinking back into the shadows. The rookie pulled out his gun and his flashlight, pointed them, and said, "All right, you. Get outa there." To the patrolman's chagrin, the suspect

[10] Harvey Schlossberg and Lucy Freeman, *Psychologist with a Gun* (New York: Coward, McCann and Geoghegan, 1974), pp. 38, 40.

turned out to be his own father carrying "a big bag of chicken cacciatore and bread and a half a bottle of wine and a napkin." His father set up a box as a table and insisted that his son, the cop, eat the food. This encounter was only one episode in a series of paternal visitations. "He cleans everything up, gives me a big kiss and goes home. Other nights, I sense a shadow following me and I know who it is. He's following me while I'm on patrol. I chase him and he runs away. How can anybody go wrong with a dad like that."[11] The long-range effect of this culinary therapy is that chicken cacciatore may take its place alongside the legendary cure-all, chicken soup.

These marital clashes and intergenerational confrontations shocked us into an awareness that in every police marriage the occupation would be a third party. Incubating over the years, that interest in the collision between family and job culminated in this study of the police family. We bring to it the knowledge and insight gained from long personal experience that has been crystallized by rap sessions, countless interviews, and questionnaires from hundreds of police officers, their spouses, and their children.

---

[11] Anthony Schiano with Anthony Burton, *Solo: Self-Portrait of an Undercover Cop* (New York: Dodd, Mead, 1973), p. 35.

The Police Family
in Literature

Living intimately within the "blue circle" for so many years tied us closely to the subject matter of this book. To balance our possible propensity toward insularity and subjectivity, we searched the literature on law enforcement for relevant sources and then turned to the standard works on the family. But they provided scant and oblique references. Occasionally, a police magazine geared for the trade produced a pertinent article; two recent books by wives of police officers approached the subject from a personal point of view.[1]

Frustrated in our quest for a more scientific vantage, we focused on the artistic vision, hoping to discover insights into police family experience from novels about the police. Just as art imitates nature, the novel mirrors reality. In fact, it often provides a deeper knowledge, an awareness of the distinction between appearance and reality, and traces the passage in life from innocence to experience. As one discerning literary critic aptly expressed it, a great novel captures life's memorabilia and instills a "fuller record, deeper exploration of realities of human character and experience." Its reality intertwines with "the reality of bourgeois life, of business and the modern city."[2]

Because the literary origins of police novels are relatively obscure, they do not fit comfortably into any mold. Perhaps, they may be classified with the adventurous folk hero sagas like Robin Hood, or they may be offshoots of the picaresque novel. Some psychiatrists, following the literary flair of Freud, have psychoanalyzed police novels and diagnosed them as restatements of archetypal myths resonating with oedipal overtones. And sustaining this line of reasoning, they identify the inevitable murder with the "primal scene."

Contemporary works on the police, such as Joseph Wambaugh's *New Centurions,* that cover the training and socialization of young law enforcement officers can with some trepidation be assigned to the hallowed category of *bildungsroman,* in which education and gradual development are traditionally the central themes. It would not be illogical to consider the police novel as a

---

[1] Barbara E. Webber, ed., *Handbook for Law Enforcement Wives* (Chicago: LE Publishers, 1974); Pat James and Martha Nelson, *Police Wife* (Springfield, Ill.: Charles C. Thomas, 1975).

[2] See, for example, Maurice Z. Shroder, "The Novel as a Genre," in Robert M. Davis, ed., *The Novel: Modern Essays in Criticism* (Englewood Cliffs, N.J.: Prentice-Hall, 1969), p. 44; Helen E. Haines, *What's in a Novel* (New York: Columbia Univ. Press, 1942), p. 18; Albert Cook, *The Meaning of Fiction* (Detroit: Wayne State Univ. Press, 1960), pp. 1, 7, 24; and Anthony Burgess, *The Novel Now: A Guide to Contemporary Fiction* (New York: Norton, 1967).

8

type of romance—escapist literature—wherein the protagonist undertakes the proverbial quest and ultimately proves himself a hero.

Fathered internationally within a few years of each other by Honoré de Balzac in France, Edgar Allen Poe in America, and Charles Dickens in Great Britain, the new literary form of police novel, detective story, or mystery tale fascinated the reading public and carved its unique niche in nineteenth-century literature. Later authors responded eagerly to the demand by creating a succession of detective heroes. Even currently, this class of fiction is more widely read than any other in the United States. One explanation for this sustained and unmatched popularity is that the reader, by identifying and empathizing with the hero detective, can escape the trap of routine existence, transcend far-ranging daydreams, and share vicariously the marvelous exploits of the hero.

From the beginning this novelistic genre mirrored society's ambivalent image of the police. In France, the term *police* conjured up the abuses of Fouché's repressive secret force. In America, the police occupied a status equivalent to watchmen. And in Great Britain, the Metropolitan Police Force, after a traumatic birth in 1829, was soon known as "Peel's bloody gang," meriting its unsavory reputation for drunkenness and brutality. But an expanding industrial society needed stability, and the second half of the century brought sweeping reforms of law enforcement that resurrected the reputation of the police. Above all, the detective—competent, intelligent, persevering, and courageous, symbolizing virtue triumphing over evil—captured the popular imagination.

Overshadowing the mechanism of personal identification, the detective has been glorified as the symbol of the significant social change and democratization that characterized the Victorian era. The appearance of the professional detective on the literary and social scene coincided "with the development of democracy and the growing acceptance of the rule of reason."[3]

These illustrations of the Manichean dichotomy disclose the polarity of society's attitude toward the police. Another critic expresses a somber caution and underscores this oscillation: "If the detective was a metaphor for the nineteenth-century's faith in man's problem solving abilities, he was just as importantly a symbol of growing nineteenth-century disillusionment with reason as a meaningful response to the human condition."[4] In support of this view, economist Ludwig von Mises offers an economic interpretation of the popularity of the detective story and crime literature. He attributes the sweeping change-over from a procapitalist point of view to an anticapitalist mentality favoring

[3] Howard Haycraft, *Murder for Pleasure: The Life and Times of the Detective Story* (New York: Appleton-Century, 1941), p. 5.

[4] Elliot L. Gilbert, "The Detective as Metaphor in the Nineteenth Century," in Francis M. Nevins, ed., *The Mystery Writer's Art* (Bowling Green: Bowling Green Univ. Popular Press, 1970), p. 287.

socialism and collectivism to the ideological crosscurrents inundating both shores of the Atlantic. In detective fiction, this engendered a story line in which the criminal frequently turns out to be the rich man, the successful bourgeois, to whom everybody has deferred. But the private detective strips the veneer of sanctimony from the dissembler and simultaneously exposes the incompetent bungling of the regular police who have been deceived by the hypocrisy and guile of the nouveau riche pretenders. And according to von Mises' theory, the common man, frustrated by society and secretly envious of those more successful, identifies with and derives vicarious satisfaction from the exploits of the amateur sleuth as he easily defeats the appointed officers and representatives of the bourgeois state.[5]

Whatever the philosophical or economic implications of their competition may have portended, it is noteworthy that both the public and the private detectives in these nineteenth-century classics were almost all bachelors who literally married themselves to law enforcement, as priests to their religion, and performed their heroic deeds unencumbered by the bonds of family life. Male chauvinists and compulsive egotists, holding women in low regard, they could not divert their attention from their obsessive pursuit of the criminal to admit a rival passion or take time out to court a potential mate. To be realistic, some of their eccentric behavior—idiosyncrasies no doubt caricatured by their creators for literary impact—would have caused their stock in the marriage market to plummet and would have precluded the formation of an intimate relationship with any woman of discernment.

Although the nearly universal absence of family life in these police novels seems to point to a literary conspiracy among writers, in actuality, they were injecting a strong element of verisimilitude into their descriptions of the police world. Historically, the police occupation defined its domain as a male territory; it was quasi-military and off limits to women, except for the occasional incursion of an Amazonian interloper. The duty schedule was prohibitive. As late as 1850 in Great Britain, members of the force were required to work 14 to 17 hours a day, seven days a week, averaging one day off every four to six weeks. Often sleeping in the barracks, the officer was uncomfortably reminded that he was more a military man than a family man. His salary—a paltry 15 to 21 shillings a week, no higher than that of an unskilled agricultural worker—could barely keep him in uniform. Interaction with outsiders was discouraged. A police officer who ate or drank with a civilian had to report these transgressions to his superior under pain of dismissal.[6] These occupational deterrents curbed marriage and family life.

Aware of these restrictions, the novelists may have concluded perceptively

[5] Ludwig von Mises, *The Anti-Capitalistic Mentality* (South Holland, Ill.: Libertarian Press, 1956), pp. 48-55.
[6] T.A. Critchley, *A History of Police in England and Wales,* 2d ed. (Montclair, N.J.: Patterson Smith, 1973), pp. 150-152.

that it would be unrealistic to introduce the complications of family life into their scenarios or even inject a romantic interlude that might detract from the dramatic intensity of the pursuit of criminals. In their search for clues to success, subsequent writers, motivated as much by the dynamics of the marketplace as by artistic integrity, patterned their craft after the pioneers. Thus it was by a natural process rather than by a fixed formula that the prototype of the celibate detective hero became the cornerstone of this literary structure for almost a century.

For some experts who have traced the genealogy of the detective story to its roots, Vidocq, the notorious French criminal turned detective, emerges as the true progenitor, and his lineage descends to Balzac, Hugo, Dickens, and Gaboriau.[7] Vidocq's *Memoires*, which appeared in 1829, record anecdotes of his metamorphosis from outlawed criminal to chief of the sûreté in a swashbuckling saga of crime, disguise, investigation, and arrests. His incredible narrative caroms from authentic autobiography to detective tale, blurring the border between fact and fiction.

When Vidocq was eighteen, he was tricked into marriage by an older woman who falsely claimed that he had made her pregnant. Within weeks he found her in bed with her lover, summarily obtained a divorce, and remained a bachelor for the rest of his life. Tiring of a life of crime, he offered his services as a police spy and within three years was promoted to commanding officer of the sûreté and remained in that post for 15 years.[8]

With the publication of *Père Goriot* in 1834, Balzac—a friend of Vidocq—introduced the arch criminal Vautrin, godfather of a powerful organization of international criminals, the Society of the Ten Thousand. Vautrin's wave of crime crested 12 years later in the novel *A Harlot's Progress.* A master of disguise, he rescues the French nobility from certain disgrace by artfully retrieving a set of compromising letters, and as a reward he is permitted to become a detective in the sûreté, eventually rising to its directorship. Balzac's evocation of Vautrin's remarkable turnabout, doffing the masks of crime and donning the robes of justice, reveals striking parallels with the legendary career of François Eugène Vidocq. Viewed in tandem, the composite of these masterworks—*Père Goriot* and *A Harlot's Progress*—constitutes the first true police novel, more for its revelatory analysis of the bureaucracy of Parisian police and the modus operandi of the minister of police and Chief Detective Gondureau than for its brief chronology of Vautrin's meteoric police career.

Against this background, Balzac silhouettes the psychology of Vautrin's bachelor status. To the broad-shouldered, muscular Vautrin, woman is an inferior animal ruled by her instincts, possessing a genius for ruthlessness and a

[7] See Edwin G. Rich, foreword to *Vidocq: The Personal Memoirs of the First Great Detective,* ed. and trans. Edwin G. Rich (Boston, Mass.: Houghton Mifflin, 1935), pp. v-ix.
[8] At that time, Paris was divided into districts, each under the jurisdiction of a sûreté. Today the Sûreté Nationale is a national police force of France.

talent for torture that would only mar men.[9] A male chauvinist, Vautrin revels so blatantly in his misogyny that this attitude is chronicled in his police dossier. When Detective Gondureau attempts to convince old Mademoiselle Michonneau to slip a knockout powder into Vautrin's drink, she counters that he ought to find a pretty young woman to beguile him. The detective answers, "Trompe-la-Mort [Vautrin] would not let a woman come near him. . . . I will tell you a secret—he does not like them."[10]

Although invulnerable to the lure of good-looking young women, the powerful criminal Vautrin displays little resistance to the charms of handsome young men. In *Père Goriot* he favors Eugène de Rastignac; in *A Harlot's Progress* his consuming passion is his youthful protégé, Lucien de Rubempré. After de Rubempré commits suicide in prison, Vautrin, mournfully reminisces:

I used to put him to bed as a nurse tucks up a child, and I made him tell me everything. . .
The best of mothers never loved an only son so tenderly as I loved that angel. . . .
At this moment they are burying my life, my beauty, my virtue, my conscience, all my powers.[11]

Vautrin's articulate and poetic outburst of emotion furnishes sufficient explanation for his unmarried status. Even if his longing for Lucien was paternal rather than sensual, taken in conjunction with his demonstrated revulsion toward women, the combination operated as an effective barrier to marriage.

Conceiving the first detective story, the American Edgar Allen Poe linked the literature of the United States and France. His contribution was the great amateur of detection, Chevalier Auguste Dupin, residing in the Faubourg St. Germain in Paris, who is as eccentric in behavior as he is brilliant in logical analysis. Poe's trilogy—*The Murders in the Rue Morgue, The Mystery of Marie Roget,* and *The Purloined Letter*—appearing in quick succession from 1841 to 1844 contrasted the genius of the private detective with the routine, lackluster performance of the regular police. Monsieur G., the prefect of the Parisian police, seeks out Dupin, that artful sleuth and fount of wisdom, for advice (in the case of *The Purloined Letter*) about a missing letter that would cause great distress to royalty if it were published. (Balzac used the same theme several years later in *A Harlot's Progress.*) Dupin recommends that Monsieur G. thoroughly search the room of the known blackmailer; but after ransacking the apartment with a team of experienced investigators, G. could not find the incriminating letter. Several days later he dejectedly returns to Dupin to report failure, vowing that he would give his check for 50,000 francs in exchange for the letter. In a magician-like charade, Dupin rises, proffers a checkbook to G., and tells him to

[9] Honoré de Balzac, *A Harlot's Progress* (New York: Bigelow, Brown, n.d.), pp. 504, 538.
[10] Honoré de Balzac, *Père Goriot* (New York: E.P. Dutton, 1907), p. 142.
[11] Balzac, *A Harlot's Progress,* pp. 500-501.

fill out the check. Whereupon Dupin, with a flourish, produces the sought-for document that he had recovered easily during a previous visit to the residence of the suspect.

In *The Murders in the Rue Morgue* Dupin even more ruthlessly and disparagingly bares his low opinion of the Parisian police, and simultaneously, he blends the actual with the imaginary by alluding to the celebrated practitioner, Vidocq.

We must not judge of the means by this shell of an examination. The Parisian police, so much extolled for *acumen,* are cunning, but no more. There is no method in their proceedings, beyond the method of the moment. They make a vast parade of measures; but, not unfrequently, these are so ill-adapted to the objects proposed, as to put us in mind of Monsieur Jourdain's calling for his *robe-de-chambre—pour mieux entendre la musique.* The results obtained by them are not unfrequently surprising, but, for the most part, are brought about by simple diligence and activity. When these qualities are unavailing, their schemes fail. Vidocq, for example, was a good guesser, and a persevering man. But, without educated thought, he erred continually by the very intensity of his investigations. He impaired his vision by holding the object too close. He might see, perhaps, one or two points with unusual clearness, but in so doing he, necessarily, lost sight of the matter as a whole.[12]

The detachment of the outsider enabled Dupin to evaluate the behavior of others objectively and incisively. But this same quality led to his defeat in interpersonal relations—the social contact so necessary a prelude to marriage.

Why was Dupin unmarried? Although a member of an illustrious family, he lived in poverty. Bookish, gloomy, and solitary, Dupin had only one close friend, the narrator of the tales. They shared a peculiar intimacy in a grotesque and secluded house to which they admitted no visitors. During the day they remained behind shuttered windows reading and writing, venturing forth only at night. Dupin was the archetypal victim of *accidie.* How could Dupin, this retreatist, ever reverse his misanthropic alienation and generate the human connections necessary for marriage?

Across the Channel, Charles Dickens, a police buff who often patrolled London streets with Detective Inspector Charles Field of Scotland Yard, quickly perceived the value of a detective as a socially mobile character who could dexterously draw together the threads of a novel by his ability to move freely to any level of the class structure.[13]

Dicken's protagonist, Inspector Bucket "of the Detective" (modeled after Field), triumphantly solves the murder mystery in *Bleak House* (1853) and is the initial representation of the professional police officer as hero, as opposed to the

---

[12] Edgar Allan Poe, *The Complete Tales and Poems of Edgar Allan Poe* (New York: Modern Library, 1938), pp. 152-153.

[13] Considering that the detective department of Scotland Yard was established in 1842 with a meager complement of two inspectors and six sergeants, it is remarkable that it spawned so many fictional heroes in so short a time.

criminal (Vautrin) or gentleman consultant (Dupin). One further distinction sets Bucket apart from all other conceptions of nineteenth-century fictional police and detectives: he is married, and, moreover, he encourages his wife to participate as a partner and active colleague in his professional career.

By coincidence or design, the murder suspect, Mademoiselle Hortense, becomes a lodger in the house that the middle-aged, stolid police couple occupies. The inspector's decision to involve his wife in the solution of the crime is carried out with singular and calculated forcefulness. Entering the bedroom, Bucket, without a word, suddenly stuffs a sheet in Mrs. Bucket's mouth, stifling any sound that she might utter that could possibly alert the sharp-eared Hortense. He then whispers his suspicions to his wife and cautions her to keep the suspect under constant surveillance. With full confidence in his spouse's effectiveness as decoy and sentinel, he energetically pursues his investigation in the field, never once returning home until he slips the handcuffs on the beautiful murderess at the dénouement. After snaring the criminal, he shares credit for her apprehension with his wife, that one woman "in a hundred and fifty thousand." The talent of Mrs. Bucket is matched by the spirit and composure of Hortense even at the moment of her downfall. When Bucket blocks her way, she arrogantly confronts him with a toss of her head, hissing, "Leave me to pass downstairs great pig."[14] (Coincidentally, this porcine epithet of contempt for the police continues to be a popular colloquialism.)

Although Dickens was certainly appreciative of marital teamwork in law enforcement, he sensed the inevitable clash between dedication to the job and commitment to the family.

It is likely that these occupations are irreconcilable with home enjoyment, but it is certain that Mr. Bucket at present does not go home. Though in general he highly appreciates the society of Mrs. Bucket—a lady of a natural detective genius, which if it had been improved by professional exercise, might have done great things, but which has paused at the level of a clever amateur—he holds himself aloof from that dear solace.[15]

Stimulated by the popularity of Bucket, real-life detectives of this era embroidered episodes of police work, glamourizing their activities to such an extent that their autobiographies unfolded more like novels than case records. Because a deluge of putative detective recollections and memoirs soon inundated the avid reading public, the authenticity of these true confessions is now open to question. One literary critic of our day has labeled them all spurious.

Some of the many volumes which appeared in London from the 'fifties onwards, purporting to be reminiscences, may actually have been genuine; but the authors of most of them were literary hacks, and it is probably safe to label the whole

[14] Charles Dickens, *Bleak House* (Boston: Houghton Mifflin, 1956), p. 558.
[15] Ibid., pp. 539-540.

class of "Revelations" and "Experiences" and "Diaries" of "Real Detectives" and "Ex-detectives" as fiction, at any rate as far down as 1890.[16]

One of the most prolific of these epigones, William Russell, who used the pseudonym Waters, cloned his Scotland Yard Detective Waters as a twin to Bucket, equally proud of the police profession, happily married, and utilizing the talents of wife and daughter as paraprofessionals to assist him in his cases.[17] But curiously, just a few years later in *Autobiography of a London Detective* (also attributed to Russell) the image of the detective had tarnished, the occupation had lost status, and the personal life of the detective has become strained.

Retired Scotland Yarder Henry Clarke recollects his 44 years on the force, idealizes the professional aspects of his career, and expresses the pain of the alienated police officer.[18] While writers of detective fiction expediently used the literary device of the detective moving fluidly between social classes to further his investigations, Clarke inadvertently exposes the harsh reality of a rigid class hierarchy that barred any semblance of actual upward social mobility, not to mention investigative mobility.

In one poignant anecdote, the veteran police officer recounts with nostalgia how he failed to hurdle the barrier of social class in a romantic and auspicious courtship of an aristocratic young woman. As a rookie detective he saves the beautiful Lady Charlotte Gray from drowning and immediately falls in love with her. After an ardent courtship, he is at the point of proposing marriage when he accidentally overhears a conversation between her brothers that effectively disrupts his plan. From their lofty social status they comment disdainfully on his arriviste pretension, hoping that Clarke "was not going to make an egregious donkey of himself about Charlotte."

Shocked by this revelation, he got away unseen, and as Clarke recalls, "There ended in a vital sense the romance of my life . . . the volume was closed." But in an ironic twist, 25 years later, he meets Charlotte again, now the mother of a prime suspect in a murder case Clarke is investigating. When the grizzled detective recognizes her after so long a separation, he nearly faints from the reawakening of passion. Because he is an experienced police officer, he is able to observe his own romantic behavior with the droll cynicism that distinguishes this calling: "Just fancy a detective police-officer, hardened, cynicized by the wear and tear of five-and-twenty years' experience in the most thoroughly disen-

---

[16] John Carter, "Collecting Detective Fiction," in Howard Haycraft, ed., *The Art of the Mystery Story* (New York: Simon and Schuster, 1946), p. 455.

[17] William Russell (Waters), *Recollections of a Detective Police-Officer* (London: J. and C. Brown, 1856). Waters' recollections have also been declared spurious by Patrick Pringle in his introduction to Henry Goddard, *Memoirs of a Bow Street Runner* (London: Museum Press, 1956), p. xxx.

[18] William Russell (Waters), *Autobiography of a London Detective* (New York: Dick and Fitzgerald, 1864).

chanting walk of life in which man can crawl to his goal, the grave, being so affected."[19]

Thoughts of love and marriage cannot penetrate the fierce commitment of Detective Inspector Javert, immortalized by Victor Hugo in *Les misérables* (1862). The implacable inspector sublimates his passion in obsessive and relentless pursuit of his criminal adversary. In the French novelist's portrait of Javert at forty—tall, gloomy, like a bulldog when serious, like a tiger when he laughed—he is obviously no love object; instead, he arouses fear in the hunted, not ardor in the fairer sex. Married solely to the job, he was

stoical, serious, austere: a dreamer of stern dreams; humble and haughty, like all fanatics. His stare was cold and as piercing as a gimblet. His whole life was contained in these two words: waking and watching. He marked out a straight path through the most tortuous thing in the world; his conscience was bound up in his utility, his religion in his duties, and he was a spy as others were priests. Woe to him who should fall into his hands.[20]

Simultaneously, Hugo deepens the shadows surrounding the detective's compulsive personality and discloses the darker implications of police work. When Javert, in pursuit of Jean Valjean, descends into the hell of the Parisian sewers, the situation becomes a confrontation between the contradictions of ethics and duty. And Javert, reaching the final solution in the lowest depths, tragically commits suicide.

Wilkie Collins, stimulated by the literary success of his friend and colleague Dickens, seized upon the sensational murder trial of Constance Kent, which had occurred just a few years before, as a source for *The Moonstone* (1868), his classic chiller—ranked by T.S. Eliot and many other critics as the greatest modern detective story ever written. Just as Dickens drew upon Detective Inspector Field for his portrayal of Bucket, Collins similarly based his character, Sergeant Cuff, upon Detective Inspector Jonathan Whicher of Scotland Yard, who earned the reputation of "the prince of detectives." Sergeant Cuff is a bachelor, and like almost all the other celebrated nineteenth-century fictional detective heroes who figuratively carried membership cards in the singles club, no unsolvable mystery surrounds the reasons for his celibate condition.

In the winter of life, the sergeant appears so desiccated, old, and grizzled that he resembles the stereotype of the elderly, lean, dried-out parson or undertaker. Cuff's steely grey eyes "had a very disconcerting trick . . . of looking as if they expected something more from you than you were aware of yourself." It is little wonder that he is more fascinated by the aroma of rose gardens than by the allure of attractive women. With poetic flair, the burnt-out detective wistfully comments, "I haven't much time to be fond of anything. But when I have a moment's fondness to bestow, the roses get it."

---

[19] Ibid., p. 100.

[20] Victor Hugo, *Les misérables* (New York: Random House, 1931), p. 144.

In a much lighter vein, Monsieur Lecoq, a less ascetic specimen of the French genus detectivus than the somber and vindictive Javert, cavorts feistily through many volumes of Emile Gaboriau's writings. Lecoq, already a bon vivant in his early twenties with a penchant for gambling and women, makes his appearance in *L'Affaire rouge* (1863). He steps down from his position as astronomer and substitutes for the study of celestial spheres the investigation of terrestrial peers when he joins the Paris police force to serve a rigorous apprenticeship under the master detective Père Tabaret. In retrospect, choosing the crowing cock as a personal symbol appears to have been a compensation for his failures rather than a seminal notch for his conquests of the opposite sex. Unrequited love is his portion. Lecoq, the bachelor, falls in love with Gypsy Nina, but when she leaves him for a rival, in desperation he contemplates suicide.

After 15 years on the force, for all his triumph and worldly cynicism, Lecoq seems to seek out unhappiness in love consciously, as this impassioned soliloquy demonstrates:

"Like every man I have my Achilles heel. I have conquered the demon of play, but I have not triumphed over my passion for woman."

He sighed heavily, with the resigned gesture of a man who has chosen his path. "It's this way. There is a woman, before whom I am but an idiot. Yes, I the detective, the terror of thieves and murderers, who have divulged the combinations of all the sharpers of all the nations, who for ten years have swum amid vice and crime; who wash the dirty linen of all the corruptions, who have measured the depths of human infamy; I who know all, who have seen and heard all; I, Lecoq, am before her, more simple and credulous than an infant. She deceives me—I see it—and she proves that I have seen wrongly. She lies—I know it, I prove it to her—and I believe her. It is because this is one of those passions," he added, in a low, mournful tone, "that age, far from extinguishing, only fans, and to which the consciousness of shame and powerlessness adds fire. One loves, and the certainty that he cannot be loved in return is one of those griefs which you must have felt to know its depth. In a moment of reason, one sees and judges himself; he says, no, it's impossible, she is almost a child, I almost an old man."[21]

Lecoq's consuming passion, no doubt, distorts his perspective in private affairs. But in his public role as the unsurpassed detective, his point of view articulates and echoes the collective conscience of the police as he explains how crime can flourish despite the best efforts of an efficient police force.

All Paris is under the eye of the police just as an ant is under that of the naturalist with his microscope. How is it, you may ask, that Paris still holds so many professional rogues? Ah, that is because we are hampered by legal forms. The law compels us to use only polite weapons against those to whom all weapons are serviceable. The courts tie our hands.[22]

[21] Emile Gaboriau, *The Mystery of Orcival* (New York: Charles Scribner's Sons, 1900), p. 120.
[22] Ibid., p. 320.

The shock of déjà vu mounts at the realization that Lecoq's defense of police, proclaimed more than a hundred years ago, strikingly resembles the ubiquitous rationalization repeated almost verbatim today in America by police flailing out at current judicial decisions.

Detective fever spreading so extensively over Europe surfaced momentarily in Russian literature and found a receptive host in Fëodor Dostoevski's *Crime and Punishment* (1866).[23] Dostoevski's brilliant detective, Porfiry Petrovitch, a master of psychological manipulation, unravels the convolutions of the mind of the murderer Raskolnikov until the guilty one cannot wait to confess his crime.

This devilish power was concealed behind a corpulent, "somewhat woman-ish figure" that seemed to be good-natured "except for a look in the eyes which shone with a watery, mawkish light" that was out of keeping with that first impression. Perhaps that peculiar expression of the eyes did not reflect his piercing insights into the tortured souls of the suspects he examined but rather opened a window into his own psychological problems reified by his bachelor status. Porfiry's alternating swings between fantasy and fear of marriage comprise a classic approach-avoidance conflict—almost a textbook case history of psychological aberration. A friend recalls Porfiry's behavior:

Last year he [Porfiry] persuaded us that he was going into a monastery: he stuck to it for two months. Not long ago he took it into his head to declare he was going to get married, that he had everything ready for the wedding. He ordered new clothes indeed. We all began to congratulate him. There was no bride, nothing, all pure fantasy![24]

What a monograph Freud might have written about a character like Porfiry.

On the American side of the Atlantic, only one real detective ever rivaled France's Vidocq—Allan Pinkerton, who emigrated from Scotland in 1842 and became the Chicago Police Department's first detective. Like Vidocq, after a career in the police service he too resigned to open his own private police agency. Pinkerton, happily married, brought his two sons, William and Robert, into the business when they were in their twenties.[25] The Pinkerton dynasty—the oldest and largest private investigative agency in the United States—still flourishes today.

Probably influenced by Pinkerton, Metta V. Victor, writing under the pseudonym Seeley Regester, devised a many-faceted detective who combined the variegated skills of the private, public, amateur, and professional police

[23] Playwrights, too, recognized the dramatic potential inherent in the detective mystery. On the stage Detective Jack Hawkshaw, "the smartest detective in the force," performed his feats of detection and spotlighted the reputation of Scotland Yard in Tom Taylor's play *The Ticket of Leave Man* (1863). But the dramatist's delineation of Hawkshaw's career omitted any inkling of the sleuth's private life.

[24] Fëodor Dostoevski, *Crime and Punishment* (New York: Random House, 1944), p. 252.

[25] James D. Horan and Howard Swiggett, *The Pinkerton Story* (London: William Heinemann, 1952).

officer. In *The Dead Letter: An American Romance* the author describes the hero, Mr. Burton, as a well-educated and aristocratic man of independent wealth who, enjoying the privilege of access to New York City Police headquarters, takes on only those cases that particularly interest him.

Equally gifted and perhaps even surpassing his prototypes on the Continent in method of investigation, Burton, the dilettante detective, stalks the criminal like "a lion about to spring" with a demeanor so fierce that other celebrated detectives seem amiable by comparison.

The light in his eye narrowed down to one gleam of concentrated fire—a steely glittering point—he watched the rest of us and said little. If I had been a guilty man I should have shrunk from that observation through the very walls, or out of a five-story window, if there had been no other way.[26]

His single-minded ferocity of purpose extended into the orbit of his family life, for Burton, a widower, exploited his older child. Gifted with marvelous powers of observation and ratiocination, Burton augmented his almost infallible technique by utilizing the mysterious forces of the occult via a personal medium, his eleven-year-old daughter Lenore, a clairvoyant. With a few passes of his hand before her eyes he induces a trance; and when he asks her what she sees, Lenore informs him where the suspects are located and what they are doing. It is a pity that she does not exorcise his enemies, because lacking her degree of wizardry, Burton dies from eating food poisoned by a criminal seeking revenge.

From the vast panoply of nineteenth-century male detective luminaries, only Bucket, Waters, Pinkerton, and Burton can be classified as family men. In each case the penumbra of the police occupation encroached upon the private life of the family, inducing the police officers to recruit immediate members of their families as aides-de-camp for the detection of the suspect and the ultimate solution of the crime.

Nowhere as commanding a figure as Mr. Burton, Ebenezer Gryce, another New York City Police Department detective, was crystallized from a formula blended by Anna Green, the first woman novelist to write a full-length detective story, *The Leavenworth Case* (1878). And although she concocts a detective with a low-key, gentle manner whose portly personage lacks the panache of more predatory and flamboyant detectives in fiction, Gryce is equally painstaking, logical, and successful in tracking down criminals.

His unassuming personality contributes to his professional competence because women find it comfortable to confide in him. But despite this ease of communication, he remains a bachelor. Consistent with his modest lifestyle, Gryce is convinced that the badge of the police officer is an emblem of social stigma that prevents him from attaining the rank of gentleman. Among all the

---

[26] Seeley Regester, *The Dead Letter: An American Romance* (New York: Beadle, 1887), p. 59.

other notable detectives in nineteenth-century fiction, only Clarke of Scotland Yard, like Gryce, experiences the class barrier; Dupin, Inspector Bucket, and Sergeant Cuff orbit gracefully in the highest stratosphere of society.

In an interesting juxtaposition, the author complements Gryce's masculine skills by introducing an amateur detective, Miss Amelia Butterworth, a genteel spinster of uncertain age, in *The Affair Next Door* (1897). Her formidable range of assets—social contacts, keen powers of observation, shrewdness, and intuition—qualified her as an invaluable associate in crime detection. But the relation between the two remains strictly business, based on mutual respect for the other's talents. Not a spark of love interest is generated.

On September 18, 1886, a momentous day in the annals of the American detective story, the exemplary Nick Carter, the all-American boy detective, appeared in a Street and Smith weekly in a story by John Coryell, "The Old Detective." Nurtured by a succession of other authors led by Frederick Dey, Nick Carter became the private-eye champion of hundreds of dime novels. Pure of heart, celibate, and hell-bent on the pursuit of criminals, he is completely indifferent to feminine charms and impervious to romance. And if there is any suggestion of romantic involvement, it is always the woman who falls in love with Nick—except once:

An aghast printer's devil at Street and Smith's discovered on perusing the latest Dey manuscript that Nick had gone and married. He rushed in consternation to the Street and Smith editors who proceeded to turn the town upside down in a search for Dey. The wife was dutifully and tragically killed off shortly thereafter. A couple of million readers would never have put up with a Nick Carter encumbered indefinitely by a wife and connubial duties.[27]

Even today, browsers in paperback book stores marvel at the impressive number of Nick Carter titles in stock that testify to his undiminished popularity through the years. And miracle of all, 90 years later this man without vices has not only maintained his youthful vigor, but also has finally mellowed enough to develop an avid interest in sex (although he still avoids marriage). His current range of cases extends more widely, scanning the international and political horizons.

Illustrious master of them all, Sherlock Holmes, stepped full blown from the mind of A. Conan Doyle into a detective story in the periodical *Beeton's Christmas Annual* (1887). One year later, Holmes took a giant step into international prominence when the magazine piece that signaled his debut was published in book form. It is fitting that Doyle's tale introducing Sherlock Holmes to a receptive world is called *A Study in Scarlet*. This most colorful of all detectives, sketched so vividly in bright strokes as an irresistible genius whose eccentricities (his Stradivarius carelessly thrown across his knee, his bouts with

[27] Richard Clurman, *Nick Carter, Detective: Fiction's Most Celebrated Detective* (New York: Macmillan, 1963), pp. xii-xiii.

cocaine, the cigar-holding coal scuttle, the Persian slipper tobacco pouch, the deer-stalker cap and Inverness cape, his distinctive lodgings at 221B Baker Street) have so personalized every aspect of his lifestyle that to millions he looms as an unforgettable figure.

Adept at highlighting the brilliant deductive powers of Holmes, Doyle contrasts his unique private consulting detective against the lackluster performance of Scotland Yard Inspectors Lestrade and Gregson—"the pick of a bad lot," according to Sherlock. With his monumental conceit, it is easy to imagine what opinion he holds of the other Scotland Yarders.

Equally disdainful of past members of his fraternity, despite their former glory, the detective bristles when his faithful companion, Dr. Watson, notices a resemblance between Sherlock and Poe's detective, Auguste Dupin. Holmes observes:

No doubt you think that you are complimenting me in comparing me to Dupin.... Now, in my opinion, Dupin was a very inferior fellow. That trick of his of breaking in on his friends' thoughts with an apropos remark after a quarter of an hour's silence is really very showy and superficial. He had some analytic genius, no doubt; but he was by no means such a phenomenon as Poe appeared to imagine.[28]

He reserves his real contempt for his renowned French rival, Monsieur Lecoq. Asked by Dr. Watson whether he has read the works of Emile Gaboriau and whether Lecoq measures up to his (Holmes') standards of competence, Sherlock sniffs sardonically:

Lecoq was a miserable bungler, he said in an angry voice; he had only one thing to recommend him, and that was his energy. That book made me positively ill. The question was how to identify an unknown prisoner. I could have done it in twenty-four hours. Lecoq took six months or so. It might be made a textbook for detectives to teach them what to avoid.[29]

Why is Holmes a bachelor? Why is love so "abhorrent to his cold, precise . . . mind"? Why should he speak of love "with a gibe and a sneer"? Could the reason be the warm relation with Dr. Watson with whom he lived so cosily and contentedly for many years? As far as can be adduced from Sherlock's adventures, no woman ever attracts him sexually, and only once did he evince a grudging sigh of admiration for a female—the adventuress Irene Adler, who outwits him in *A Scandal in Bohemia*. It is interesting that this attraction does not develop until Dr. Watson marries and leaves the Baker Street establishment that the odd couple had shared.

[28] A. Conan Doyle, "A Study in Scarlet," in A. Conan Doyle, *The Complete Sherlock Holmes* (New York: Garden City, 1938), p. 14.
[29] Ibid., p. 15.

Lending credence to this conjecture, the redoubtable American detective story writer, Rex Stout, shocked a meeting of the Baker Street Irregulars, a group of Sherlock Holmes aficionados, with an after-dinner speech, "Watson Was a Woman." The faithful listened outraged to Stout's verbal emasculation of the heretofore impeccable confidant of Holmes. To these cognoscenti it was blasphemy to hear "Watson's sturdy sentiments interpreted as sentimentality, his manly self-sufficiency read as domesticity, and his loyal companionship transformed into wifely fidelity."[30] This snide innuendo implicating Holmes and his loyal retainer, Dr. Watson, is a later-day manifestation of the erosion of the sacrosanct theme of the hero detective in fiction.

Far more defamatory and devastating to the reputation of the career police officer was the sensational device contrived in 1892 by Israel Zangwill in *The Big Bow Mystery*. In a stunning plot reversal, almost a parody of the traditional delineation of the detective's role, the hero and the villain merge in the dual personality of retired Scotland Yard detective George Grodman. In order to humiliate his successors at the Yard by demonstrating their inefficiency, Grodman cunningly plans and executes the perfect crime; he cuts the throat of a fellow lodger who is subsequently discovered in a room securely bolted from the inside with no other means of egress, to the mystification of the detective assigned to the case (none other than Grodman's hated rival). Thus the former Scotland Yard mastermind, by means of the classic locked-door mystery, achieves his purpose—to baffle his successor. Who would ever suspect that the respected retired detective could be the ruthless murderer? And with an ironic twist, the circle has closed. Instead of the criminal turned detective, the detective has turned criminal.

Ignoring the murderous impulse in the character he created, Zangwill in a laudatory comment attributes Grodman's failure to marry as the one tragic flaw in his investigative competency: "Grodman is a bachelor. In the celestial matrimonial bureau a partner might have been selected for him, but he had never been able to discover her. It was his one failure as a detective."[31] On the contrary, it is rather fortuitous that he never consummated a "marriage made in heaven," for any man who could formulate such a Machiavellian scheme of violence to prove his professional expertise and shame an imagined rival manifests a diabolic rather than an angelic personality.

No review of the nineteenth-century police literature can be complete without a discussion of the distaff side. Did female detectives in the fiction of this era rival the accomplishments of their male colleagues or add to our knowledge of the police family? In 1861, the first fictional Scotland Yard woman detective, Mrs. Paschal, appeared in *The Experiences of a Lady Detective*, by Anonyma. Perhaps to avoid the complications of a husband

---

[30] Michele B. Slung, *Crime on Her Mind* (New York: Pantheon, 1975), p. xv.

[31] Israel Zangwill, "The Big Bow Mystery," in Israel Zangwill, *The Grey Wig: Stories and Novelettes* (London: William Heinemann, 1903), pp. 107-224.

hovering in the background, her creator described her as a widow in her late thirties. The heroine's forte, like that of most other woman detectives of this period, was intuition rather than deduction.

It took until 1883, however, for the Metropolitan Police Force in London to open its doors a crack and appoint two women, not as detectives to be sure, but as matrons to oversee female prisoners. Spurred by even this begrudged foothold, at least 20 fictional women detectives burgeoned by the end of the century.

In the neomythic period of the detective story in America only one woman detective, Clarice Dyke, had a helpmate. Equally as clever as her detective husband, Clarice matched her spouse's powers of deduction. The two, apparently happily married, skillfully dovetailed their talents in the solution of mysteries, although we are not permitted by the author, Harry Rockwood, to penetrate the curtain of domesticity in *Clarice Dyke, the Female Detective* (1883).

As a result of this encompassing shield of privacy, the women characters in the Victorian era provide little insight into police family life. Most of them were single, and a few turned sleuth to prove the innocence of a husband or sweetheart. But generally, the female detective was an anomaly:

The authors themselves seem never to be quite certain of their creations, intent as they are on playing up the novelty of such a peculiar figure, often abandoning her in mid-career and finishing her off, not at the Reichenbach Falls, but at the matrimonial altar, in order to reassure the Victorian public of her ultimate femaleness.[32]

A male critic, in a rather superficial appraisal, blankets the whole female detective genre with a cloak of mediocrity, asserting, "Lady detectives are uncommon and, on the whole, undistinguished."[33] But despite their scarcity in number, in the early 1900s, at least two London representatives excelled in this predominantly masculine calling: one demonstrated her power by capturing a renowned detective and leading him to the altar, and the other performed so brilliantly in detection that the chiefs of Scotland Yard turned to her instinctively when the male detectives became stymied.

Dora Myrl, who handled cases competently as a private consultant, soon found herself in competition with the "rule of thumb" Detective, Paul Beck; ultimately, they consolidated their rival talents in a conjugal merger. No doubt this partnership of career and marriage meshed effectively, for not much later their originator, M. McDonnel Bodkin, produced genealogical evidence in his

[32] Slung, *Crime on Her Mind,* pp. xix-xx.

[33] John Carter, "Collecting Detective Fiction," in Howard Haycraft, ed., *The Art of the Mystery Story* (New York: Simon and Schuster, 1946), p. 47.

sequel, *Young Beck: A Chip Off the Old Block,* in which Paul, Jr., a boy sleuth, outdid his famous parents.[34]

The queen of detectives must be Lady Molly, attached to the "Female Department" of Scotland Yard, who "has worked her way upwards, analyzing and studying, exercising her powers of intuition and deduction, until . . . she is considered, by chiefs and men alike, the greatest authority among them on criminal investigation."[35] Her origins were mysterious. Her secret marriage to Captain Hubert de Mazareen was consummated tragically because her husband was sentenced to 20 years in prison for a crime he did not commit. Lady Molly's efforts finally cleared his name.

Although surprisingly few of the nineteenth-century detective protagonists of fiction were family oriented, from a psychoanalytic point of view the detective story connects with family life via the agency of the reader. Some psychoanalysts, contending that the detective story actually recapitulates the primal scene in which the reader as a young child once watched his parents having sexual relations, assert that the criminal represents the parent and the detective the alter ego of the reader:

By participating in the detective story version of the primal scene, the reader's ego need fear no punishment for the libidinal or aggressive urges. In an orgy of investigation the ego personified by the great detective, can look, remember and correlate without fear and without reproach in utter contrast to the ego of the terrified infant witnessing the primal scene.[36]

But there is a complication, because "in the ideal detective story the detective or hero would discover that he himself is the criminal for whom he has been seeking."[37] According to this theory, the reader is the detective and at the same time he or she is the criminal who stands for the parent. That truly is a very close, if complicated, family relation.

With a sinister twist, uncannily anticipating psychoanalytic exegesis, Gaston Leroux, the French mystery story writer, synchronized the detective-murderer and the classical locked-door themes, gruesomely embellishing them into an ultimate unhappy police marriage in *The Mystery of the Yellow Room* (1908).

---

[34] Ellery Queen labels the Becks the first detective family, although the Buckets (Dickens) and the Dykes (Rockwood) preceded them by a good many years. See Ellery Queen, *In the Queen's Parlor* (New York: Simon and Schuster, 1957), pp. 45-46.

[35] Baroness Emmuska Orczy, "Lady Molly of Scotland Yard," in Slung, *Crime on Her Mind,* p. 90.

[36] Geraldine Pederson-Krag, "Detective Stories and the Primal Scene," *Psychoanalytic Quarterly* 18 (1949):213.

[37] Charles Rycroft, "A Detective Story: Psychoanalytic Observations," *Psychoanalytic Quarterly* 26 (1957):230.

Behind the closed bedroom door, the great French detective Fredric Larsan, really the vicious American criminal Ballmeyer, devises a nearly successful scheme to murder his wife, Mathilde.

Just about this time, across the Channel, the Polish-English author Joseph Conrad broke with his regular pattern of writing about seafarers and wanderers to pen a classic thriller, *The Secret Agent,* blending all the ingredients of the best-selling spy stories seasoned by the chief detective's domestic difficulties. A cell of terrorists controlled by enemy agents, an innocuous-appearing bookstore operated by a "sleeper," (a spy who surfaces after a prolonged period of inaction), a bomb that explodes too soon, and a conflict between two high-ranking Scotland Yard police officers are combined into a work of art that the noted literary critic F.R. Leavis has praised as one of Conrad's masterpieces.

The officer assigned to the investigation of the explosion is the assistant commissioner in charge of the special crimes branch. Through instinctive detective brilliance, fortuitously nurtured by a marriage to a politically influential woman, he attains his exalted position. At first, he considers it an excellent match, but his wife soon reveals herself as "a woman devoured by all sorts of small selfishness, small envies, small jealousies."[38] The same quasi-facetious explanation that Zangwill offered for Grodman's remaining unmarried is repeated by Conrad in excusing the assistant commissioner's failure to pick a wife who could bring him contentment: "He was a born detective. It had unconsciously governed his choice of a career, and if it ever failed him in life it was perhaps in the one exceptional circumstance of his marriage—which was also natural."[39]

Has Conrad put his finger on it? Does the infallible intuition of even the born detective fail him naturally in the all-important quest for the perfect wife? Does this blind spot explain the overwhelming tendency of detectives and police officers of fiction to fail to find the right mate, so that they either remain bachelors or end up married unhappily to the wrong woman?

Appalled by the lack of direction, the loss of tradition, and the contradictory trends in police literature, S.S. Van Dine, a master of the mystery form, engraved a tablet of laws for detective story writers. Of particular interest are numbers three and four:

3. There must be no love interest. The business in hand is to bring a criminal to justice, not to bring a lovelorn suspect couple to the hymeneal altar.

4. The detective himself, or one of the official investigators, should never turn out to be the culprit, This is bald trickery.[40]

---

[38] Joseph Conrad, *The Secret Agent* (New York: Doubleday, 1953), p. 100.

[39] Ibid., p. 105.

[40] S.S. Van Dine, "Twenty Rules for Writing Detective Stories," in Haycraft, *Art of the Mystery Story,* pp. 189-190.

For a considerable time the Van Dine credo operated as an automatic editor to regulate the detective fiction of the 1920s and 1930s. The rigid formula prescribed that primary emphasis be placed on the puzzle, the clues, and the trick dénouement to challenge the reader within the limits of fair play. The price paid was superficial character development. In order to produce taut thrillers, authors could not divert their attention to extraneous matters like the families of police officers. Thus the fictional detective even well into the twentieth century still functioned as a solitary searcher grasping at a clue—but never at a woman.

The list of asexual detective heroes born before World War II and never permitted by their progenitors to consummate the act unfolds like a literary hall of celibate fame: Gilbert K. Chesterton's priest detective Father Brown (his asceticism needs no explanation), Leslie Charteris's Saint, who lives up to his name. These bachelors were matched by Agatha Christie's Hercule Poirot, past the age of peccadilloes, and the Queens' Ellery Queen (the name is evocative).

As war encroached, with families everywhere disrupted and once-stable marital relations threatened by a new sexual permissiveness, the golden age of the detective story dimmed. Van Dine's rules no longer seemed appropriate or feasible in the face of the new zeitgeist. Some authors resisted and attempted to inject a sense of stability by chronicling the adventures of happily married detectives who would reappear with members of their families in book after book. For the most part, the couples depicted functioned more like business partners than lovers; sex was still a forbidden subject.

Dashiell Hammett coupled the urbane Thin Man—Nick Charles, the former ace detective of the Trans American Detective Agency—with a smashing young wife, Nora. Together, they flashingly solved their murder mysteries between rounds of martinis, supper engagements, and attendance at posh social and cultural events. At this frenetic pace, they managed to ration their affection by calling each other "dear" or "darling."

Another dashing duo, Pamela and Gerald North (his actual profession, a book publisher), effervescent members of the tennis set, seem to stumble artlessly over dead bodies. They reveal their more sophisticated talents by assisting the police authorities in uncovering the murderers. Frances and Richard Lockridge, their literary parents, expanded the Norths' harmonious marital teamwork into a series of almost 30 books.

Concurrently in France, Georges Simenon conceived his celebrated detective, Maigret, whose marriage to Madame Maigret epitomized the typical French bourgeois virtues. Her behind-the-scenes role in a myriad of cases as sounding board and dispenser of domestic and secretarial services—from delivering his telephone messages to waking him up for appointments—defined her relationship to Maigret as efficient concierge rather than as intimate helpmate.

The absence of any overt reference to sex in this school of fiction became so apparent that it raised questions in the minds of students of the detective story, so much so that once when Dashiell Hammett introduced the equally famous detective story writer Ellery Queen[41] to a class of adults studying the mystery story, he began by asking, "Mr. Queen, will you be good enough to explain your famous character's sex life, if any?"[42] Queen's candid response obviously did not "skirt the issue" but confirmed the pervasive power of literary traditions: "The truth is, the sex life of a gentleman detective is a perplexing problem . . . we are forced to skirt the problem with almost puritanical delicacy."[43]

Julian Symons, a well-regarded exponent of the art, trenchantly interpreted this dialogue, linking it to changing standards:

Such a question could not have been asked before World War II. Holmes could then be accepted as a misogynist, Poirot as an aging bachelor, Queen as a figure susceptible to feminine beauty but above or outside emotional entanglement; but with the acceptance during the fifties and the sixties of the fact that everybody has some kind of real and/or fantasy sex life, such easy answers would no longer do. It now appeared suggestive of impotence to fall in love with lovely ladies in a purely platonic way like Ellery. . . .[44]

There is no doubt that the horror of World War II exposed the sinister, brutal, and passionate vein of man, displacing the view of life and morals that had been dominated by society's superego so unabashedly during the Victorian age and its aftermath. With crime rampant and law-enforcement officers the only identifiable group manning the barricades, public interest swelled concerning the character of the men and women fighting crime.

Realizing the precious lode of novelistic gold still unmined, enterprising writers definitely cast off the Van Dine formalism and capitulated to the newly emerging mores, delineating this new breed as fully rounded human beings rather than as merely logical automatons programmed to act on the signal of a clue. Consequently, the rational, ego-controlled Apollonian police-detective, who previously had been accepted unequivocally because he represented the conscience of society and its holy triumvirate of God, country, and the triumph of virtue yielded to a more appropriate protagonist: the Dionysian hero. To exceed television's glamourized stylization of the police officer, the more radical authors transformed the remorseless bloodhounds sniffing after clues into indefatigable womanizers, swinging satyrs, more stud than nailer of criminals. To be realistic, it would be implausible to project an image of a powerful, adventurous leading character who would risk his life for a trifle and break laws when he wished but who would not reach out sexually to the vulnerable women thrown into his orbit.

---

[41] Ellery Queen is a pseudonym for the combined efforts of Frederick Dannay and Manfred B. Lee.

[42] Julian Symons, *Mortal Consequences* (New York: Harper and Row, 1972), p. 152.

[43] Ellery Queen, *In the Queen's Parlor* (New York: Simon and Schuster, 1957), p. 47.

[44] Julian Symons, *Mortal Consequences* (New York: Harper and Row, 1972), p. 152.

In the postwar period dramatists and novelists experimented with the police officer-detective as the central focus of the story rather than as a mechanical auxiliary to the solution of a puzzle. And as writers poked into the viscera of their subjects, dissecting their inner secrets, family ties were ventilated as well. Under the old conventions, a police family detracted and distracted from the dénouement of a crime novel; in the contemporary treatment, the tension between the family and the job heightened the drama. Authors of the caliber of Sidney Kingsley, Arthur Miller, Graham Greene, and Alan Paton guaranteed literary respectability for the police novel; just as a century before, Balzac, Dickens, and Dostoevski had performed the same type of service for the early classic form.

The result was a cascade of books about the police family. The lifting of this curtain on the private world of the police officer's families unfolded a diorama of disaster, with destructive episodes and tragic scenes of chronic malaise, infidelity, alienation, incompatibility, and unhappiness shattering family relationships. The spotlight starkly illuminated a stage set of warped and melancholy tableaux with the leading men's lives scarred by chicanery, brutality, and lechery.

Contemporary dramatists cannot resist injecting the certified crowd pleaser—the police officer satyr or pervert—into their dramas. In adaptations of classic plays this character is frequently introduced among the dramatis personae even when the role deviates from the spirit of the original. In one of the hits of the 1977 Broadway season, *Sly Fox,* a modern version of Ben Jonson's seventeenth-century satire *Volpone,* a chief of police appears in the second act courtroom scene and briefly upstages the rest of the company. Unable to resist the charms of the chastely beautiful female witness for the prosecution, he removes his jacket in a quick motion suggestive of a "flasher," leaps to ravish her, and has to be restrained forcibly. The chief blames his outburst of passion on his sexual deprivation, moaning, "My wife died yesterday, and it's been hell!"

Evidently, modern architects of the police novel have designed their blueprints on a foundation of troubled marriages. The sampling in table 2-1, below compressing the themes of 26 contemporary novels and 2 plays (many of them best sellers) in which male police officers and their families predominate, presents convincing evidence that the depressing common denominator of police family interaction in literature is a lifetime of tragedy.[45] Sexual incompatibility emerges as the main problem—typically revolving around the lack of desire on the part of the wife or the impotence of the husband. Homosexuality of the police husband varies the sexual motif. Another cause of marital disaster is miscegenation between a white police officer and a black prostitute. A final gulf separating a police couple yawns wider over the years because the wife cannot adjust to the extraordinary demands of the police occupation.

[45] We apologize to devotees of Agatha Christie, John Creasey, Ian Fleming, Ed McBain, Ross Macdonald, Dell Shannon, Georges Simenon, and Rex Stout, to mention a few. As a matter of expediency we eliminated from consideration two categories of books: those in which the crime and the criminal rather than the police officer occupied the center of interest and those in which the police officer-detective remained unmarried.

28

Table 2-1
The Police Family in Contemporary Fiction

Book	Police Officer and Affiliation	Rating of Marriage	Description
Graham Greene, *The Heart of the Matter* (Viking, 1948)	Police Major Henry Scobie, West Africa	Unhappy	The major and his wife, Louise, grow apart. She prefers poetry. Their daughter dies at an early age. He commits adultery with a young girl, Helen, and is blackmailed.
Sidney Kingsley, *Detective Story* (Dramatists Play Service, 1951)	Detective James McCleod, NYCPD	Unhappy	During the investigation of a case, McCleod learns that his adored wife, Mary, was formerly the girl friend of a racketeer and has had an abortion. Losing concentration, he is shot by the criminal he is interrogating.
Alan Paton, *Too Late the Phalarope* (Scribner's, 1953)	Lieutenant Pieter Van Vlaanderen, South Africa	Unhappy	The lieutenant's wife, Nella, does not provide him with enough sexual gratification. In violation of the Immorality Act, he has sex with a black prostitute, Stephanie. He is caught, disgraced, and sent to prison.
Richard Dougherty, *The Commissioner* (Doubleday, 1962)	Police Commissioner Anthony Russell, Detective Daniel Madigan, Detective Rocco Bonaro, NYCPD	Unhappy / Unhappy / Happy	No longer in love with his wife, Margie, the commissioner has an affair with socialite Tricia Bentley. Star detective Madigan, also unhappily married, takes a mistress. He is killed in a shoot-out. With lots of kids, cooking, and loving, Rocco Bonaro's marriage to Catrina blooms.

Author / Title	Character	Status	Description
Roderick Thorp, *The Detective* (Dial, 1966)	Detective Lieutenant Joseph Leland, Port Smith PD	Unhappy	Leland's marriage is shaky because of his wife Karen's infidelity and neurosis.
Arthur Miller, *The Price* (Viking, 1968)	Sergeant Victor Franz, NYCPD	Unhappy	After twenty-eight years of police work, the sergeant, a bitter and frustrated police officer, still resents his lack of status and nostalgically reminisces about his thwarted youthful ambition to become a physician. His wife, Esther, is an incipient alcoholic.
William Johnston, *Barney* (Random House, 1970)	Police officer Barney Scanlon, NYCPD	Unhappy	Barney's marriage to Kate is miserable because of his impotence, stupidity, and prejudice. He blinds his little son in a fit of rage, kills a man without proper cause, and is arrested.
Joseph Wambaugh, *The New Centurions* (Little, Brown, 1970)	Police officers Roy Fehler, Gus Plebesly, Andy Kilvinsky, Los Angeles PD	Unhappy Unhappy Unhappy	Fehler's marriage ends in divorce, while Plebesly's is on the verge of breaking up. Kilvinsky, already divorced for many years, commits suicide.
William Harrington, *Trial* (McKay, 1970)	Detective Lieutenant Clement Yacobucci, Cleveland PD	Initially happy but ends in tragedy	The detective lieutenant's wife, Anne, is killed in an auto accident. When Yacobucci's homosexual relation with his captain, Paul Chichester, is exposed, the captain commits suicide; Yacobucci resigns and bears the disgrace.
Peter Ustinov, *Krumnagel* (Little, Brown, 1971)	Police Chief Bartram Krumnagel, Deputy Chief Al Carbide, a midwestern city	Unhappy Unhappy	Evidently, Police Chief Krumnagel's wife, Edie, is infatuated with police officers. But all of her six marriages to police officers, including both Krumnagel and Carbide, end unhappily because of sexual problems.

Table 2-1 (cont.)

Book	Police Officer and Affiliation	Rating of Marriage	Description
Henry Kane, *The Moonlighter* (Bernard Geis, 1971)	Detective Joseph Blake, NYCPD	Unhappy	Detective Blake is unhappy and impotent with his wife, Mamie. But he regains his virility in a homosexual relation with an interior decorator, Anthony Donovan.
Joseph Wambaugh, *The Blue Knight* (Little, Brown, 1972)	Police officer Bumper Morgan, Sergeant Cruz Segovia, Los Angeles PD	Unhappy / Initially happy but ends in tragedy	Police officer Bumper Morgan is already divorced from his wife, Verna. When his sickly five-year-old son, Billy, died, the marriage soon disintegrated. His former radio car partner and best friend, Sergeant Cruz Segovia, a Chicano, is happily married to Socorro, and they have many children. But the job ineluctably spells tragedy when Cruz is shot and killed during a holdup.
Donald Westlake, *Cops and Robbers* (Evans, 1972)	Police officer Joe Loomis, Detective Tom Garrity, NYCPD	Happy / Happy	Radio car buddies and neighbors in suburbia, Joe is married to Grace and Tom to Mary. The men contrive a plot to steal $1 million. But it is not only money that Joe covets because "the only one he really wanted to ball was Tom's wife" (p. 30).
John Gardner, *Sunlight Dialogues* (Knopf, 1972)	Police Chief Fred Clumly, Batavia, NYPD	Unhappy	Alienated and bitter, Chief Clumly is married to a blind wife, which increases his misery.
Frank Yerby, *The Girl from Storyville* (Dial, 1972)	Detective Lieutenant Bill Turner, Shreveport, La., PD	Unhappy	When the detective catches his wife in flagrante, he beats her up and divorces her. Finding his daughter, Fanny, the star of a brothel operated by his former wife, he dies of apoplexy.

Author / Title	Character / Role	Marital Status	Description
Lawrence Sanders, *The First Deadly Sin* (Putnam's, 1973)	Police Captain Edward X. Delaney, NYCPD	Initially happy unti tragedy strikes	Captain Delaney, nicknamed "Iron Balls," is very happily married to wife, Barbara. But they learn that she is dying of cancer.
Paige Mitchell, *The Covenant* (Atheneum, 1973)	Police Chief Otis Simmons, Sergeant Maynard Taylor, Holmesdale, Miss., PD	Unhappy / Unhappy	After three marital fiascos, Chief Simmons becomes the lover of the wife of Sergeant Taylor who was impotent.
Noel Gerson *State Trooper* (Doubleday, 1973)	Lieutenant Red Martin, Connecticut State Police	Unhappy	Red, a basically decent person, and his wife, Emily, have grown apart because of the demands of the job.
L.H. Whittemore, *The Super Cops* (Stein and Day, 1973)	Police officer David Greenberg, NYCPD	Unhappy	Officer Greenberg, one of the Batman and Robin pair, married to Irene, moves in with a young girl living near the precinct, ostensibly so that he can have more time to devote to the job.
Jimmy Breslin, *World Without End, Amen* (Viking, 1973)	Police officer Dermot Davey, Sergeant John O'Donnell, NYCPD	Unhappy / Unhappy	Alcoholic, impotent, and at the point of suicide, both officers have sex with a black, male, transvestite prostitute.
Robin Moore, *The Fifth Estate* (Doubleday, 1973)[a]	Detective Pat Kenney, NYCPD	Unhappy	Detective Kenney "left his wife after finding out she was screwing an Italian who he knew damned well was a mafioso" (p. 87).
Dorothy Uhnak, *Law and Order* (Simon and Schuster, 1973)	Sergeant Brian O'Malley, Deputy Chief Inspector Brian O'Malley, NYCPD	Unhappy / Unhappy	Father and son desired more sex than their respective wives would give them. The sergeant, forcing himself upon his black prostitute mistress, is emasculated and killed. The son, the DCI, takes a glamourous mistress.

Table 2-1 (cont.)

Book	Police Officer and Affiliation	Rating of Marriage	Description
Joseph Wambaugh, *The Onion Field* (Delacorte, 1973)	Police officers Ian Campbell, Karl Hettinger, Los Angeles PD	Initially happy but both end in tragedy	Criminals ambush radio car partners Ian and Karl, murdering Ian and confiscating Karl's gun. Karl suffers a breakdown, becoming alcoholic and impotent.
Peter Benchley, *Jaws* (Doubleday, 1974)	Police Chief Martin Brody, Amity, Long Island, PD	Unhappy	Chief Brody's marriage to Ellen is unhappy because she is dissatisfied with the boring life and low prestige of a police officer's wife. She resists sex with her husband but has an affair with marine biologist Matt Hooper, brother of an old flame.
Joseph Wambaugh, *The Choirboys* (Delacorte, 1975)	Police officers Spermwhale Whalen, Sam Niles, Calvin Potts, Roscoe Rules, Spencer Van Moot, Willie Wright, Tom Garrity, Los Angeles PD	Unhappy Unhappy Unhappy Unhappy Unhappy Unhappy Unhappy	The roll call includes alcoholics, sadists, neurotics, deviates, and suicides. Their grim marital statistics toll a dirge of repeated divorces and misery.
Jerome Charyn, *Marilyn the Wild* (Arbor House, 1976)	Inspector Isaac Sidel, NYCPD	Unhappy	Separated from his Catholic wife, Kathleen, the Jewish inspector joins his mistress, Ida. His daughter, Marilyn, is a wild nymphomaniac who has thrown over three husbands.

Robert Daley, *To Kill a Cop* (Crown Publishers, 1976)	Chief of Detectives Earl Eischied, Police officer Martin Delehanty, Police officer Agnes Cusack, NYCPD	Unhappy Initially happy but both end in tragedy	Although the chief is divorced from his wife, Betty, he depends on her to provide an alibi when he is accused of illegally accepting gratuities. Assigned as radio car partners, police officers Martin Delehanty and Agnes Cusack fall in love. Both are married but not to each other. When their attraction is inadvertently revealed on a television program, Agnes's husband beats her up. Soon after, Martin is killed by an assassin.
Dorothy Uhnak, *The Investigation* (Simon and Schuster, 1977)	Detective Sergeant Joe Peters, NYCPD	Unhappy	Facing retirement and a dead marriage to his wife, Jen, Peters is assigned to investigate the brutal murder of two young children. He is seduced into an affair with the chief suspect, Kitty Keeler, the children's mother.

[a]Few moviegoers can forget the hair-raising chase by NYCPD Detectives "Popeye" Doyle and his sidekick "Cloudy" in *The French Connection*, based on Robin Moore's popular novel of the same name. Although the two detectives in the book are single (thus not meeting the criterion for inclusion in this listing), the real-life detective who was the model for Popeye is now on his fourth marriage. His third wife, is reportedly trying to "make a connection" in family court for child support. See *Newsday*, March 19, 1974, p. 6.

Our thumbnail condensations in table 2-1 illustrate that writers rarely diverge from the pattern of recording disastrous family relationships. One marriage, however, glows euphorically, although its aura of empathy is darkened by a terminal illness. During 31 years, Police Captain Delaney in *The First Deadly Sin* so intimately constructed a tapestry of love and respect with his wife Barbara—now dying of cancer—that she becomes his confidante and sounding board to whom he regularly reports "intra-departmental feuding, the intrigues and squabbles of ambitious men and factions."[46] And the captain, who in the department wears the sobriquet "Iron Balls," depends upon "her sharp, practical, aggressive female intelligence to weigh motives, choices, possibilities, safeguards."[47] It is ironic that this relationship, one of the few that is admirable in detective fiction, violates a fundamental credo of the real world of the police: most police officers would recoil in horror at the captain's standard practice of sharing department confidences, personalities, and decisions with his wife.

Although the two radio car partners Joe Loomis and Tom Garrity in *Cops and Robbers* seem content in their marriages, they are so deeply involved in the planning and execution of the perfect crime—a heist of more than $1 million—that they can be only peripherally occupied with family life. The question can be raised about Loomis of the roving eye, "If a police officer husband becomes corrupt, commits a serious crime and covets his partner's wife, how much fallout rains upon the marriage?"

When writers did lighten this leitmotif of gloom with a happy couple, the pair was conceived as secondary characters acting out the stereotype of an ethnic old-country marriage, with the wife joyfully cooking great pots of food and the police officer returning from his labors to be greeted and treated like a king by his large brood of kids. A typical homecoming for Italian Detective Rocky Bonaro in *The Commissioner* captures this essence:

The smaller kids would hug his legs, and Momma would smother him with kisses. The tub would be drawn and waiting; the smell of pasta and tomato sauce would reach through the whole house from the steamy kitchen. Rocky would start talking the minute he entered and the interminable review of the day would continue through the half-opened door of the bathroom and, after his bath, right up to the end of dinner.

The kids would be hushed and reverent, Catrina would be full of interest and love.[48]

Bonaro, who incorporates the ultimate male chauvinist viewpoint, eulogizes his wife Catrina as "the best woman in the world—a perfect wife and mother and as good in the bedroom as she was in the kitchen. She was a listener and an

[46] Lawrence Sanders, *The First Deadly Sin* (New York: Putnam's Sons, 1973), p. 128.
[47] Ibid., p. 122.
[48] Richard Dougherty, *The Commissioner* (New York: Doubleday, 1962), p. 71.

admirer, a builder-upper and not a complainer—the kind of woman a man should have to come home to."[49]

Similarly, when Police Officer Bumper Morgan, *The Blue Knight* of Wambaugh's best seller, visits Mexican Sergeant Cruz Segovia, father of nine kids, the dinner guest is entranced by aromatic cooking and the zestful good looks of Cruz's wife—in that order:

I sniffed. . . . Chile relleno, carnitas, cilantro and onion . . . some enchiladas, some guacamole. . . .

I went through the big formal dining room to the kitchen and saw Socorro, her back to me, ladling out a huge wooden spoonful of rice into two of the bowls that sat on the drainboard. She was naturally a little the worse for wear after twenty years and nine kids, but her hair was as long and black and shiny rich as ever, and though she was twenty pounds heavier, she still was a strong, lively-looking girl with the whitest teeth I'd ever seen.[50]

Even a novelist who attempts to evade the mainstream of misery so fashionable in current police fiction may be thwarted. In a revealing glimpse behind the scenes into the writing of his best seller, *Jaws*, Peter Benchley describes how he was maneuvered into established literary channels. Apparently, his original conception was to restate the theme of *Moby Dick* in modern terms, substituting a great white shark for the great white whale, and a captain of police, Martin Brody of Amity, Long Island, for the captain of the *Pequod*. Benchley's knowledgeable editor, Tom Congdon of Doubleday, realized the potential for suspense of a man-eating predator playing the lead but vetoed the depiction of a normal sex life between the police chief and his wife: "I don't think there's any place for wholesome married sex in this kind of book."[51] So the author revised his scenario: the police chief's compatible marriage of 15 years is threatened by his wife's growing restlessness, and the couple's relation begins to fall apart.

Summers were bad times for Ellen Brody, for in summer she was tortured by thoughts she didn't want to think—thoughts of chances missed and lives that could have been. She saw people she had grown up with: prep school classmates now married to bankers and brokers, summering in Amity and wintering in New York, graceful women who stroked tennis balls and enlivened conversations with equal ease, women who (Ellen was convinced) joked among themselves about Ellen Shepherd marrying that policeman because he got her pregnant in the back seat of his 1948 Ford, which had not been the case.[52]

---

[49] Ibid., p. 147.

[50] Joseph Wambaugh, *The Blue Knight* (New York: Dell, 1972), p. 122.

[51] Ted Morgan, "Sharks," *New York Times Magazine*, April 21, 1974, p. 86.

[52] Peter Benchley, *Jaws* (New York: Doubleday, 1974), pp. 21-22.

Ellen becomes Madame Bovary transplanted to our time. Painfully aware and resentful that the best part of her life is behind her, restricted in status and opportunity by her husband's occupation, she refuses to have sex with him. Ripe and vulnerable for a liaison, she takes a lover. By adding infidelity to unhappiness in a police marriage, both editor and author follow the popular line. The fantastic acclaim accorded the novel attests to their intuitive feeling for what would be appealing to mass-market tastes.

Conversely, while the male rogue and strife in family life may be in vogue in contemporary police fiction, the female detective escapes relatively unscathed. In conformity with the traditional framework established more than a century ago, her marital status for the most part is still either single or widowed, unfettered by family ties. Completely career oriented, she performs her police duties in such an exemplary fashion that she maintains professional parity with her masculine co-workers.

Miss Jane Marple, the indomitable white-haired, aged spinster, a true armchair speculator, unravels crimes expertly while she sits knitting placidly without even dropping a stitch.[53] Mrs. Emily Pollifax, a widowed grandmother, escapes from a boring suburban life to act in the capacity of an unofficial CIA agent.[54] Christie Opera, first grade detective in the NYCPD attached to the district attorney's special investigative squad, more than holds her own in competition with her male colleagues, despite the tragedy of having lost her husband, a plainclothesman, in a shootout with a narcotics addict and having to bring up a young son without a father.[55] In a curious way, these female sleuths created by women writers seem to have anticipated the thrust of the feminist movement, carrying the banners of female equality and demonstrating their professional competence time after time in a predominantly male occupation.

When male novelists write of the nonpareil female detective or secret agent, however, they activate male chauvinistic fantasies. The sexually intriguing heroine becomes the female counterpart of the satyric superman. Secret agent Modesty Blaise, a bachelor beauty, should more appropriately have been named "Nailer" because of her potent mesmerizing technique of stripping to the waist before entering a room, a weapon "guaranteed to nail a roomful of men, holding them frozen for at least two or three vital seconds."[56] Perhaps her only equal is the "Baroness," the voluptuous widow of an Italian nobleman who orchestrates her irresistible feminine charms in bed or demonstrates her matchless martial skills as a secret agent on the field of honor.[57] Like praying mantises, these two often copulate with their intended prey before dispatching them. Nevertheless,

[53] Agatha Christie, *Thirteen Problems* (New York: Dodd, Mead, 1973).

[54] Dorothy Gilman, *A Palm for Mrs. Pollifax* (New York: Doubleday, 1973).

[55] Dorothy Uhnak, *The Witness* (New York: Simon and Schuster, 1969).

[56] Peter O'Donnell, *Modesty Blaise* (New York: Doubleday, 1965), p. 22. Her fleeting marriage of convenience to gain British nationality can be discounted.

[57] See, for example, Paul Kenyon, *Death in a Ruby Light* New York: Pocket Books, 1974); and Paul Kenyon, *Flicker of Doom* (New York: Pocket Books, 1974).

lurking below the overt admiration of the authors for their nubile creations, one can detect the nervous trepidation of the male confronting the liberated woman who may prove to be the Venus trap.

Although the profiles of these fictional leading ladies may be caricatures of real-life policewomen, the contrast of their personalities—the exaggerated roles of the professionally competent bachelor lady versus the seductively attractive dragon lady—articulates authentic concerns of the feminist movement. However, when female writers make the effort to synthesize this dichotomy for police-women in more realistic terms, they translate it into a prosaic conflict—career versus marriage—ending with the marriage victimized by the job. For example, against the advice of her father, Detective Sergeant Norah Mulcahaney of the NYCPD homicide squad marries swinger Lieutenant Joseph Capretto. When Joe becomes her commanding officer, their marriage begins to deteriorate. Working on different phases of an important investigation, they come into further conflict; after he pulls rank on her, they decide to separate. With the solution of the case, the possibility of a reconciliation materializes.[58]

In contemporary fiction, then, this irresolution in the feminine role, this vacillating between independence and sexual objectivity, may in reality be the male novelist's candid reporting of life according to his concept of the modern woman. Therefore, it becomes a relevant and typical commentary on the syndrome of the real policewoman and her interaction with her family.

For the male police officer the perplexing question remains, Why has the cult of the twisted and alienated antihero and his tormented family become the fundamental postulate of a literary myth? Table 2-1, which sampled this stockpile of fiction on law enforcement families, graphically charts this direction. Oddly enough, for the opportunistic writers of these melodramas of marital misadventures, the perpetuation of the theme of the policeman's miserable lot may produce a bonanza. On television, the policeman hero is exemplified as noble and infallible. Since books must compete with the excitement of television, it becomes strategic to sensationalize plots. In the guise of entertaining the public, authors can pander to the popular taste for sex and violence and also cater to the fact that it is human nature to take delight in pushing paragons of authority from their pedestals. Thus the artisans of the police novel, straining to exceed the glamourous or the kinky, succumb to the pressure and concentrate on constructing a sordid and macabre social landscape strewn with casualties among police and their families.

On television, however, it is only in the exceptional case, when the image of the police officer as paragon is satirized, that he appears as less than demigod. When the iconoclastic television producer Norman Lear contrived the format of the sexually oriented soap opera series "Mary Hartman, Mary Hartman," he studded it with a cast of weird characters. A good share of the wild popularity of

<hr />

[58] Lillian O'Donnell, *Leisure Dying: A Detective Norah Mulcahaney Novel* (New York: Putnam's Sons, 1976).

the syndicated series, could be tracked to the married Mary's dalliance with her lover, the "libidinous lawman" Police Sergeant Dennis Foley, whose lust loomed larger than his heart. The preliminary preparations for a longed-for sexual encounter with Mary may have precipitated his massive heart attack. But his recuperative sojourn in the cardiac intensive care center did not prevent him from "scoring," as Mary slipped into his hospital bed to administer the therapy that cardiac patients must of necessity only dream.

But what is the rationalization for the specialized core of writers, formerly members of actual police departments, who record accounts of unhappy policemen and report family relationships of misery? Because of the inside position of these people, it is logical to assume that they are providing us with unique access into the secret world of the police.[60] And with unerring verisimilitude they document police experiences, replicate recognizable police types, capture the nuances of police patois—and hurl expletives at the police occupation.

Two high-ranking former law enforcement officers, Robert Daley, a deputy commissioner of the New York City Police Department, and Joseph Wambaugh, a veteran sergeant in the Los Angeles Police Department, insinuate that the police occupation is a whore who seduces its members, gradually destroying them and their marriages as well. Daley's fictional hero Chief of Detectives Earl Eischied

cursed a system which sucked rough, ill-educated young men in at the bottom, which exalted and promoted them for physical bravery, but which then informed them as they approached middle age that entirely different qualities suddenly were necessary. Men . . . were being destroyed by the very whore they had given their lives to. It happened every day, and was in no way remarkable. It was as normal as a stickup. It was as normal as a victim dead on the floor. The Police Department was a whore.[61]

In Wambaugh's *The Blue Knight* the police officer's beat is dubbed *la puta,* the whore, by Cruz and Bumper. When Bumper decides not to retire and not to marry again, he feels a sense of freedom because he has returned to *la puta:*

I felt as though a tremendous weight was lifted from my shoulders. . . . I felt somehow light and free like when I first started on my beat. There's nothing left now but the *puta.* But she's not a *puta.* . . . You couldn't tell a whore from a bewitching lady. I'll keep her as long as I can.[62]

[59] *New York Post,* April 27, 1977, p. 44.

[60] In fact, Joseph Wambaugh assures his readers that *The Choirboys,* chronicling nearly a dozen unhappy marriages and unsavory family situations, "is the truest novel I've ever written."

[61] Robert Daley, *To Kill a Cop* (New York: Crown, 1976), p. 58.

[62] Joseph Wambaugh, *The Blue Knight* (New York: Dell, 1972), pp. 314-315.

Afterward Bumper "felt like the most vigorous and powerful man on earth, a real *macho*."[63] What wife, what marriage could compete with that remarkable whore?

Whatever the motivation of laymen or veteran police authors, their writings echo an adamant conviction permeating law enforcement in America. The fictional and the real merge indissolubly in the succinct comments by Andy Kilvinsky, Wambaugh's counselor cop (*The New Centurions*), who philosophizes, "This job isn't conducive to stable family relationships." Most members of police forces would agree because they are convinced that sinister occupational stresses hammer at their personal lives and that unhappiness and divorce are the natural conditions of their existence.[64] Is there a justification for these denigrators to attack the job as an oppressive intruder corroding family relationships? Or are they embracing a myth—the job as scapegoat—to use as a perfect defense mechanism to camouflage personal and familial deficiencies?

[63] Ibid., p. 315.
[64] See Howard D. Teten and John W. Minderman, "Police Personal Problems—Practical Considerations for Administrators," *FBI Law Enforcement Bulletin* (January 1977):8-15.

3

Power, Status, and the Family: The Policeman and the Physician

The backdrop at social gatherings varies, but whether it is a house party, cocktail hour, or an after-ski supper, as soon as new acquaintances learn that Arthur was formerly a policeman, he becomes the target of conversation. A psychological barrage escalates. It usually starts with scattered requests for advice from individuals with personal problems. Then unfailingly, the fusillade detonates a chorus of venomous jokes ridiculing policemen and malicious anecdotes about police corruption, brutality, and inefficiency.

In conversations with other police officers we confirmed the universality of this syndrome. Sensitized to these encounters, we discovered that this pattern is not only endemic to the police profession but that physicians also are magnets for "sick" jokes and verbal assaults. Radiating from this common center of interest, many overlapping lines of resemblance between the roles of policemen and physicians and their families can be traced. This similarity exists, although the public accords the highest status to the physician and a relatively low status to the policeman.

Each calling can point to a long and honorable tradition. The local constable and the family doctor tower as quasi-folk heroes in the growth of our country. Television capitalized on their universal appeal and romanticized the physician and the professional police officer as contemporary knights of chivalry. Ideally, each role demands altruism. The practitioners are expected to be available night and day to serve the public with loyalty, responsibility, and commitment when trouble, be it sickness or crime strikes. As soon as conditions return to normal, their services become expendable.

From the very beginning of their occupational careers, both police officer and physician must come to terms with the shock of their daily experience. In their preliminary training they learn to keep their equilibrium in an environment where blood, excrement, and death are normal conditions. Constantly, they are exposed to the backside of humanity with all its sordid and guilty secrets. To keep their sanity, and even to survive, most of them build a protective shield of cynicism around themselves as insulation against this human misery.[1] Without it, many would crack under the battering. Many do go under. Others feel guilt as a result of the frequently necessary lapses from professional ethics and idealism. Drug addiction, alcoholism, and suicide become occupational hazards.

[1] For the growth of cynicism among police recruits, see Arthur Niederhoffer, *Behind the Shield* (Garden City: Doubleday, 1967), pp. 46-47; for a parallel study of cynicism among medical students, see Howard S. Becker and Blanche Geer, "The Fate of Idealism in Medical School," *American Sociological Review* 23 (February 1958):51-53.

The social reality and the evolution of their roles confer upon physicians and police a peculiar combination of power that belies the humility of their oaths. Each promises to serve the people faithfully as he protects and preserves life. But as they gain experience and confidence, their duties frequently translate into a harsh type of regulation. While serving, they order their clients, they threaten them, they control the behavior of others.

The need for authority and control by the police is obvious. The essence of their duty calls for them to regulate, direct, and secure compliance. The art of police work consists in large measure of techniques to maintain authority and control, to gain compliance from the public without the necessity of resorting to force.

From the doctors' perspective the issue of control may be equally vital. In one model of the physician-patient relation, control was the nucleus around which the other dimensions revolved. Control meant the power of the doctor to direct the patient's behavior and, like the police officer's control, was best when it was rational and legitimate.[2] A subsequent study of doctors' views supported the model in many respects.

What police and physicians dislike most is challenge to their control and authority.[3] Yet challenges are unavoidable because the practitioners veil their real power by representing themselves as servants of the public. But when a client or patient accepts this facade as reality, both the doctor and the police officer resent being treated as a servant.

Several alternatives are available to restore control. Punishment for those who refuse to obey may be incarceration, either in a hospital or a prison. Or a doctor may decide that the case is not so drastic after all and write a prescription rather than send a patient to the hospital. In a comparable situation, the police officer writes a summons instead of arresting the challenger. But in severe cases they may choose to operate on the person, one with a scalpel, the other with a nightstick. Lurking behind this demand for control is a sense of fear. The policeman fears attack from his client, the criminal; the doctor fears attack by the sickness of his client, the patient.

One of the unpleasant but fundamental requirements is the necessity and obligation to ferret out secret, often unpleasant, and guilty knowledge from their clientele.[4] Each fulfills his responsibility best when he is cynical and

---

[2] Amasa B. Ford et al., *The Doctor's Perspective: Physicians View Their Patients and Practice* (Cleveland: Case Western Reserve Univ. Press, 1967), pp. 28-30, 144-145.

[3] Several studies have emphasized this point. For example, see Howard S. Becker et al. *Boys in White: Student Culture in Medical School* (Chicago: Univ. of Chicago Press, 1961), pp. 320-321; Victor G. Strecher, "When Subcultures Meet: Police-Negro Relations," in S.A. Yefsky, ed., *Law Enforcement, Science and Technology*, Vol. 1 (London: Academic Press, 1967), p. 704; and James Walsh, "Professionalism and the Police: The Cop as Medical Student," in Harlan Hahn, ed., *The Police in Urban Society* (Beverly Hills, Calif.: Sage Publications, 1970), p. 227.

[4] See, for example, Everett C. Hughes, "The Study of Occupations," in Robert K. Merton, Leonard Broom, and Leonard S. Cottrell, eds., *Sociology Today* (New York: Basic Books, 1959), p. 448, where in speaking of the police and the classical professions such as medicine, he states, "All of them must have license to get—and, in some degree, to keep secret—some order of guilty knowledge."

suspicious, when he checks statements carefully and probes deeply before deciding what action to take. If his action does not turn out to be the proper one, the client has legal remedies:—suits for damages for false arrest or abuse of civil rights, and suits for damages for malpractice.

The law recognizes that a patient must tell the physician the most intimate details of his or her life as part of the treatment process. Rules of evidence protect the confidentiality of these doctor-patient revelations. A doctor testifying in court is not permitted to divulge any statements made by the patient, even those admitting a crime, unless the patient expressly waives his or her rights. The police officer also radiates a mystique that impels people to confide in him and to ask for advice. A young recruit is often amazed when an experienced professional reveals secrets and complex problems that the novice can barely comprehend and then hangs anxiously on every word of guidance the younger officer offers, no matter how trite or noncommittal.

The Supreme Court has recognized this aura of psychological power that drives people, especially when they are in custody, to reveal anything. In effect, by its *Miranda* decision, the Court recognized the confidentiality of such confessions unless the person expressly waives his rights after being warned that he has a right to remain silent. Otherwise the policeman, like the doctor, cannot in testimony disclose the confession even if it did admit a crime.

When Studs Terkel went out into the streets a few years ago to record the daily lives of the workers of America, he taped one articulate and sensitive New York City policeman's reactions to his job. Bob Patrick, assigned to emergency service duty, described movingly his feelings of shock. He spoke vividly about the cases to which he had to respond almost daily: the cars folded like accordions from which he had to carry out a mangled girl with no face, adolescents with hands pulverized in meat grinders, people smashed to pieces under trains. Then Bob talked about his family.

You look across the breakfast table and see your son. My wife plenty times asked me, "How can you do that? How can you go under a train with a person that's severed the legs off [sic], come home and eat breakfast, and feel. . . ?" That's what I'm waiting for: when I can go home and not feel anything for my family. See, I have to feel.[5]

Doctors during their years of study work rotating shifts in hospitals; and like policemen, who also must maintain a schedule of work around the clock, they discover that natural rhythms are disrupted by this interference with their biological clocks. Although they may be experiencing peculiar physiological and psychological departures from the normal, both must develop a bearing to inspire comfort and confidence in people who are at the breaking point.

The stereotyped image of the policeman as law enforcement officer and crime fighter dominates and distorts our perception of his actual duties in society. Many studies repeatedly attempt to dispel this unrealistic portrait.

[5] Studs Terkel, *Working* (New York: Pantheon Books, 1974), p. 574.

Actual police work can be portioned into one-quarter crime prevention and three-quarters service to the community, much of it demanding the counseling and therapeutic skills of the officer as he assists people in trouble.

The idealized view of the physician popularly focuses on the doctor deeply involved in strictly medical practice—operating, injecting, examining, and prescribing. But an analogous identity crisis exists in medicine. As one doctor aptly described it:

In medicine, it is the same. A general practitioner handles more than 70% social kinds of inter-personal problems and 15 or 20% are of organic functions. The same sort of identity crisis goes on. Should we spend our time talking about somebody and his personal life, or should we be giving injections or doing surgery?[6]

It does not require a subliminal probe to perceive the affinity between the two occupations. In many respects, the police act as the paraprofessionals of medicine. Because so much of police work demands service rather than law enforcement duties, a sizable share of that service will involve saving lives and administering first aid to the injured or sick. Often a policeman on the beat spends a significant amount of his shift in hospitals and in the company of interns and residents who inhabit the emergency rooms.

When Arthur was assigned to the radio car, he and his partner frequently stayed at Bellevue Hospital for as many as three hours in an eight-hour tour of duty in the course of processing aided and accident cases, investigating suspicious injuries, identifying unconscious persons, and conveying prisoners who needed medical treatment. Occasionally, when the radio car team was ordered to report to Bellevue at 3 A.M., they would convivially bring along a pizza and sodas for the staff of doctors in the emergency room.

All these threads are woven into an occupational self-image. The police are not so naive that they dream of themselves as doctors in blue uniforms patroling the streets of the cities looking for patients to operate on. But when they are asked to rate police on many traits and then compare these ratings with other professions, they rate medical doctors closest to the police.

Nearly 500 midwestern city and state police officers were given a semantic differential questionnaire in which they were asked to rate 13 groups, including police, ministers and priests, lawyers, medical doctors, businessmen, women, and college students. The police had a very positive self-image, rating themselves high in the following traits: "sane, clean, honest, trustworthy, dependable, healthy, law-abiding, safe and sincere."[7] The point that interests us most in this study

[6] Forest Hospital Foundation, Report of the Fifth Annual Police Seminar, Des Plaines, Ill., 1969, pp. 46-47.

[7] Dae H. Chang and Charles H. Zastrow, "Police Evaluative Perceptions of Themselves, the General Public and Selected Occupational Groups," *Journal of Criminal Justice* 4 (1976):24.

was the ranking of the groups. In first place came the priests and ministers. It was followed by the "I am," which indicates self-concept. In third place were the police. Closest to the police, separated by a mean only 0.007 lower, were medical doctors.[8] So there is some connection in the minds of the police with the medical profession.

The wives of these practitioners cannot escape the vicissitudes of their husbands' work: not for them a nine-to-five routine with quiet evenings spent watching television with their husbands. They learn to cope with revolving and unpredictable schedules. Emergencies become a regular pattern. Eventually, they reach a point where they no longer burst into tears when their husbands are called away just when the roast is ready to be served. Even lovemaking must be interrupted when duty calls. The wives have to grow accustomed to sleeping alone those nights when their husbands are working. Every time the telephone rings, the blare arouses a sense of anxiety. Will that call destroy the plans for a pleasant family activity? What emergency does it signal? How long will the doctor or the police officer be away from home? Where other types of families can plan events long ahead, these families learn from experience that the exigencies of the occupation will more than likely disrupt schedules. One bright-eyed youngster, a doctor's son, asked to draw a picture of his father, responded by sketching two scenes of his father—one sleeping and the other on the telephone.

The children share some of the special status. They are identified by their peers as children of doctors or police officers. Occasionally, in school, teachers will chide the children of police officers by saying, "You shouldn't act that way. After all, your father is a police officer." And what are two of the most popular children's games if not "cops and robbers" and "playing doctor"?

Wives, guardians of precious moments of privacy, learn the skills of diversion and diplomacy to barricade their homes and husbands from the frequent intrusions of neighbors and friends demanding assistance. At a rap session one harassed policeman's wife exclaimed, "He's really not on block patrol; I just say he's not home." This type of annoyance seems ubiquitous. A police constable's wife from Queensland, Australia, complained:

I continually have neighbors and friends coming to my door enquiring if my husband is at home and if not I am expected to answer their queries on anything from where to pay a ticket to how they go about reporting a stolen car. Even a leisurely Sunday afternoon drive can be spoiled by the fact that my husband is unable to relax from his job.[9]

[8] Ibid., pp. 17-27. In contrast to the high rank the police assigned to doctors was the low rank accorded to lawyers (10), college students (11), politicians (12), and prison inmates (13 and last). It is an interesting coincidence to find that college students, years before, had responded to the same type of semantic differential questionnaire. They rated police eleventh out of fifteen occupations and described them as sour, dishonest, and unsuccessful. Joseph R. Gusfield and Michael Schwartz, "The Meanings of Occupational Prestige: Reconsideration of the NORC Scale," *American Sociological Review* 28 (1963):269.

[9] Monica M. Amos, "Views from Down Under," *FBI Law Enforcement Bulletin* 45 (March 1976):15.

Doctors' wives block similar invasions via telephone from those seeking medical advice. Their acquaintances soon learn that there is no hot line to the doctor. One wife repeats interminably, "He's asleep. I can't awaken him now. He's been up all night." Others decisively terminate these middle-of-the-night intrusions by sending out bills for the emergency calls.

A source of permanent anxiety for the family is the ever-present accoutrement, the identifying symbol: in one case, the doctor's bag of instruments and medicines, in the other, the leather holster holding his instrument, the .38 Special police revolver. There is no way to escape the necessity of eternal vigilance in guarding these tools of the trade. A moment of forgetfulness or a careless lapse may result in tragedy when a curious child fingers his father's gun. How many children have accidentally shot themselves with their father's police revolver because in a moment of forgetfulness he neglected to lock it up? How many children have been poisoned by eating the pills on their father's desks when he forgot to lock them up in his bag?

Another gnawing problem is what to do about that secret fascinating information picked up automatically in the course of a day's work. How much should they tell their wives? Can they be true to their occupational codes that demand total confidentiality and fulfill the trust they owe their wives to share with them their inmost thoughts? To confide too much might create a legal or criminal responsibility for improper revelation. At the same time, they may have a compelling emotional need to relieve tension by rehashing some of the traumatic episodes. At one o'clock in the morning, how receptive a listener will a wife be?

Although doctors' wives have much higher prestige than police wives, each is marked for special attention by the other women in the community. There is even a similarity between them when they drive. The wife of a doctor whose car sports M.D. plates may possibly take more liberties with the traffic regulations than her doctor husband will. For example, she may double-park her car when she goes shopping, expecting that the special license plate will protect her from a traffic summons. Wives of police officers may not hesitate to display Police Association cards on their windshields, expecting to be passed over when the police officer comes around to ticket illegally parked cars.

Despite the disparity of policemen and physicians in class and status, their marriages suggest striking parallels.[10] In each, the husband tends to be conservative in ideology, authoritarian, and patriarchal in interpersonal relationships. His wife is likely to be vexed by nagging concerns about his job: the unpredictability of his schedule, loneliness and insecurity when he works nights,

[10]On the North-Hatt Scale of Occupational Prestige (1963) physicians ranked second among the 90 occupations included. Policemen filled the forty-seventh position, two slots below the midpoint of the scale. Although policemen are on the verge of middle-class status in their lifestyle, sociological textbooks still relegate the police occupation to the lower echelons. For example, see George Ritzer, *Man and His Work* (New York: Appleton-Century Crofts, 1972), pp. 249-251.

resentment that he places his occupation ahead of his family (when an emergency call can supersede their convenience), and finally, a sense of isolation because he communicates and confides so little about his career.

Her underlying tensions may surface into anxiety about her husband's possible temptations with other women. As in most other occupations, physicians and policemen will have many occasions to interact with female co-workers. The closed circle of the hospital world and the sensual insulation of the radio car can bind the members of the team with chords of intimacy. Medicine and law enforcement radiate power and authority and generate thankfulness and dependence from their clients. As a concomitant of this professional relationship, social controls are frequently lowered or even erased. Wives worry and twitch with jealousy that this release of sanctions may be a prelude to a switch to intimacy.

Interestingly, Frank Slaughter, a doctor himself, analyzed this situation in a popular novel, *Doctors' Wives,* depicting five unhappy marriages. The blurb on the dust jacket charted the etiology of the conjugal epidemic:

Doctors' Wives' Disease is not an imaginary ailment. For, in the closed, inbred society of a great medical center, these women, wives of superbly successful physicians are driven by loneliness, boredom, and frustration along forbidden pathways. And alcohol, drugs, and promiscuity become their alternatives to despair.[11]

Although the medical novel trails police fiction in quantity, variety, and popularity, the two genres match each other in maligning the marriages of their protagonists.[12] Nevertheless, to a middle-class girl (and her mother) a medical student, or even better, an established physician, is the ultimate conjugal catch. After matrimony the stresses of a profession that infiltrate her private life so intensely may cloud this initial euphoria. Her husband's high status and power may be a handicap and place her at a disadvantage in any internecine conflict. This syndrome of disenchantment and discontent may incubate from vague complaints into the "doctors' wives' disease," described and diagnosed by Dr. Robert T. Taubman, a psychiatrist at the University of Oregon Medical School. He analyzed the causes and traced them to "differences in maturity between doctors and their wives, the strains imposed by the husband's long and intense work schedule, and the wife's resentment over being left alone at home."[13]

[11] Frank Slaughter, *Doctors' Wives* (Garden City: Doubleday, 1967).

[12] A brief survey of medical novels reveals that doctor and wife are favorite subjects. Almost every marriage in the following books is an unhappy one: Elizabeth Seifert, *Doctor Takes a Wife* (New York: Dodd, Mead, 1952); Frank Slaughter, *Doctors' Wives* (New York: Award Books, 1968); Benjamin Siegel, *Doctors and Wives* (New York: David McKay, 1970); Milton Bass, *The Doctor Who Made House Calls* (New York: Putnams Sons, 1973); Brian Moore, *The Doctor's Wife* (New York: Farrar, Straus and Giroux, 1976); Hugh Miller, *The Dissector* (New York: St. Martin's Press, 1976).

[13] *Time,* November 6, 1972, p. 100. See also Irving Rosow and K. Daniel Rose, "Divorce Among Doctors," *Journal of Marriage and the Family* 34 (November 1972):588.

To avoid a high divorce rate among doctors and their wives, Taubman suggests a course of treatment: attendance at a therapeutic session in which the participants view an hour-long videotape of interviews with four psychiatrists who discuss the causes and symptoms of the wives' distress. Realistically, however, a doctor's troubled wife who is experiencing intense emotional problems will not be reached by a superficial seminar. In fact, the best remedy for her malaise would be to have her husband in constant attendance. Since this is an impossible dream, she gropes for an equivalent prescription.

One private psychiatric hospital admitted so many doctors' wives for treatment that it sponsored a research project to investigate the relationship between the husband's professional activity and the wife's illness. The 50 wives in the sample manifested characteristic symptoms: depression, addiction to drugs or alcohol, and somatic disorders, especially persistent pain. They accused their husbands of being cold and undemonstrative, of failing to fulfill their responsibilities as husbands and fathers, of being dependent and passive, of behaving in a compulsive or perfectionistic manner, and of excluding wives from their professional lives. But the chronic complaint was the husbands' absence.[14]

The policeman's wife is not hampered by a sense of inferiority because she is well aware that society has relegated her spouse to a middle rung on the status ladder, and she accepts the position. The internal frictions in the police family instead revolve around the husband's status and role. He must resolve the contradiction of a divided self-image that vacillates between his occupational role: cop as master or cop as servant of the public. Can he divest himself of this dichotomy of personality when he doffs his uniform?

This type of problem aggravates the many concerns the police wife shares with the wife of the physician. But with less status, less money, less leisure, and less commitment to the medical profession, the police wife is not inclined to seek solace in medicine or psychiatry. She hopefully looks in the direction of the police department for a more immediate, less sophisticated source of guidance. Many of our police wife respondents pleaded for sessions of orientation and training to help them cope with their problems. In response to this need, the Los Angeles County Sheriff's Department foresightedly developed a spouses' training program and an annual seminar for wives of law enforcement personnel (always oversubscribed) that "emphasizes the importance of the wife and family in the life of a law enforcement officer. It provides an opportunity for the women to express their concerns, ideas, and ways they can improve their relationships."[15]

Paradoxically, although the wives reach out for counseling from the department, their mates resist it fiercely. Informal conversations with policemen confirmed that even when confronted with marital discord, they would refuse to

[14] James L. Evans, "Psychiatric Illness in the Physician's Wife," *American Journal of Psychiatry* 122 (August 1965):159-163.
[15] John Stratton, "The Law Enforcement Family: Programs for Spouses," *FBI Law Enforcement Bulletin* 45 (March 1976):21-22.

seek help from the departmental psychologists. A generalized suspicion of psychological testing and counseling pervades the job, particularly among the lower ranks. The men are afraid of being labeled as stupid or stigmatized as psychotic. The underlying fear is that such denigration may lead to dismissal. Ordered by his superior to report to the psychological services unit for testing, one New York City police officer felt so threatened that he instituted legal action to challenge the command.[16] Once again the parallel with physicians emerges: a progress report of the American Psychiatric Association's Task Force on Suicide Prevention stresses that doctors generally are resistant to and delay as long as possible in seeking psychiatric counseling.[17]

The familial contours of policeman and physician continue to match in marital patterns, literally to the breaking point, the disruption in divorce. Even when there is breakdown and dissolution, the two groups maintain symmetry. Large-scale surveys of physicians and police completed independently in 1968 supported the conclusion that their respective rates of divorce ranked comparably low: 16.4 per thousand or 1.64 percent for doctors and 2 percent for police, compared to a national rate of 2.6 percent for adult men in the United States. Significantly, the correspondence holds for marriage as well as divorce. Detailed analysis of the surveys pointed to a higher incidence of marriage: 87.4 percent for physicians and 93 percent for policemen, each surpassing the national rate of 75.6 percent for adult males.[18]

Nonetheless, in our conversations with physicians and policemen, many vehemently denied and disparaged these statistical conclusions of the social scientists. They insisted that divorce rates were very high. This prevailing opinion is based on the assumption that the pressures of the work situation must inevitably undermine marriage stability. We suggest, parenthetically, that perhaps the emotional impact of personal involvement in the trauma of a particular friend's or relative's marital malaise metastasizes into this subjective and intuitive projection of a divorce epidemic. (We explore the subject of police divorce in depth in chapter 7.)

The Forest Hospital Foundation's Fifth Annual Police Seminar in December 1969 was mainly devoted to an analysis of problems associated with the family of the police officer. Throughout the workshops, conducted by Dr. Karl Wilbrich, director of the Family Therapy Service at Forest Hospital in Des Plaines, Illinois, the participants strongly supported their contention that the rate of divorce for police officers continues to soar. They projected the experience of a small department into a generalization about the larger world of the police.

---

[16] *New York Post,* January 16, 1976, p. 2.

[17] Mathew Ross, "Physicians Who Commit Suicide: The Deck Is Not Stacked," *Psychiatric Opinion* 12 (May 1975):26-30.

[18] For divorce and marriage rates of physicians, see Rosow and Rose, "Divorce Among Doctors," pp. 587-589. For the comparable rates of policemen, see Nelson A. Watson and James W. Sterling, *Police and Their Opinions* (Washington, D.C.: International Association of Chiefs of Police, 1969), pp. 26, 105-119.

Typical comments by police discussants in the family workshops reinforced their convictions:

I recall, reading "Cop," recently, and I think it was in that book that it was brought out that one of the highest divorce rates in the entire country revolves around law enforcement officers.[19]

A police officer's wife attending the workshop underscored the popular view that the police divorce rate is astronomical:

...the divorce rate is staggering. Even on our small town police force it is staggering, and it is just awful. Really, percentage-wise it is really bad. I feel that maybe some of this could be averted if maybe they had something for the wives, because their ability to speak out against the job is practically nil. I feel that maybe if there were some outlet for the wives, where they could get together and have a jam session and really knock it against the wall and really get out all those inhibitions within you then sometimes I think that would be more helpful. There has got to be a reason for these divorces. I think a policeman's wife is a very lonely person basically.[20]

Another wife traced the causes of "divorce fever" to unavoidable exposure to a machismo infection on the job.

I think that the divorce rate that bothers you is always going to be high, for the simple reason that every new man who comes into our department has to walk the beat. Now we have two or three all-night restaurants and I don't know of a man who has come on in the last few years and has walked that beat, that some gal doesn't shine up to him. This particular man has to have enough moral character not to get involved, and if he does get involved it ends up in a divorce.[21]

Countering this explanation, the rejoinder of a self-assured wife revealed her husband's antidote to temptation.

My husband has a wonderful way of telling me about these women who he tries to give these tickets to, and their skirt is up to here and all of a sudden the blouse becomes unbuttoned. He'll tell me, "You know what I told her? Don't bother, I've got better at home." Now what more can a man say to you? He's

[19] Forest Hospital Foundation, Report, p. 20. Although *Cop!* by L.H. Whittemore (New York: Holt, Rinehart and Winston, 1969) recounts the lives of various police officers in New York, Chicago, and San Francisco, most of whom are divorced, some more than once, there is no actual statistic or statement about the alleged high rate of police divorce. We are grateful to the Forest Hospital Foundation for granting us permission to quote from the report.

[20] Ibid., p. 29.

[21] Ibid., p. 37.

telling you his experience with this other woman, and at the same time he's flattering you.[22]

And finally, one husband's diagnosis shattered the spell of high divorce rates:

I don't question the statistics on the divorce rate of police officers, because I myself feel that it is no higher than the average person living in a metropolitan area. I don't feel the policemen have any higher divorce rate at all. I think the policeman has more contact with the opposite sex but I don't feel that their divorce rate is higher.[23]

But that astute policeman's acute perception is a solitary voice. Fully two-thirds of the police respondents in our survey expressed the conviction that their families experienced more problems than others. Because of this sensitivity and pessimism, they magnify the tremors of marital stress into a domestic earthquake—divorce.

Actually, there are occupational restraints upon an officer's freedom to become involved in extramarital situations that might lead to divorce. He lacks the curtain of privacy that other citizens can draw over their personal lives and family problems. Functioning in a total institution and conforming to the demands of a quasi-military code that has lagged considerably behind the current patterns of permissiveness, the police officer's sphere of action has circumscribed limits. The expectations of an above-reproach model of conduct place him in double jeopardy from his commanding officer on the job and from his wife in the home. If the policeman husband transgresses, the wife often complains to the police department.

Curiously, the same police departments that seem callous and uncaring in the treatment of their members (demanding long hours of work without relief or denying fires to warm the cold feet of officers on frigid, fixed posts) will often extend themselves to cooperate with complaining wives to straighten out a marital problem. If the wife reports that her husband gambles away his paycheck, the department may permit the wife to pick up the check herself. If she communicates a suspicion that her mate is showing too much interest in a woman who lives on his post, the officer may be transferred to another post or even another precinct. When the gossip about the amatory exploits of a police sergeant Lothario reached the ears of his superior, he found himself contemplating his peccadillos in pastoral solitude in a Siberia of precincts, a lonely park.

The police officer carrying on an affair may also face the possibility of double trouble. If his wife does not complain, his mistress may appear at the station house to demand what she sees as her rights. When this occurred in the

---

[22] Ibid.

[23] Ibid., p. 54.

Nassau County Police Department, a police sergeant was brought up on charges and dismissed for committing the crime of adultery. The sergeant has appealed his dismissal in federal court on the grounds that

the statute against adultery had not been enforced in the state for more than fifty years regardless of the standing of the persons in the community.
... that adultery was no more uncommon in the personal, private lives of policemen than it was in the personal, private lives of persons in other professions.
... that the alleged crime of adultery did not in any way violate the standards of morality of either Nassau County or the State of New York.[24]

The threat of punishment, ranging from a mild reprimand all the way to dismissal, may be an immediate deterrent to promiscuity and other forms of misbehavior undermining the stability of marriage. But the long-term problems of unhappy family situations dammed up in this fashion may build up explosive pressure.

Dr. Paul Friedman, one of the few researchers granted access to the full case histories of more than 90 suicides among New York City police officers, concluded that marital discord was a leading cause of the very high suicide rate at that time, and that in many of the cases, suicide was a symbolic act of extreme aggression against the wives: "Of the men who were married, 50 percent manifested varying degrees of hostility toward their wives during their last days—restrained hostility which culminated in impotent anger at the time of the suicide."[25] One case Friedman described was neither a symbolic nor impotent act. The police officer, known as "king of the beat" and called "stud horse" by his co-workers, was threatened with exposure by his wife because of his liaisons with several mistresses. He shot her and then turned his gun on himself.[26]

Once it became clear that family dynamics could have some relation to suicide, we searched for reliable data about suicide rates of police and physicians. We communicated with the National Center for Health Statistics of the Department of Health, Education and Welfare. Its only national study linking occupation, mortality, and cause of death occurred in 1950 and concluded that policemen, sheriffs, and marshals had a high suicide rate, nearly twice as high as the national average for males, which hovered at that time around 18 per 100,000. That would place the rate for police at 35 per 100,000. Figures computed on physicians' suicides were just slightly higher than the national average of 18.[27]

[24] *New York Times,* July 20, 1976, p. 35.

[25] Paul Friedman, "Suicide Among Police: A Study of Ninety-three Suicides Among New York City Policemen 1934-1940," in Edwin S. Shneidman, ed., *Essays in Self Destruction* (New York: Science House, 1967), pp. 434-435.

[26] Ibid.

[27] Correspondence from the National Center for Health Statistics, February 19, 1976.

But only 15 years later, in the period 1965 to 1967, the rate of suicide among physicians had almost doubled, reaching 37 per 100,000.[28] That rate has remained high over the intervening period. Alarmed at this trend, the American Psychiatric Association established the Task Force on Suicide Prevention for the purpose of reducing suicide rates among physicians. Its research confirmed the high rate of suicide among physicians, particularly psychiatrists and female physicians.[29]

Was this distressing surge in physicians' suicides paralleled by the police? Literature on police suicide is sparse. More than half focuses on the New York City Police Department, the largest in the country and one of the very few that publishes its suicide statistics in its annual reports (at least it did so until 1970).[30] Because the statistical picture of police suicide in the last 25 years is based on studies that are 10 to 20 years old, extrapolated from small numbers[31] and therefore leading to inconsistent interpretations, they are inapplicable to the current scene.[32]

Table 3-1, which summarizes the reports on police suicide, confirms the anachronistic and inconsistent elements. Utilizing 1950 as the cutoff year and going back, we can see that most of the cities reported high suicide rates for their police. Yet, the minuscule totals for St. Louis and Denver cannot be charted as high. The pattern of police suicide becomes more complex after 1958. Niederhoffer computed a figure of 22.5 as the suicide rate for the New York City Police Department from 1950 to 1965 which was one and one-half times as great as the rate for the New York City white male population.[33] Lewis reviewed that series and showed that in each five-year period the rates became smaller.[34] Heiman carried the investigation to 1973 and reported the rate of suicide for New York City police at 19.1. He recognizes that the rate is lower than in past years, and he attributes the decline to better selection of police candidates and a more progressive attitude toward mental hygiene. But Heiman considers a rate of 19.1 too high: "Yet, it is disquieting to observe a rate almost twice as high as that for the general population of New York City. The etiology

[28] P.H. Blachly, William Disher, and Gregory Roduner, "Suicide by Physicians," *Bulletin of Suicidology* (December 1968):1-18.

[29] Ross, "Physicians Who Commit Suicide," pp. 26-30.

[30] The following studies of police suicide concentrate on the data for the New York City Police Department. See, for example, Friedman, "Suicide Among Police," pp. 414-449; Niederhoffer, *Behind the Shield*, pp. 96-97; Rodney Lewis, "Toward an Understanding of Police Anomie," *Journal of Police Science and Administration* 1 (December 1973):484-492; Michael Heiman, "The Police Suicide," *Journal of Police Science and Administration* 3 (September 1975):267-273; and Michael Heiman, "Police Suicides Revisited," *Suicide*, 5 (Spring 1975):5-20.

[31] Zane Nelson and Wilford Smith, "The Law Enforcement Profession: An Incident of High Suicide," *Omega* 1 (November 1970):293-299.

[32] Pow-meng Yap, *Suicide in Hong Kong* (Hong Kong: Hong Kong Univ. Press, 1958), p. 33.

[33] Niederhoffer, *Behind the Shield*, pp. 96-97.

[34] Lewis, "Toward an Understanding," p. 486.

Table 3-1
Police Suicide

Location of Police Force	Period	Number of Police Suicides	Rate of Suicide	Reporter
New York City	1928-1933	51	High	Friedman
New York City	1934-1939	91	High	Friedman
Chicago	1934-1939	18	High	Heiman
Denver	1934-1939	0	Low	Heiman
St. Louis	1934-1939	2	High	Heiman
San Francisco	1934-1939	4	High	Heiman
All United States	1950	95	High	National Center for Health Statistics Department of Health, Education and Welfare
New York City	1950-1965	81	High	Niederhoffer
New York City	1960-1973	74	High	Heiman
State of Wyoming	1960-1968	7	High	Nelson and Smith
Hong Kong	1958	—[a]	Low	Yap
London	1960-1973	16	Low	Heiman

Source: Paul Friedman, "Suicide Among Police: A Study of Ninety-three Suicides Among New York City Policemen, 1934-1940," in Edwin S. Shneidman, ed., *Essays in Self-Destruction* (New York: Science House, 1967); Michael Heiman, "The Police Suicide," *Journal of Police Science and Administration* 3 (September 1975); Personal communication from the National Center for Health Statistics of the Department of Health, Education and Welfare, Washington, D.C., February 19, 1976. Arthur Niederhoffer, *Behind the Shield* (Garden City, N.Y.: Doubleday, 1967); Zane Nelson and Wilford Smith, "The Law Enforcement Profession: An Incident of High Suicide," *Omega* 1 (November 1970); and P.M. Yap, *Suicide in Hong Kong* (Hong Kong: Hong Kong University Press, 1958).

[a]Not tabulated by Yap.

of this discrepancy as well as contrast to the rate found for London are subjects for further inquiry."[35]

In another study comparing New York City and London police suicide rates from 1960 to 1973, Heiman found the London police suicide rate to be 5.8: "Thus the London suicide rate is virtually no different from its white-male urban population; whereas the New York City police suicide rate is almost twice that of its white-male urban population."[36]

Heiman's figures for the 10-year period from 1964 to 1973 show that the suicide rate for the New York City Police Department was only 17.2. Once again there is a problem of interpretation. Heiman is right in declaring that the rate is

[35] Heiman, "Police Suicides Revisited," p. 19.

[36] Heiman, "The Police Suicide," pp. 270-271.

twice as high as that of the general New York City population, which was 8.3 in 1973.[37] The rate for males in the city would be a little higher—about 11. But when any expert extrapolates from these local rates to the national scene, as most do, they must reconcile the 17.2 rate, which may be high in New York City, with the national rate of suicide for adult males, which was about 18 in 1973.[38] Are they willing to accept the statistics and conclude that the rate of police suicide is about the same as that for the national adult male population?

The Nelson and Smith study is no more convincing. There were only seven police suicides in Wyoming during an eight-year period, fewer than one per year. How much credence can we attach to a rate based on not even one case a year, which the authors of the study admit to be statistically inconclusive? At the opposite end of the spectrum are the low rates for Hong Kong and London. We are entitled to ask how high the actual rate of police suicide is.

The instrument of death was the police revolver in most cases. Since the British police do not carry revolvers, this may be the crucial variable associated with the low suicide rate of the London police.

The conclusion seems inescapable that police suicide is far more complex a phenomenon than experts have assumed. It requires more research at the primary level, a gathering of valid figures of suicide from many police departments. Nevertheless, there is a logical, although tragic, inference that can be drawn. Since there are converging patterns among the large urban police forces in the United States, predictably they will be infected with the same suicide producing viruses: the quasi-military system, the presence of the revolver, job stress, alienation from the community they serve, and an occupational ideology pervaded by cynicism. There is reason to believe that if the data were available, the rates of police suicide throughout the country would be comparable to those of the New York City police.

The data on physicians' suicide, more specific than those concerning the police, include relevant figures for the medical specialties. We explored the possibility that there might be a positive correlation between the rates of suicide and divorce despite the realization that the differences among the various categories were not very large. Table 3-2 ranks 15 medical specialties for which data were available. Rank 1 is reserved for the highest rate, and rank 15 is the lowest. Although there was a small positive correlation between the rankings for suicide and divorce, the figure was so small that no significance could be attached to it.[39]

[37] Personal communication from the New York City Health Department, Bureau of Health Statistics and Analysis, July 13, 1976.

[38] Personal communication from the National Center for Health Statistics of the United States, Department of Health, Education and Welfare, February 19, 1976.

[39] We correlated the rankings of suicide and divorce using Spearman's coefficient for ranked data:
$$P = \frac{1 - 6\Sigma D^2}{N(N^2 - 1)} = .19$$

Table 3-2
Suicide and Divorce Rates Among Physicians

Medical Specialty	Physicians' Suicide in the U.S., 1967		Physicians' Divorce in California, 1968	
	Rank	Rate	Rank	Rate
Psychiatry	1	61	2	19.1
Opthalmology and Otolaryngology	2	55	8	14.0
Preventive medicine	3	54	15	3.3
Anesthesiology	4	52	13	5.5
Neurology	5	38	4	15.7
Administrative medicine	6	37	5	14.8
Obstetrics/gynecology	7	36	6.5	14.4
Orthopedic surgery	8	35	1	22.6
Internal medicine	9.5	34	11	11.2
General practice	9.5	34	3	16.6
Urology	11	30	12	8.6
Radiology	12	27	10	12.9
Surgery	13.5	25	9	13.4
Pathology	13.5	25	14	4.2
Pediatrics	15	10	6.5	14.4
Average rate		37		14.3

Source: Adapted from the data reported in P.H. Blachly, William Disher, and Gregory Roduner, "Suicide by Physicians," *Bulletin of Suicidology* (December 1968):5; and from Irving Rosow and K. Daniel Rose, "Divorce Among Doctors," *Journal of Marriage and the Family* 34 (1972):595. The average of 14.3 for the rate of physicians' divorce was derived by Rosow and Rose.
Note: The rate for suicide is rate per 100,000, and the rate for divorce is rate per 1,000. The divorce rate for purposes of comparison will translate into 1.43 percent, a very low rate, far below the national average.

The comparison of the physicians' rates of divorce and suicide did provide some interesting insights. For example, the specialty of pathology was low in both scales, while obstetrics-gynecology, administrative medicine, and neurology were all concentrated in the middle of each scale. But the most fascinating and distressing statistic of all is the rate for psychiatry, that specialty of medicine to which troubled patients threatened by suicidal impulses or marital conflicts come for help. Psychiatrists tallied the highest suicide rate and placed second highest in divorce.

The authors of the studies speculate that the most convincing explanation for physicians' suicide is the extremely high level of stress in the profession. One often overlooked element of that stress is the sensitive physician's knowledge of the pain and suffering his patients endure and of how little he can do to relieve them. One authority on suicide suspects that this sensitivity to pain accounts for many euthanatic suicides among physicians. Aware of their own serious, perhaps terminal illness, anticipating the prolonged, painful, hopeless future course of events, they take their own prescription of quick-acting lethal drugs to escape the agony.[40] This, of course, is an unconfirmed hypothesis. But in the tabulation of the means of suicide of 200 doctors, 72 were attributed to drugs. The second leading cause, accounting for 65 of these suicides, turned out to be gunshot wounds.[41] Ironically, police officers and physicians, both sworn to preserve life, not only violate their oath when they take their own lives, but also choose the same instrument of self-destruction—the gun.

[40] Jacques Choron, *Suicide* (New York: Charles Scribner's Sons, 1972), p. 105.

[41] Blachly, Disher, and Roduner, "Suicide by Physicians," p. 3.

4

The Police Mystique: From Station House to Ranch House

Whether you color the uniform the midnight blue of the New York City Police Force or the forest green of the Menlo Park (California) Department, the aura of the police officer becomes intensified when he is in full regalia. The men on patrol generally project the image of strength, virility, good looks, and eligibility.

Thus it did not require visual aids to convince a graduate class of female elementary and high school teachers that policemen might be excellent marital prospects. Lecturing about the police to that class, Arthur described the many attractive qualities that distinguished policemen. At the close of the session, seven young women in the class inquired how they could join the police force, their interest probably motivated by the anticipation that such a move might be the checkmate in the marriage game.

Detective Harvey Schlossberg, who heads the psychological services unit of the New York City Police Department, supports the view that policemen patrolling in uniform exude a unique pheromone that attracts women. Relying on personal data tempered with a sprinkling of Freud, he explains:

But when I became a cop, no woman rejected me for another man, older or younger. It was difficult to keep the women away. A man in a policeman's uniform seems very seductive to women. It isn't a policeman's face or body but his uniform that women respond to. And the gun and the nightstick. All sex symbols. In the policeman you find id and superego combined—an unbeatable combination. Women not only are fascinated by a policeman, but consider the conquest of a cop a great challenge. He is to them the most powerful man of all, the big daddy of childhood.[1]

What is more, their official powers clothe the police with license to enter homes without arousing suspicion when husbands are away at work. Their legal authority produces situations where they have influence or control over women. A classic example is that of the officer who stops a woman driver for a traffic violation. A frequent response of many women in such incidents is to try to avoid the service of a summons or an arrest by using their sexual wiles, ranging from almost unconsciously seductive body language to more overt propositions. Clearly, where there is potent physical capacity, temptation, and opportunity, there will be some officers who succumb.

The police have yet to reach the height of popularity of rock and roll stars

[1] Harvey Schlossberg and Lucy Freeman, *Psychologist with a Gun* (New York: Coward, McCann and Geoghegan, 1974), p. 50.

60

or professional baseball and football superjocks who have to contend with groupies. There are invariably, however, a few women who seem to enjoy sharing their sexual favors with the complement of a specific police precinct.

In an autobiographical novel, a psychiatrist reports that a friend of hers worked "her way through nearly an entire police precinct" to stave off loneliness. Then, realizing that it was ridiculous to sleep around and still be miserable, the friend decided that she might just as well get paid for it. Curiously, her experience as a prostitute only made her appreciate her former police lovers.[2]

On a more cosmopolitan scale, a young lady from Arkansas called a press conference to report that she liked and respected officers of the law to such a degree that she indulged in interstate sexual relations with a large number, possibly up to 200, of policemen of all ranks but concentrated her erotic efforts in the states of Arkansas and Tennessee. How different from the strict constructionists in other departments was the police director in Tennessee who confirmed that news flash with an investigation of his own. He announced publicly that he would not discharge any of the 24 subordinates and 15 commanding officers on his force for their excessive zeal in forging interstate amity. That director was merciful "because he learned that some illicit sexual activity by police officers had not been seriously frowned upon in the past."[3]

Traditionally, machismo reaches its peak in the culture of the locker room. The police are no exception. As the squads change in and out of uniform within the privacy of the locker room, the most outrageous claims of sexual prowess are stridently proclaimed. In the ambience of the changing room, studded with the confidentiality of this closed society, married policemen enter into the spirit of licentious banter on equal terms with the benedicts. And knowing that there is no tape recorder about to immortalize their phallic verbal jousting, the group enjoys the camaraderie of its intimate sanctum, all experiencing vicariously the lurid scenarios of a few stalwarts. Their embroidered tales of sexual dalliance act as a safety valve for unwinding tension before and after their tours of duty.

In their own locker-room stories, officers talk tough. They brag about the criminals, cheats, and other nasty folk they deal with. A few become gun freaks. Others are superjocks. Many more are superstuds. The irregular hours, the opportunity to meet women while on the job, the bragging of fellow cops, and the freedom of movement all lead to playing around.[4]

But for the most part, there are few superstuds on the beat. Instead, the average patrolman is a family man whose sexual fantasies never materialize,

[2] Judith Benetar, M.D., *Admissions: Notes from a Woman Psychiatrist* (New York: Charterhouse, 1974), p. 202.

[3] For an account of this incident see *New York Post,* October 30, 1973, p. 67; and *Hartford Courant,* December 15, 1973, p. 2.

[4] Georgette Bennett-Sandler and Earl Ubell, "Time Bombs in Blue," *New York,* March 21, 1977, p. 50.

whose thoughts are occupied with more mundane problems, whose once erect posture now curves into a little paunch, whose aching feet plod protestingly through the tour's routine activities as he conscientiously performs his duties. Nevertheless, the policeman gradually absorbs the occupational mystique, composed of traditional police conservatism and a typical male chauvinist point of view about the nature and role of women and the proper form of marriage.

Feminists have been sensitized to and become deeply resentful of this aspect of male chauvinism. They are convinced that this veneer of masculine supremacy conceals a layer of suspicion and denigration of the female that in its most moderate form postulates that women's place is in the home and that women are making a mistake by their invasion of masculine occupations like law enforcement.

College-educated police officers in particular respond with guilt feelings when they are accused of being male chauvinists. But they can accumulate supporting evidence to deny the allegations of the militant women's movement from the official evaluation of male police officers' attitudes toward policewomen on patrol. Researchers have concluded that initially, about half the men advocated equality for policewomen, and that after a year's experience working with their female counterparts, the attitudes of the men improved slightly, although not significantly.[5]

Probably a majority of the patrol force would acknowledge, albeit somewhat begrudgingly, that it was only fair to allow policewomen to break out of their cloistered confinement of clerical, juvenile, and matron duties to attain parity in pay, work assignment, and promotion. But when the specific issue arose of policewomen riding in tandem with the men in radio cars, a lively controversy ensued whose reverberations are still echoing through many police forces, dredging emotions and feelings that had been kept in check up to that time.

Wherever police administrators attempted to introduce policewomen as partners to the men in the radio cars, explosions occurred. Vociferous wives of police officers attacked this female incursion with every weapon in their arsenal. Not even a temporary training program was permitted to operate unobstructedly. In New Orleans, six policewomen, after graduation from the police academy, were assigned to radio cars with male officers as chauffeurs to familiarize them with a range of police duties. A roomful of angry wives protested indignantly against the co-ed cars.[6] (How incidents such as this one set off a chain reaction among police wives has been delineated in chapter 5.)

Counteracting this opposition, policewomen, backed by the vigor of the women's movement and favorable court decisions, pressed for equality of opportunity in police work. And in spite of direct objections by police wives and a more lethargic resistance by the occupation itself, male police officers had to move over to make room for policewomen.

---

[5] Peter B. Bloch and Deborah Anderson, *Policewomen on Patrol* (Washington, D.C.: Police Foundation, 1974), pp. 38-44.

[6] Catherine Milton, *Women in Policing* (Washington, D.C.: Police Foundation, 1972), p. 50.

What the men really think about women riding alongside them in the cars turned out to be a more practical and personal issue than the rather abstract question of whether women should be allowed equality in police work. When we talked informally with male police officers, at first their off-the-record comments tended to be superficial or facetious. They parroted the chauvinistic clichés about women, commenting on their driving inadequacies, their lack of mechanical ability, their helplessness to fix a flat or make a minor motor adjustment or repair. Some quipped about future protocol asking, "If the female partner is a beautiful blonde, should the male hold the door open for her?" But as the conversations continued, they turned more serious, and a deeper dissatisfaction surfaced. The men recounted many cases where policewomen could not provide adequate backup support for their male partners. Our informants told us that they believed that some of the official statistics demonstrating that women were doing the job as well as men were inflated. They claimed that the men often made the arrests and did the physically arduous police work, sharing half the credit and half the arrests with their female partners as a matter of chivalry, although their contribution was not commensurate.

Superior officers, close friends of ours, confided to us that in several departments scandals involving pregnancies among female police officers and broken marriages had been suppressed. One commanding officer remarked that whenever there was an opening in the radio car to partner an especially attractive policewoman, he was besieged with requests from male officers eager to ride with her. As we reminisced about former times, he closed the conversation epigrammatically, "In the old days my problem with radio cars used to be cooping. Now it's screwing."

In Washington, D.C., policewomen have complained about sexual harassment, especially by superior officers who punish policewomen who refuse to have sex and reward those who do submit with better assignments. One remarked plaintively, "You've got to make love to get a day off or make love to get a good beat."[7]

In our survey (see Appendix A) we asked police officers how they would react if they were assigned to radio car patrol with a policewoman as a steady partner. Of the 182 American respondents, a slight majority 92 (51 percent) opposed the assignment, 61 (33 percent) remained neutral, but only 10 (5 percent) favored the assignment.

An analysis of the data brought out an intriguing cross-cultural difference of opinion toward the introduction of women into the once exclusively male enclave. In contrast to the majority of the Americans who reacted negatively to feminine encroachment into radio car patrol, only 5 (17 percent) of the 29 British and Australian police officers expressed disapproval. British constables themselves put their finger on the most feasible explanation for the disparity of

---

[7]*New York Post,* October 14, 1975, p. 77.

views between the two cultures. With their characteristic reserve and brevity they admitted, "We don't really think of policewomen . . . as females."[8]

Utilizing an open-ended format for the next item in the questionnaire, we asked our respondents to elaborate on the reasons for their answers. In doing so, we must have touched a sensitive occupational nerve, because this question released a stream of comments. In addition, it became obvious that for American policemen, irrespective of location, length of service, rank, or size of force, their opposition to co-ed assignments fell into two emotionally charged categories: sexual attraction and potential danger. The following statements relating to gender indicate that this highly combustible element, when compounded, would heat up the chemistry of mixed sexes in the patrol car.

A sergeant on the Michigan State Police Force with 14 years of experience said:

Most women talk too much about the wrong things. Lack of trust in stress situations. Vehicle enclosure is too close for eight hours with a female.

A sergeant on the Hartford (Connecticut) Police Force with 20 years of experience said:

I would be conscious of her femininity in a tight situation and would be concerned with her safety.

A captain on the Williston (North Dakota) Police Force with 13 years of experience said:

I would be worried about physical contact with the violator with a female as a partner. I would also be concerned about the relationship with my wife if I had a female as a partner.

A sergeant in the South Australian Police Department with 25 years of experience said:

Work is work; play is play; they don't mix.

A lieutenant in the Orange (New Jersey) Police Department with 23 years of experience said:

Leave a male and female together and something is bound to happen.

A patrolman in the New York City Police Department with 19 years of experience said:

[8] Maureen Cain, *Society and the Policeman's Role* (London: Routledge and Kegan Paul, 1973), pp. 116-117.

My wife realizes the close relation I now have with my male partner. Close relations such as RMP patrol with a female may tend to be embarrassing.

A patrolman on the New Jersey State Police Force with 8 years of experience said:

I'm prejudiced. If she was a good looking chick I'd be driving the back roads a lot. If she was a dog I'd be calling in sick. Just wouldn't feel safe with a woman partner.

Judging from the following on-the-spot interviews with policemen from Long Island, New York, sexual attraction appears to be a prevalent reaction to the innovation of policewomen on radio car patrol:[9]

Eventually I'd want to get friendly if I had a female partner.

Let's face it. If she's an attractive woman, she's going to make the day pleasant, but disconcerting. And we have to have our wits about us.

You couldn't spend eight hours a day together without the conversation getting around to sex. and once that happens, well . . .

Can you imagine my coming home and saying I had a couple of drinks with my partner after work, if it were a "her."

Every police officer lives intermittently in the clutch of fear, although there are countless rationalizations and subterfuges to help him sublimate his concern for his own personal safety. No official departmental survey will convince him that a policewoman can back him up properly in any of the critical police incidents requiring physical strength, such as taking a powerful male "psycho" into custody, arresting a belligerent six-footer, or breaking up a fierce fight. The policeman is more than willing to be fair; he will concede all the capabilities of policewomen: their potential for defusing violence, their talent for settling family fights, their ability to deal with female clients. But at bottom is a basic anxiety about personal danger on patrol that motivates opposition to policewomen in radio cars. And this fear is consistently pointed out in the responses to our poll.

A constable in the South Australia Police Department with 16 years of experience said:

I have an open mind on the female ability. However, it gives me a little concern. I have minor doubts on the female to withstand direct violence.

[9] *Long Island Press,* May 10, 1972, p. 1.

A patrolman in the New York City Police Department with 1 year of experience said:

Women are not physically or emotionally capable of handling certain circumstances which do occur on patrol. I want a partner that I can feel confident in when those circumstances occur.

A sergeant on the Mamaroneck (New York) Police Force with 13 years of experience said:

I find it hard enough to find a fellow male officer that's not a ding a ling, as a partner. I may deal in violence only once a year, but I must be able to meet it head on at that time.

In a debate between rival candidates for the presidency of the New York City Patrolmen's Benevolent Association, both made the campaign promise to resist the assignment of policewomen to radio cars

Mr. McKiernan: I'm absolutely opposed to women riding around in radio cars. There are so many other functions they can serve, but they do not have the physical strength needed for this kind of patrol. We will do everything in our power to show that it is detrimental to patrol.

Mr. McFeeley: A policewoman can do everything a policeman can do. She's great on patrol—with one exception: she doesn't have the physical ability to protect herself, her partner or the one who called her without resorting to her gun.[10]

No matter how persuasively the police justify their case for men only on the basis of self-preservation, many women reject their brief as legal sophistry aimed to disguise an egregious example of male domination of the occupation. They back up their claims with convincing logic. First, statistics confirm that three-quarters of police work involves service calls to assist people in need of help, with only the remaining portion related exclusively to law enforcement and crime prevention. Second, policewomen have been rated as equally competent as their male counterparts in performance on service calls. They conclude, "Why should policewomen be barred from duty in radio cars?"

Today's active patrolmen are certainly cognizant that service is the vital part of police work. (In our survey, the majority of respondents concurred with this assessment of their duties.) The male officers' rebuttal to these accusations of discrimination, however, is that even if violent encounters occur infrequently, they weigh more in terms of potential seriousness. And to dispel the allegation

[10] *New York Times,* June 2, 1974, p. 60. McFeeley won the election.

of bias against women, the men also point out that they are fighting just as forcefully against the change from two-man to one-man radio cars, for the same reason—increased danger.[11]

But feminists revert to another line of argument to shore up their condemnation of police behavior, charging that even when women in distress come as supplicants, policemen consistently maintain their chauvinistic stance. This is especially apparent in cases involving battered wives and rape victims, where the reluctance of the police to take action against the husband or rapist is notorious.

There are cases in which policemen really identify with the perpetrator [the husband] and they feel that the wife is the property of the husband and if he needs to punch her around a little bit to teach her a lesson he's entitled to do it.[12]

The victims themselves allege that the police treat them like violators rather than the violated. One abused wife flailed out at the injustice of the system:

The police simply do not understand the total terror you're in . . . and they will do nothing. If you have a husband of stature they feel that his reputation is more important than your health.[13]

Complainants—frightened, humiliated, shocked, and sometimes severely injured—are often subjected to unsympathetic questioning and manipulation by the police to discourage them from proceeding with the case.

[Police] arguments cover a wide range: "Who will support you if he's locked up?" "He could lose his job." "You'll have to spend days in court." "Why don't you kiss and make up?" "Why'd you make him slug you?" "If you make trouble, think of what he'll do to you next time?"[14]

A recent move in this continuing confrontation was the filing of a class action on behalf of 59 battered wives against the New York City Police Department and family court personnel in which the wives detailed the serious beatings at the hands of their husbands. They accused the police of unlawfully refusing to arrest their spouses in these cases.[15]

But the policemen defend themselves vigorously. They point out the frequent occasions where the supposedly injured wife turned like a fury to

[11] Ibid., June 22, 1977, p. B4.
[12] Ibid., October 21, 1974, p. 38.
[13] Ibid.
[14] Ibid., October 7, 1975, p. 35.
[15] Ibid., June 12, 1977, p. 48.

attack the police officer when he did try to arrest the husband. The police know from experience that most of their clients' domestic battles are sporadic and, if given a chance, the husband and wife will make up and resume their normal style of life. The police are also aware that most of the time the men are the breadwinners, and if they are jailed, there will be no income—a sad punishment for wives and children. Most convincingly of all, the job teaches members of the force that family disputes are best handled by patience and fortitude rather than radical police action; given time, the majority of family fights will settle themselves without the necessity of arrest.

Rape cases are the second cluster that incite denunciation of the police. If the rape victim in her distraught state, so traumatized by this most horrible nightmare come true, is courageous enough to report the assault to the authorities, at the least she expects compassion from them. Instead she is often subjected to embarrassing questioning, prodding and routine cross-examination by policemen and detectives, and, she feels degraded and drained. One female complainant lamented, "It's like being raped all over again."[16]

The police rationalize their blunt probing as the only way to gauge how the case will stand up in court. From a legal frame of reference, it becomes imperative to ascertain whether there has been any penetration, whether the woman can identify the rapist, whether she has been injured, whether she cried out, whether sodomy has been committed, whether she has ever had any sexual relations with the rapist at any other time, and even whether she is of chaste character. Many state penal codes require this kind of evidence if there is to be a chance of conviction.

Finally, the police excuse themselves by referring to the highly emotional state of the victim. Some anguished rape victims have condemned physicians who examined them soon after the assault because they administered massive doses of penicillin to avert the possibility of venereal disease. In their distress, the women resented being considered the sick ones.

Perhaps policemen are too readily disposed to follow official thinking on this subject, such as these cynical admonitions proffered by a California police manual:

Forcible rape is one of the most falsely reported crimes. The majority of "second day reported" rapes are not legitimate. Rape calls often result when a husband leaves town on business and a wife takes the opportunity "to go out on the town," with later remorse.[17]

Indeed, if the following observations of a New York City detective accurately reflect the attitudes of his colleagues toward the rape victim, then

[16] Carol V. Horos, *Rape* (New Canaan, Conn.: Tobey, 1974), p. 80.
[17] George T. Payton, *Patrol Procedure* (Los Angeles: Legal Book Corp., 1967), p. 312, cited by Susan Brownmiller, *Against Our Will: Men, Women and Rape* (New York: Simon and Schuster, 1975), p. 364.

most certainly women across the country are right in demanding family crisis intervention units and rape investigation squads staffed by a complement of well-trained officers of both sexes.

A lot of officers, especially the oldtimers, believe that unless a women comes in bruised, there's no rape. They also say, "Unless a woman's a virgin, what's the big deal?" But I wonder if one of these guys was suddenly jumped and forced to commit sodomy at gunpoint, wouldn't he be pretty upset? And wouldn't he submit?[18]

Feminists, in their insistent clamor for specialized units staffed principally by women, are making the assumption that female victims will be more compassionately treated by members of their own sex. These activists may be capitulating to and perpetuating the belief (which they contend is a myth) that there are inherent differences between the sexes other than the obvious anatomical ones.

Male chauvinism is the subcutaneous layer of the police mystique. But feminists may be making a serious mistake in condemning it in every one of its manifestations. Police male chauvinism operates according to a contemporary code of chivalry that has in large measure protected women from the full force of aggressive police action. It has been a factor in police discretion and decisionmaking that has often saved a female from arrest or the application of force. In fact, one popular explanation for the currently escalating number of arrests of women is that the police, in response to the feminist campaign for equal treatment, are gradually giving up this chauvinism and making no distinction between male and female when duty calls for an arrest or the use of force.

Thrown into the hopper of the police occupation, members of the force are practically cloned with a police genetic code that imparts an occupational personality and ideology composed of male chauvinism, conservatism, authoritarianism, and cynicism. Although within the liberal academic community these traits carry a pejorative connotation, within the occupation these characteristics constitute the vital ingredients to help the police officer cope with its stresses and made a successful adjustment to a demanding calling.

There are less anxiety-producing, less ideological, but more work-oriented descriptions of law enforcement. Police officers could find solace in the *Dictionary of Occupational Titles* under the section devoted to investigating and protecting occupations, where police work is defined as protecting the citizenry from harm and defending the person, property, or rights of individuals. The composite police officer is the person who can adjust to fluctuating conditions

---

[18] Nancy Gager and Cathleen Schurr, *Confronting Rape in America* (New York: Grosset and Dunlap, 1976), pp. 94-95.

and maintain equanimity in the face of danger, who possesses motor coordination, honesty, dependability, tact, and diplomacy.[19]

Anxiety, nonetheless, is the policeman's albatross. Almost every action he performs retains a residue of apprehension. The potential for trouble flows by in a constant stream of psychodrama in the theater of the street. What if the irate citizen the officer has just ordered to move along goes into the station house to complain about abusive language? Suppose the feuding husband and wife that the patrolman has just managed to separate before they seriously injured each other join forces against their common enemy, the cop, and register a complaint against him for police brutality. How about that bit of bad luck when that gossipy neighbor, by coincidence, just happened to be in the coffee shop when the officer was acting too friendly with a good-looking waitress?

On post, the most innocent activities and routines of life—chatting with people, stopping for a coffee break, calling the wife to check out how things are at home, and even going to the bathroom—are tinged with anxiety because unless the officer goes through the tedious process of obtaining permission from a superior, he may be violating police rules.

At a more threatening level, the police officer may find himself in a state of nerves over a small gratuity that he had, in a moment of weakness, accepted from the bookie, a motorist, or a storekeeper for looking the other way. The situation often grows desperate when a vindictive superior is on the prowl to "throw the book" at the first subordinate he finds unable to fulfill every technicality in the manual of procedure. Worst of all is the panic that spreads through the ranks during a large-scale investigation of corruption.

The police officers' level of stress and anxiety is heightened by the frustration and lack of recognition that is sustained outside the job as well. They feel that they are performing a vital societal function (which indeed, they are), and they resent the public's lack of appreciation. In our sample of 211 policemen, 87 (41 percent) thought that the public rated the police low in prestige; 91 (43 percent) felt that the public rated the police average in prestige; and only 33 (15 percent) said that the public granted high prestige to the police. Wherever and whenever we spoke to policemen, this sensitivity to rejection by the community surfaced and generated a great deal of psychological stress. For no matter how hackneyed it sounds, everyone needs a pat on the back for a job well done.

In both formal research and rap sessions, members of the force complained about the revolving-door policy of the juvenile and criminal courts. Bitterly, they echoed the accusation that when a police officer brings a prisoner to court for arraignment, even for a serious crime, there is a strong probability that the prisoner will be back on the street before the arresting officer returns to his post. To make a mockery of hard work and dangerous risks aggravates tension.

[19] *Dictionary of Occupational Titles,* Vol. 2, 3d ed. (Washington, D.C.: United States Department of Labor, 1965), pp. 416, 427.

To the rookie, these psychological blows can be almost lethal, for he enters the career with a sense of idealism and even naiveté. Within the perilous first three years he is apt to fall into a Slough of Despond, a state of psychological conflict that immobilizes. With one sphere of his personality the neophyte comes to think of the occupation as his new world, his new family, and feels a transcendent pride and loyalty to it. But the baleful effects of the job become all too apparent to him and contradict his more idealistic yearnings.

For the veteran members of the force, these conditions engender discontent, disenchantment, and a sense of failure. Shortchanged by the occupation and bothered by doubts, they wonder if they should have chosen another career with less arduous schedules, less strain, and fewer burdensome restrictions of the private realm. Of course, many of them carry their traps within themselves. They are bound to the job by the magnetic allure of the pension. Then, too, common sense tells them that their lack of skills locks them out of a job with higher prestige or commensurate salary.

When policemen are asked what bothers them most, their immediate response is to fault the administration.[20] At a Police Wives Association meeting, several of the police officer husbands who had accompanied their spouses voiced their fears that the militancy of the wives on such issues as co-ed radio car patrol and adverse changes in schedule would cause the department to take punitive action. They did not want their wives to irritate the hierarchy. Others lamented, "The department is out to 'get the men' in the lower ranks." Some filed a verbal brief against the administration's lack of loyalty, alleging, "They will never back up a policeman in trouble." Underlining this generalized suspicion, one of the participants confronted Arthur demanding identification because he suspected that Arthur who had been taking notes of the proceedings, might be a spy from the department checking for troublemakers.

The truth is that for all their vaunted machismo and physical courage, many members of the force mistrust and fear the large police department and its administrators. The police officer projects a paradoxical picture—in the foreground, strong, assertive, and courageous in his interaction with his clientele, the public, and yet submissive, even supine, in confrontations with the department as represented by the omnipresent superior officers. Perhaps it is a police variety of working-class consciousness, a realization that the worker and the boss are fundamentally opponents, even enemies, and the bosses always hold the top cards. The feeling of powerlessness is a component of police alienation, one additional source of stress.[21]

---

[20] See, for example, William H. Kroes, Bruce L. Margolis, and Joseph J. Hurrell, Jr., "Job Stress in Policemen," *Journal of Police Science and Administration* 2 (June 1974):145-155; and James Hillgren, Rebekah Bond, and Sue Jones, "Primary Stressors in Police Administration and Law Enforcement," *Journal of Police Science and Administration* 4 (December 1976):445-449.

[21] For example, see Carl P. Wagoner, "Police Alienation: Some Sources and Implications," *Journal of Police Science and Administration* 4 (December 1976):389-403; Tom Denyer, Robert Callender, and Dennis L. Thompson, "The Policeman as Alienated Laborer," *Journal of Police Science and Administration* 3 (September 1975):251-258; and Arthur Niederhoffer, *Behind the Shield* (Garden City, N.Y.: Doubleday, 1967).

Less Marxist and more psychological is this explanation offered by a psychiatrist:

This seeming contradiction, i.e., the curious amalgam of conforming and aggressive behavior, is particularly present in upward-striving working-class youths. . . . The conforming individual, who is a policeman, is selective. He can express his direct feelings of aggression freely to subordinates, somewhat to equals but never to superiors. This behavior is reminiscent of what the French call the "bicyclist personality"—one who bows his head above and kicks below.[22]

It would be impossible for the police officer to maintain his psychological equilibrium under this battering if there were no defense mechanism available to him. He copes by forging a shield of cynicism toward the job, toward the public, and toward life in general. This cynicism, for which the police are usually criticized, serves as a potent tranquilizer, reducing the impact of the shocks in police work, alleviating frustration and stress, and soothing anxiety.[23] On the beat, if the officer fails to incorporate a cynical attitude, then the penal worm of his own self-judgment will sentence him.

The married officer is trapped in an additional set of satellite stresses related to family life that even an umbrella of cynicism cannot repel. And the pressure mounts as the married recruit works his post. A study of a small sample of married rookies in a large county police force found that the new men considered the job a benign, rather positive institution that could not adversely affect their personal and social lives. But in the scant span of three years their attitudes had changed significantly. The same group that in 1974 was favorably disposed to the job, in 1977 condemned it as a pernicious source of personal and social problems ranging from the ultimate disruption, divorce, to difficulties in dealing with their children. The patrolmen blamed the job for damaging the conjugal relation and encouraging sexual infidelity.[24]

In a more comprehensive study of stress in the first three years of the police career, Reiser emphasizes the strength of opposing forces: on one side, the development of identification with and loyalty to the peer group, and on the other, the growth of an ideology of cynicism, emotional coldness, and authoritarianism. He speculates about the possible effect of this phase of the career upon the police family:

He may become emotionally cool and lose some of his "love" for his wife. Consequently, she feels rejected, alienated, and reacts in ways that significantly influence their total relationship, including communication, sex, and value systems.[25]

[22] Martin Symonds, "Policemen and Policework: A Psychodynamic Understanding," in Arthur Niederhoffer and Abraham Blumberg, eds., *The Ambivalent Force: Perspectives on the Police*, 2d ed. (Hinsdale, Ill.: Dryden Press, 1976), p. 75.

[23] See Niederhoffer, *Behind the Shield* pp. 90-102, 187-242.

[24] David C. Murray, "Police Divorce: The Effects, Causes and Treatment" (Master's thesis, C.W. Post College), 1977, pp. 29-32.

[25] Martin Reiser, "Some Organizational Stresses on Policemen," *Journal of Police Science and Administration* 2 (June 1974):156-159.

Married police officers can point to the problem areas endemic to the job that upset them: retards nonpolice friendships; don't see enough of the children; miss weekends and holidays with family; pressures of job taken home; wife worries for safety of husband.[26] Nearly every gripe on their list can be traced to a common base: the schedule or the danger.

But the schedule and the danger are the two unique factors that are impervious to every effort to control their interference in family life. Nothing can stop a loving wife from worrying about the safety of her policeman husband when he is at work. And there is no escape from the imperious demands of the rotating duty chart.

Behavioral scientists who specialize in the study of biological rhythms and human deprivation have only recently discovered the powerful negative effects of shift work upon the individual. These specialists have missed an obvious candidate: the policeman who works in conditions of fatigue, isolation, deprivation, and time shifts in the natural setting of the city streets. With its concentration on the mutual interaction of fatigue, isolation, anxiety, and time shifts, this core of scientific research could be highly relevant for an understanding of the police officer on patrol. Instead, ingeniously contrived laboratory situations all but immolate the subjects in dark, damp, secret caves or immerse them in underwater domiciles so that the experimenters can study their reactions. These controlled observations indicate that night workers show definite signs of physiological disturbance when compared to the normal day-worker populations. If the biological clock is disturbed, hormonal activity is impaired, performance on a variety of tests is poorer, and there are other deleterious consequences on mind and body.[27]

Presumably, policemen can adapt to steady night work and can compensate for the change in circadian rhythms despite the fact that "a person who sleeps by day and works by night is physiologically 180 degrees out of phase with the people who work by day."[28] A constant change of shift may eventually have a devastating effect over a prolonged period of time, however. The typical pattern of a police officer's career charts a course of stress scarred by his collisions with physical ailments, depression, and a host of other psychosomatic conditions. Many municipalities have recognized heart disease as a policeman's occupational hazard. As a result, they are permitting early retirement with service-connected disability for members of the force with heart conditions.

The best the married police officer can hope to do is to protect his family from the stress by drawing a thick blue line to separate the two sectors, the public zone from the private sphere. A policeman-student in Arthur's class

---

[26] Kroes, Margolis and Hurrell, "Job Stress," p. 151.

[27] See, for example, Wallace Bloom, "Shift Work and Human Efficiency," in Edwin A. Fleishman, ed., *Studies in Personnel and Industrial Psychology* (Homewood, Ill.: Dorsey Press, 1967), pp. 572-580.

[28] Gay G. Luce, *Body Time* (New York: Bantam Books, 1973), p. 24.

submitted a report in which he explained why it was so necessary to erect a
barrier between the station house and the ranch house:

Policemen generally lead a dual life—public and private. Care is usually taken to
isolate or cushion the private family life from the public one, with little success.
The writer and those officers he has been closely associated with seldom bring
their work home. That is to say, we seldom tell of the many sordid affairs we are
confronted with. Only the witty, light-hearted stories are ever repeated in the
presence of the children and great care is taken to hide the perverted, even from
our wives.

Members of the force try to insulate their families from the dark side of the
occupation. One reason is that family security takes the highest priority for the
policeman. The results of a psychological research project in which members of a
medium-sized police force were compared to a representative national sample of
males definitively bore out this predilection. Not only did the police group
consider family security the highest terminal value, but they attached more
importance to it than did any other segment of the national sample.[29]

For the corrupt cop, however, self-interest rather than altruism motivates
him to screen his wife and children from his wrongdoing. A police officer who is
"on the pad" lives under a cloud of anxiety and guilt that may shower a torrent
of retribution and disgrace upon him at any moment. He realizes that it would
be indiscreet and dangerous to use as a confidante a family member who is
inexperienced and naive in matters of this kind and who might in casual gossip
divulge damaging evidence.

In an odd juxtaposition, the conventional wisdom of the oldtimers on the
job, passed down for generations to the rookies, "Tell your wife nothing if you
want to stay out of trouble," has become incorporated as a basic tenet of the
corrupt officer's way of life. William Phillips, the turn-coat cop who testified at
the widely publicized Knapp Commission investigation into New York City
police corruption, phrased it crudely:

I don't trust women. I don't tell women shit. . . . Nobody, not my wife, my
sister, my brother-in-law, nobody. Nobody knew I made a dime. As far as they
were concerned I was Johnny good guy who was completely honest. That's one
reason I never brought my wife to policemen's affairs. Because policemen's wives
talk about the money their husbands make.[30]

That the less wives know the better off they are constitutes judicious advice,
because many wives have been subjected to questioning by prosecutors about
their husbands' financial affairs, the existence of joint bank accounts, safe

[29] Milton Rokeach, Martin G. Miller, and John A. Snyder, "The Value Gap Between Police
and Policed," *Journal of Social Issues* 27 (1971):161.
[30] Leonard Schechter, *On the Pad* (New York: Berkley, 1974), p. 103.

74

deposit boxes, and even their own personal involvement in the corrupt activities.[31]

How effectively can the improprieties of policemen be concealed from their wives? Edward Droge, another policeman who became a cooperative witness for the Knapp Commission in its exposé of police corruption, contends that if police officers take graft steadily, then their spouses must necessarily be aware of it: "My wife knew. All policemen's wives must know. You cannot keep the reaction away from your home."[32]

Droge's insight is sharp. For a corrupt police officer to hide his transgressions from an observant wife for any length of time would seem an incredible feat of legerdemain. She may find bills of large denomination in his pockets, a deposit slip for a secret bank account, or a safe deposit key, or he may flash a roll of cash at the wrong time. When she does make the discovery, she may be shocked at the revelation; but as much as she may wish to reform him, she hesitates to risk public exposure. With resignation, she realizes that once her husband has become involved, it is very difficult to pull out. Usually she capitulates, accepts the situation, and assimilates his code of police values.

In fact, of the police wives in our sample, 112 (52 percent) rated the acceptance by a police officer of gratuities such as a free meal or a Christmas present as no violation at all. The wives' tolerance for the acceptance of gratuities exceeded by far that of the police officers themselves; only half as many policemen in the sample, 54 (25 percent), evaluated the acceptance of those gratuities as no violation at all. The wives' lenience stands in marked contrast to the position of New York City police officers, who, at an ethical awareness workshop, condemned the acceptance of any gratuity at all, even a cup of coffee, because it might affect the officer's performance of duty, it might be demeaning to a professional police officer, or it might precipitate a slide into corruption.[33]

Whatever the wife's code of ethics may be when she finally knows all, a subtle change in the relation between husband and wife takes place. Although the wife, in a sense, participates as a kind of accessory after the fact by profiting from the extra money her husband makes, her faith in her spouse has been badly shaken. His badge of honor has corroded. And with her knowledge comes permanent anxiety. In compensation, she achieves potential power over her husband. He must be careful not to anger her to a point where, in a fit of vindictive or jealous rage, blind to the destructive consequences to the family, she writes a letter to the department detailing the corrupt activities. Legendary in the occupation is the stockpile of anecdotes about philandering husbands who, seemingly secure in office jobs or promoted to higher rank, have been

[31] See, for example, *New York Times,* June 13, 1974, p. 47.
[32] Edward F. Droge, Jr., *The Patrolman: A Cop's Story* (New York: New American Library, 1973), p. 16.
[33] *Knapp Commission Report on Police Corruption* (New York: George Braziller, 1973), pp. 181, 240.

transferred, demoted, or even dismissed as a result of disclosures by vengeful wives.

Conceivably, then, for a wife to act as a hedge against police corruption, her influence would have to be proactive, not reactive. In other words, she could help her husband resist corruption before he falls, but rarely after. One state trooper was probably saved from a prison term because he thought about his wife's reaction before he got involved. At a trial in New York City, held in October 1974, a tape recording obtained by a turnaround cop was introduced in evidence against three detectives who had been members of the safe, loft, and truck squad. The testimony disclosed that the detectives, searching for a hijacked truck, found it abandoned in New Jersey loaded with color television sets. They rented a truck and loaded the stolen sets into it. One of them tried to persuade a New Jersey state trooper, present at the scene, to take a set for himself. The trooper refused, citing his wife's ethical principles: "My wife comes from Italy—she's very religious."[34]

When the threat of exposure becomes imminent, some corrupt police who have experienced this worst of all possible fates many times in their nightmares reach a point where death—either their own or that of the person responsible— would be preferable to public disgrace. When Droge learned that the investigators had tapes proving his guilt, he immediately thought of suicide: "For the first time in my life I thought seriously of committing suicide. I could picture myself jumping from a rooftop."[35] Dreading the moment of truth, a plainclothesman who suspected that Frank Serpico might be an informer tried to intimidate him with a veiled threat of death:

I got a lot to lose. Maybe you don't, but I do. If it ever came to where I could get indicted, and I thought somebody was going to talk about me, I mean before I'd shame my wife and family, it'd be worth a couple of grand to me to have that somebody taken care of.[36]

Customarily, the egocentric need for self-protection that drives corrupt officers to try to mislead their wives becomes secondary to the overwhelming compulsion to safeguard their families at all costs from the disgrace and destruction that public exposure would bring.

Honest officers, too, have been thwarted in their strategies to repel vindictive adversaries threatening to invade their family's private terrain. Recently, a New York City detective working with the department's internal affairs division in exposing corruption within his own command discovered that even the full protection of the police department could not prevent reprisals against his family. Menacing telephone callers anonymously vowed to throw lye in the

---

[34] *New York Times,* October 5, 1974, p. 29.

[35] Droge, *Patrolman,* p. 20.

[36] Peter Maas, *Serpico: The Cop Who Defied the System* (New York: Viking, 1973), p. 219.

face of his sixteen-year-old daughter; his wife had been followed home from work; and he himself had been warned that he would be killed.[37]

Law enforcement officers are also apprehensive that the smoldering hostility that a small fraction of the public harbors toward the police may penetrate the sanctuary of the home. Above all, they fear harassment of their families. It is not paranoia when a police officer asks to have his home phone changed to an unlisted number after he and his family have received innumerable obscene and threatening phone calls. In fact, in 1974, when the administrators of the New York City Police Department decreed that members of the force had to wear name tags on all outer garments of the uniform except raincoats, policemen protested vehemently that it was tantamount to placing a coin for a poison phone call to a police family in the hands of a disgruntled person.[38]

In other places and at other times, distressing episodes of intimidation of police officers and their families have occurred. In Glasgow, Scotland, detectives were afraid to walk down the streets with their families in their home towns for fear that shady characters might identify their wives and children and then later try to molest them. And in some sections, their youngsters were subjected to such a degree of victimization by their peers that the worried police parents had to guard them on their way home from school.[39]

The police grapevine buzzes with similar cases of persecution. Thus, for the ordinary policeman, it is sensible policy to be cautious, and some members of the force have invented artful subterfuges of "bluelining" to keep their career a secret from their neighbors. It is annoying for a police officer, off duty, to be treated like the official policeman in residence on his block. Most police officers to whom we have spoken would wholeheartedly empathize with the following graphic description:

He is a kind of "watchdog." This added duty often causes him discomfort, a certain loss of freedom and an additional stage on which to role play. He is called to settle petty arguments; to investigate a "suspicious" car parked several days; give advice relative to drugs or marital problems. All this, while that same neighbor asks, "Are you off today?, off again?", etc. At times their requests are greatly resented. But to refer a neighbor to dial 911 is rather a cold thing to do; so he does his thing again, and again, and again.

I find it extremely distasteful to be ever On Stage. So many stories have been repeated so many times. A lesson has been dearly learned, and resolve has been made. My planned move to Croton-on-Hudson will include an introduction to my new neighbors as Bill ———, the shoemaker, accountant, or bookkeeper, NEVER the policeman.[40]

[37] *New York Times,* July 3, 1977, pp. 1, 33.

[38] Ibid., December 28, 1974, p. 27.

[39] Michael Banton, *The Policeman in the Community* (New York: Basic Books, 1964), pp. 204-208.

[40] Personal communication from a police officer friend, 1976.

Some police officers who find it too onerous to keep up this facade of deception against their neighbors' intrusions move their families to enclaves where other policemen and firemen live—where they do not have to dissemble, and they can relax and be themselves. That cop's house in 1977 sells for $48,000, and compared to the 1962 version:

The 1977 "cops and firemen's house" is still semi-attached, but it is on a lot 20 feet wide instead of 25. Inside the width of the house is 12 feet instead of 16. There is 1,100 square feet of living space instead of 1,200 square feet.[41]

Ordinarily, policemen prefer to maintain their social distance from other police families unless they are working partners or close friends, but evidently this normal pattern of separation is replaced, under conditions of stress, by a deeper reflex of consciousness of kind that brings the police together. In our sample, two-thirds of the police officers confirmed the more typical inclination to keep to themselves by admitting that they seldom or never socialized with other police couples.

Through the years police acquaintances of ours have outlined to us the many artifices they had to engineer to conceal their police identities. Many boasted to us that they had lived in the same neighborhood in New York City for several decades without neighbors ever having any inkling that they lived next door to a cop. To maintain this anonymity, members of the force concocted involved schemes to avoid wearing their uniforms to and from work. Police officers commonly kept a spare uniform at home so that when they were called for emergency duty after midnight at some distant precinct, they would not have to lose time by first going to their own station house locker room to change clothes. To camouflage their identity from passersby who might be walking the streets at that hour, the officers would either cover their uniform with a long coat or carry the uniform in a valise.

During the Korean War an order came down requiring members of the New York City force to wear their uniforms commuting to and from their precincts in order to increase their visibility and make them more available should an alert be called. The elaborate and inventive ploys the police officers devised to circumvent this regulation could match the most intricate game of strategy an ingenious tactician might plot. One determined group of officers rented lockers in a tailor shop around the corner from their precinct where they could surreptitiously enter, remove their police uniforms, and exchange them for sets of outer civilian garments that effectively disguised their police identity. Certainly, this violation of procedure was a dangerous gamble, because the shop

---

[41] These figures are from the builder who started in 1962 in Staten Island, New York, to cater to this special market. He is still concentrating on the basic model in that borough. See *New York Times,* February 13, 1977, Real Estate Section, pp. 1, 6.

was so old and flimsy that it almost invited a burglar to push in the door to steal the uniforms. What's more, the location was so near the station house that the officers were completely vulnerable to discovery by the parade of superiors who constantly passed by.

Apparently this type of subterfuge is not confined to the local gendarmerie, for British policemen are just as reluctant to publicize their calling to the populace. " 'I always go home in civies; you don't want to advertise the fact that you're a copper, do you?' 72 percent of men interviewed said they did not like to be recognized as policemen while on holiday."[42]

Sometimes the exigencies of police work preclude this guise of secrecy. How one patrolman's efforts to foil his inquisitive neighbors boomeranged made an amusing anecdote. Once, after making an arrest, he found himself detained in court. To save time, he decided to go directly home from the courthouse without changing out of uniform, since the court was located much nearer to his residence than the station house where he usually slipped into civies. Despite his cautious approach, someone spotted him entering his home in uniform but did not recognize him, since he had succeeded so adroitly in keeping his occupation a secret. The concerned neighbor immediately called up the patrolman's wife to find out what had happened, assuming that only an emergency could bring the police to the door at such a late hour.

Detectives and undercover officers find it particularly difficult to lock out their "details" from the family circle. Because of the nature of their work, they must develop a network of informers whose identities for obvious reasons must be kept secret. Tradition has it that a detective or plainclothes officer is only as good as his informers. To build such a relation requires a mixture of skill, patience, and credibility on the officer's part; and for helpful information, he will pay the informer on a sliding scale. After trust has been established, the officer will sometimes give the informer his home telephone number so that he can call in vital information, no matter what the hour.

In one incident, a police officer assigned to a federal strike force obtained a reliable informer who dug up many productive leads. In time, the detective gave him his home telephone number. One day the informer needed money quickly, looked up the officer's name in the directory, checked it with the phone number he had, and soon after rang the doorbell of the officer's home while the officer was at work. His appearance and demeanor so frightened the detective's wife that when he asked where he could get in touch with her husband who was on a roving assignment, she panicked. Managing to reach her husband by telephone, she told him about the disreputable visitor. The officer, recognizing who it was from his wife's description, soothed her fears. But later, enraged at the audacity of the informer who had so complacently broken the unwritten rules of the relationship, the officer warned him that if he ever came to the house again, he would shoot him.

[42] Maureen Cain, "The Life of a Policeman and His Family," in Benjamin Whitaker, *The Police* (London: Eyre and Spottiswoode, 1964), p. 164.

In another case, a useful informer suddenly found himself threatened by a criminal who suspected him of passing information to the police. He appealed to the police officer who had recruited him and reminded him of his original commitment to protect him if anything went wrong. The officer tried to get the police department to provide a guard but discovered that, although the department recognized the necessity of informers to the extent that it would allocate funds to buy information, it refused to acknowledge the actual existence of informers by assigning a police escort. Because the officer felt that the informer might be killed, he took him to his own home for several days as a safety precaution while he searched for a safe house. Meanwhile, the officer's wife nervously had to maneuver her inquisitive young children from contact with the unexpected guest. When we asked the officer why he chose to bring the informer to his own home to hide out and whether he was worried about the safety of his wife and children with the informer in his house, he shrugged and answered that there was no alternative. Evidently, on balance, his sense of obligation to the informer weighed heavily, even at the cost of inconvenience and possible risk to his family.

The police family, in its struggle to maintain its privacy, may be able to resist direct attack, but it can hardly be expected to withstand the blandishments of subtle seduction. Thus, in Prince George County, Maryland, the department easily infiltrated the life space of its members by introducing a personal patrol car program. Officers receive a police radio car for their personal use when off duty, but they must use the cars to commute to and from work. At all times they have to keep the police radio in operation and respond to police incidents in their immediate areas, even when they are not on duty. On these emergency calls, they must drop off their families in a safe place.[43] During the first year of operation, through October 1972, 365 members of the force received cars and responded to 12,800 incidents (an incredible number).

A police officer contrives to cover every base to barricade and insulate his family from the vagaries of the job: he can conceal his identity from the neighbors, he can make sure that his family does not socialize with other police couples; he can turn down the offer of a personal patrol car; he can forgo the assistance of informers; he can even beat the tyranny of the rotating schedule and lift the worry from his wife by landing a coveted day detail. But the officer understands viscerally that these are only the physical manifestations. Over the years, he has internalized the occupational values, and his personality has been forged in the mold designed by the occupation. The real problem is psychological and sociological. How can he transform the culture of the job as he steps across the threshold into his home, and switch the current to activate a set of values more responsive to the institutional imperatives of the contemporary family?

The police officer in the home incarnates a Picasso profile, looking both

---

[43] Roland B. Sweitzer and Giacomo San Felice, "The Personal Patrol Car Program," *FBI Law Enforcement Bulletin* (September 1973):16-20.

ways. Which side will control? If the occupational personality dominates—conservative, chauvinistic, authoritarian, suspicious, and cynical—the family is headed for trouble. In extreme cases, a situation may fester, as it did for this patrolman carrier who infected his family relationships. He felt compelled to write his autobiography as an object lesson for other members of the force.

I took my short temper and my cruelty home to my family. I contaminated my wife and children with dirty, foul-mouthed talk. . . . When I came home from work, I yelled incessantly and listened to no pleas or excuses. I was a madman at times, ranting and raving through the house, screaming at the most insignificant things and barking at my children for the little mistakes that children are supposed to make.[44]

Rather fortunately for the wives and children of police officers, such destructive and frenetic behavior symptomizes the deviant and defines a personality pattern of an oddball among law enforcement personnel. Yet it would be ingenuous to believe that the job does not implant a series of land mines within each member, set to detonate under provocation in the future.

In the main, the turbulence of the occupation subsides in the climate of the home because members of the force have learned that they act out their roles as husbands and fathers more efficiently and comfortably when they are flexible and modern in their policies rather than conservative and rigid, fairly egalitarian rather than authoritarian, supportive of women's right to personal fulfillment rather than chauvinistic, and trusting and open rather than suspicious and cynical. And as the police family climbs up the rungs in its quest for middle-class status, wives and adolescent children are increasingly pressing for a larger voice in the decisionmaking process.

Our sample of police officers showed that they recognized and upheld these fundamentals of contemporary family lifestyle. For example, two-thirds categorized their style of child rearing as flexible rather than strict or permissive, corroborating this flexibility in their response to our question about what career they would prefer for their son or daughter by opting for whatever career he or she prefers. Moreover, 75 percent confirmed the egalitarian relation with their wives by noting that the important decisions in the family were made jointly with their spouses. Finally, almost as many policemen stated that they were favorably disposed to the women's movement as the number who were opposed to it.

The embourgeoisement of the police family permeates the lifestyle with powerful repercussions. One of the first signs is the pressure to own a private home rather than to live in a rented apartment, and this desire is succeeded by a yearning to leave the city for the space, status, and safety for the family that the suburbs represent. Our sample included 182 American police officers; 142 of

[44] Droge, *Patrolman*, p. 176.

them (nearly 80 percent) owned their own homes, and 101 (almost 60 percent) lived in the suburbs.[45]

In order to reach the next stage of the journey to middle-class status, thousands of police officers have applied for the official card of admission, the college diploma. The magnitude of this educational revolution—enthusiastic members of the force flooding into the more than 1000 college degree programs offered particularly for them in criminal justice and police science—can be truly evaluated only when it is compared to the mutual antagonism that existed between the police and the academic community as recently as 10 years ago.

The police officer's wife catches the rings of the academic carousel once the father becomes the scholarly role model for the family. She enrolls in college courses and may even matriculate for a degree. Perceptibly, the relationship between husband and wife shifts toward a more democratic, egalitarian, middle-class standard. She craves more involvement in her spouse's work and demands more communication between them.

The thrust of the upward social movement pushes the children along as well. Caught in the middle-class orbit, competing with their more affluent neighbors, police parents soon assimilate the values of the truly socialized bourgeoisie. They have high aspirations for their children, and they encourage them to participate in pursuits that ensure their competence in a wide range of skills. The police mother becomes the official pilot, ferrying the children from one extracurricular activity to another; or if she is lucky, she becomes one of many chauffeurs in a community car pool. When dad is available for driving chores, he loads up the family station wagon with Little Leaguers or Midget Footballers and spends the day cheering or sulking, depending on the vicissitudes of his offspring's team.

Police parents have taken a giant step into the ranks of the middle class. But their lifestyle exhibits observable cultural lags, suggesting that these families have not yet freed themselves completely from their former working-class allegiance. From our questionnaire we ascertained that about 70 percent of the police officers and wives provide lessons in religion, team sports, skating, swimming, or tennis for their children, but most of them shy away from such middle-class esthetic pursuits as music, art, dancing, and dramatics. Consistent with this lack of interest in the arts, police couples prefer visiting friends or seeing a movie to going to concerts or plays as a popular choice for an enjoyable evening of relaxation.

Like their middle-class models, police parents, if given the opportunity, unquestionably would select professional careers for their sons and daughters. However, their police background intervenes to channel their choices along conventional gender lines—law and medicine for the sons, teaching and nursing for the daughters. But the vanguard of the middle class has advanced to a more

---

[45] About 50 percent of the New York City police force lives outside New York City. *New York Times,* July 16, 1977, p. 9.

liberated platform, encouraging their daughters to vie equally with their sons for coveted positions in the top professions. At the same time, they acknowledge the democratic spirit of the middle-class family by quickly amending their own arbitrary preference with the observation that they would accept any choice of career that would make their children happy. Ironically, the one career for both sons and daughters that most police parents would object to strenuously is police work. In our sample, not one parent indicated that he or she wanted a daughter to be a policewoman. And out of a total of 426 officers and wives, only 9 policemen and 6 wives approved of police work as a career for their sons.

Parents understand that to become a professional in today's competitive society, the child must start preparing at an early age. Because admission to a highly rated college and graduate school is predicated upon a solid record of scholastic achievement, police parents meticulously monitor their children's progress in school.

Almost every religious and social organization in the larger police departments grants scholarships to its members' gifted children. Departmental and organizational newsletters devote prominent columns to broadcast the academic achievements of the younger generation, with special accolades for those who have entered or graduated from law, medical, or dental school or who have earned advanced degrees.

Convinced of the unique power of education as the springboard to success in American society, police officers can make no sense of and are outraged by young middle-class radicals who demonstrate against the administrations of the prestigious universities they attend. An observant reporter at the Columbia University student uprising of 1968 captured the disappointment and frustration of one police father whose son had been denied a place in that renowned institution of learning: "The classic case . . . was that of a sergeant who stood outside of Columbia after the riots . . . with tears streaming down his face. All he ever wanted was to get his son into that school."[46]

Even while concentrating on his children's development, the police father is impelled to fortify his position in the family by mobilizing the qualities that distinguished his occupational role. In their growing years, his youngsters depended on him for control and comfort, looking up to him as the impeccable, benign protector. To a great extent, he had been the dominant figure within the family because of his police role and personality. Although regulated by a psychological rheostat, that occupational mystique personified power.

By the time his children have reached puberty, however, the police father recognizes that they are rapidly moving from a position of lower status to one of new-found strength, freedom, and heightened self-esteem. At this point, the family enters a period of confrontation and subtle struggle for power between the generations. The police officer, more than other fathers, finds it disturbing

---

[46] A. James Reichley, "The Way to Cool the Police Rebellion," *Fortune* (December 1968):111.

to be challenged by his children, who are asserting their independence and sovereignty at the expense of his authority within the family. The revolt of the rising generation demolishes at one blow the traditional pattern of interpersonal relations that the father had built up so laboriously over the years. Now his adolescents are defying him, breaking away from his control, and criticizing him for acting like the policeman he is.

Part of the future shock of our postindustrial era has been the unnatural prolongation of adolescence that forces young people into limbo. Frustrated by the enforced delay in attaining their goals, many adolescents in every social group—from lower-class gangs, middle-class hippies, to upper-class college demonstrators—have had run-ins with the police. Whether it is youthful crime, adolescent drug abuse, rock-and-roll mob scenes, or college sit-ins, it is the police officer who becomes the adversary as he regulates, defuses, and/or arrests adolescent lawbreakers. So when the police father looks at his own teenagers, he can envision an army of young people who epitomize defiance of lawful authority. As his children declare their emancipation, he worries that without his firm guidance they may get into serious difficulty or fall in with the wrong crowd when the peer culture takes over.

To make the situation more volatile, the police father is not without his own personal problems; for coinciding with the time that his youngsters reach adolescence, he is experiencing his own traumatic passage from vigorous adulthood through a mid-life transition that can be as disturbing to him and his family as the adolescent *rite de passage* faced by his children. The police parent veering through his forties is in reverse gear, braking toward a gradual diminution of power, reduction of opportunity, and a crisis of self-esteem. This mid-life transition, especially for the policeman whose physical vigor and self-confidence are so vital to his self-image, raises the anxiety level. At the minimum, it brings intimations of mortality, "the sense of bodily decline . . . and the sense of aging, which means to be old rather than young."[47]

About this time, the police officer hits the 17- or 18-year marker of his police career, and an impending crisis concerning retirement darkens the horizon. His reward for all those working years—a pension of half-pay—turns out to be more mirage than reality; for with inflation and escalating college tuition costs, even the full police salary is inadequate. And it becomes an impossible dream to expect to retire and live on a pension that amounts to about 50 percent of one's police paycheck.

Our sample of policemen realistically evaluated the economics of their retirement alternatives. Very few planned to retire completely and live on the pension when they became eligible to do so. Of the 23 (11 percent) who chose this option, only 12 were American police officers, and the 11 others were

[47] See, for example, Daniel J. Levinson et al., "The Psychosocial Development of Man in Early Adulthood and the Mid-Life Transition," in David Ricks, ed., *Life History Research in Psychopathology* (Minneapolis, Minn.: Univ. of Minnesota Press, 1974), 3:253-255.

British or Australian. It is a reflection of either the hardship of contemporary police work or of low morale that only 36 (37 percent) considered staying on after they reached the retirement point. Instead, more than two-thirds of the 211 policemen expressed a desire to leave police work but felt compelled to start a second career.

In the larger American cities, where the great majority of policemen work, conditions for the older members of the force have deteriorated so much that they feel that their best move would be to retire as soon as possible. The enterprising officer, then, a few years before the time of retirement, begins to search for possible employment outside the police field. Disappointingly, in the economic recession of the 1970s, good jobs for a retired policeman have all but disappeared. All the skills he had developed as an experienced police officer, or as a college graduate with a degree in police science or criminal justice, have little transfer value in the current employment market. Self-esteem takes a beating when an officer is told by interviewers that he is too old for most jobs, too unskilled or inexperienced for others, and unsuited for positions with some companies because of his police background. He may find police-correlated opportunities in security work as a bank guard, store or hotel detective, bonded messenger, or night watchman. Some insurance companies make a practice of hiring retired police officers as insurance claims investigators and adjusters, but the salaries offered are exceedingly low.

For a fortunate few policemen who had continued their education, a master's degree in criminal justice supplemented by their years of police experience enabled them to obtain positions in teaching or planning and research with the hundreds of criminal justice educational programs and agencies that sprang up and were fostered by the billions of dollars the Law Enforcement Assistance Administration (LEAA) distributed. But now, with retrenchment under President Carter, LEAA has closed many of its regional offices and cut back its financial support across the board. Thus, many worthwhile opportunities for highly educated officers have become increasingly rare.

Having struggled up the social scale successfully, the now disillusioned officer begins to wonder why he should step down to a job that is much lower in prestige and with a salary that, combined with his police pension, is no more than what he earned as a police officer. The usual decision is to stay on the job a few more years to build up the pension and get the children through college. But although it is a rational compromise, it is not a happy one. The job of pounding a beat is too arduous for a man past the age of retirement. The eyes are not as sharp for the search at night, the heart is not as strong for the long chase or the winding flights of stairs, the aches and pains of rheumatism and arthritis plague the older man. Worst of all is the depressing realization that there is no place for him to go; he is tied to the job.

Inexorably, when the moment of truth occurs and the police officer retires, he discovers that there is no real escape from the job. He may try to forget his career as a policeman, but he is still propelled by the magnetic force of the occupation. Many retirees harbor a nostalgia for the old life and, unable to accept the divorce, visit precinct station houses week after week, seeking out old buddies. At one extreme is the legend of the pensioned police officer who for many years after his separation from the force conscientiously continued to patrol his old post in uniform.[48] At the other are those who continue their association in a less concrete but more symbolic pattern. Members of this relatively small group immortalize their police adventures in autobiographical and idealized versions that whitewash their careers or write police novels that sometimes sensationalize or vitalize the essence of police work. In between is a large cadre of former policemen who belong to a wide variety of social and welfare organizations for retired police officers. Their meetings are largely devoted to reminiscences of the good old days in uniform.

It is a hallowed ritual for the colleagues of a retiring officer to present him with a gold shield, a replica of his badge of office, which he treasures almost as much as the real tin because it is a memento of his former occupational clout and charisma. The retiree will unhesitatingly flash this facsimile gold shield when he is stopped by a radio car for a traffic violation. Out of a sense of solidarity, many times the men in the radio car will wave him on with a warning instead of issuing a summons.

In our personal life we have observed that although Arthur retired from the police department many years ago, acquaintances still persist in identifying him as a policeman. After five years of teaching at Hofstra University, Arthur was finally beginning to think of himself as a professor of sociology until he passed two students on campus and heard one say to the other, "There goes the old cop." When our older son, Victor, became a national champion in squash racquets, he became the subject of many articles that appeared in well-known magazines and newspapers. Invariably, the write-ups would mention that his father was a New York City policeman, although Arthur had been a professor for many years.

That the brand of the policeman cannot be erased completely, even after 30 years of an illustrious second career as a physician, came vividly to our attention at a recent conference on police stress. This symposium, attended by high-ranking police officers, also included a cross-section of faculty and practitioners. A practicing psychiatrist, who many years before had been a member of the police force and had resigned to study medicine, delivered a stimulating paper outlining his views on stress. At the conclusion of his talk, an assistant chief inspector of the police department, impressively weighted with the stars of his office on his jacket and with heavy gold braid on his hat, approached and respectfully prefaced a question to the psychiatrist by addressing him as, "Sir." Later, the physician admitted sheepishly to us that for the moment he still felt like a policeman and had to make an effort to hold back his initial reflex action to salute the superior officer and stand at attention.

[48] *Spring 3100* (September 1975):14.

The job controls a police officer's life when he is on the force, and it haunts him when he leaves. Once a cop, always a cop.

Policemen's Wives: The Blue Connection

Under the romantic umbrella of courtship and idyllic love, the police shield radiates the illusion of a valorous knight wooing his fair lady. For the affianced couple this idealized view of the law enforcement officer as chivalrous protector and provider complements mutual emotional needs. But the exigencies of the occupation soon filter through this layer of euphoria. Even on her wedding day, no doubt chosen expediently to conform to the groom's unconventional work schedule, the bride of the police officer senses that she has married not only the man, but also his job. Nevertheless, she would have to possess extraordinary powers of ESP to envisage that this invisible member of the wedding party could become as oppressive and intrusive as any stereotypical mother-in-law.

The shadow of the job darkens normal conjugal routines. The rhythm of existence switches abruptly every week, reminding the policeman's wife that she is a Cinderella with midnight the pivot around which the family schedule rotates. Generally, a member of the force must work around the clock, with tours of duty that alternate each week from midnight to 8 A.M. (the late tour or night shift) to 8 A.M. to 4 P.M. (the day tour) to 4 P.M. to midnight (the evening shift) and then repeat the cycle.

Because the revolving chart does not conform to the conventional work week, weekends and days off rarely coincide. A police officer may have to wait 15 years to accumulate enough seniority to warrant a vacation during the summer months. One shift out of three a wife may wait up past midnight in order to greet her husband. But the timing is bad: he's all keyed up, and she's half asleep.

The most difficult adjustment for the wife grows out of the late tour (midnight to 8 A.M.). Every third week she sleeps alone while her husband works the "graveyard" shift. Especially in these times of high crime rates, her imagination has been traumatized by the gory tales spotlighted by television and screaming newspaper headlines. As a result, many police wives lie awake nights for hours, lonely and fearful, translating the night sounds into threats against her, her children, and even her spouse. If she is a sensual person, her sexual cravings remain unsatisfied during those long nights.

When police officers return home after a late tour, some are eager for sex. But their individual marital clocks are set to a different meridian. The wife may not be in an amorous mood or a seductive pose after spending an insomniac night. She may be unwinding from the frenetic experience of packing the kids off to school and may be morosely contemplating the unpleasant chore of cleaning the house or getting dressed for work.

A marriage counselor we know managed to resolve this incompatibility of one frustrated police couple on the verge of divorce. The husband was convinced that his wife had no real feeling for him because whenever he came home from a late tour, his wife immediately fell into a deep sleep, forestalling any possibility of sexual relations. At a joint therapy session the wife explained that she worried so much when her husband worked the late shift that she could not sleep at all. But, when she heard his key turn in the door, the sound soothed her and acted like a powerful sleeping potion. As soon as the couple discovered that the reason for their sexual impasse was concern rather than indifference, together they plotted a more coordinated sexual timetable.

Other policemen, exhausted by the night's duty, may look forward to falling into bed in a quiet room. The wife tiptoes about, shushing the younger children, pulling the shades on the sun to simulate night, in order to facilitate his sleeping by day. But the exuberant spirits of preschoolers cannot be turned down by drawing the curtains. The responsibility and the pressure are on the wife. A final group of officers has learned to avoid any type of family confrontation—sexual or other—by stopping off on the way home for a few beers with the boys so that they will be drowsy enough to fall asleep as soon as they hit the bed.

Moreover, the realities of law enforcement, necessitating overtime duty in emergencies, unanticipated court appearances, extra hours for changing into and out of uniform, and time for commuting long distances to out-of-the-way precincts for special assignments extort onerous demands of her husband's already tight and intermittent swing-shift schedule. And the wife twists in the whirlpool of the job as well; her biological rhythms are distorted and social interaction becomes disorganized as she struggles in frustration to juggle engagements and to rearrange upset plans. After many broken dates, even close friends give up.

Contrary to the lyrics of the folk song that joyfully proclaim "everybody loves Saturday night," that last evening of the week can be interminably long and depressing to those sitting home alone. Typical domestic vignettes, although reported to us by police wives in a bantering and accepting tone, point up some of the inconveniences of forced accommodation to an arbitrary police work schedule when family life is involved:

Serving at 6 P.M. a breakfast special of orange juice, bacon and eggs, and "pouring coffee over the head" of a heavy-lidded husband, half-awake after his unsuccessful attempt to sleep during the day after a late tour.

Gaining 15 pounds sharing midnight snacks in a spirit of camaraderie with her husband after his 4 P.M. to midnight shift.

Coordinating the sexual timetable with the rigidity of the duty chart.

Missing the school picnic, the event of the year, and trying to console the children.

Drinking champagne alone on New Year's Eve.

Serving Thanksgiving dinner at an 11:30 A.M. brunch because one wife remembered wistfully her own childhood disappointment when her father, a train engineer, missed festive family occasions.

In recent books by police officers, the disruptive effect of the changing shift is a target of concern, as in this perceptive analysis by a police officer-psychologist:

These changing hours take a large toll of a man. About seventeen times a year you are asked to change your pattern of sleeping and eating, as well as your sexual pattern. Police are subject to strange sexual patterns because of this change of hours, and their wives also must get accustomed to the change. The shifting hours bring an added hazard to marriage, which holds hazards enough. The average wife's routine is upset when her husband sleeps during the day and she must keep the children quiet, sometimes an impossible task. A wife who feels insecure may look on the late tour as a threat to her marriage if her husband fails to come home from work, seeking relaxation elsewhere. The shift that ends at midnight, when he is still wound up from the excitement of the day and wants companionship and gaiety, is the one that may lead to trouble for both the bachelor and the married Don Juan.[1]

This accumulation of grievances against the evening and late tours explained why two-thirds of the wives answering our questionnaire preferred the 8 A.M. to 4 P.M. tour over the other two, and why a scant 10 percent favored the late tour. In an interesting variation, the wives correctly perceived their husband's preferences for the 4 P.M. to midnight tour.

Despite this dearth of prime time for family togetherness, it came as quite a surprise to us that most police wives have learned to adapt to their vexations. When we assessed their attitudes toward the schedule, the majority (nearly 60 percent) of the group was convinced that the schedule had little effect on family living. In fact, 18 percent asserted that the duty chart actually strengthened family life, and only 23 percent believed that it weakened family life.

In theory, when a police wife has a job outside the home, a side effect might be that the inflexibility of the police clock would complicate family logistics. Indeed, in a television documentary on a black police family, the working wife did complain to her husband, "If we see each other ten hours a week, it's a lot. When I'm going, you're coming."[2] But only a minority of the working wives,

---

[1] Harvey Schlossberg and Lucy Freeman, *Psychologist with a Gun* (New York: Coward, McCann and Geoghegan, 1974), p. 47.

[2] The George Family, "Six American Families," WNET Channel 13, April 25, 1977.

both on our questionnaire and in personal discussions, would endorse her objections. When we analyzed the findings on the item, "How does your husband's police work schedule affect your family life?" 65 percent of the working wives disclosed that the schedule did not affect their lives much. This statistic was 10 percent higher than the figure tallied by their nonworking counterparts. The opinion of the two groups was in close harmony on the possible weakening effect of the schedule; 25 percent of the working wives (a mere 2 percent more than nonworking wives) felt that the schedule did weaken family life. The percentages for English and Australian wives parallel these results. Perhaps, for a wife in pursuit of a career or an education, it may be an asset to have a police officer husband whose peculiar schedule permits him to be home with the children, do some marketing, or start dinner preparation while she is at work or school.

Regardless of how she responds to the erratic tempo of the police timetable, the truth is that for the police wife it is never an easy accommodation. As a police officer friend of the Georges—the family so candidly screened on television—succinctly commented, "It's harder to be a cop's wife than a cop."

Of necessity, a police wife must cope with pressing problems endemic to her husband's work. In her situation the ring of the doorbell or the telephone does not signal a pleasant interlude but portends an ominous alarm—a threat of another crisis or emergency that wrests her husband from her while proclaiming the absolute power of the job. She lives with the frightening awareness that her husband on patrol is virtually a soldier on the firing line. Her role must be that of the rear echelon backup suffused with the attendant anxiety, unnerved by the shriek of every siren, distraught at each snatch of crime news on radio or television. It is this apprehension that is the common denominator binding police wives together.

Are you scared to death? The one thing police wives have an excess of is fear: fear of the other woman, fear of the gun, fear of the criminal, fear of the husband being killed, fear of being alone late at night, etc. You name it and we all have it. You may not verbalize it, but it's there.[3]

The wife's fear is the mirror image of the sense of danger that sociologist Jerome Skolnick found to be the vital force shaping the police officer's working personality. For the man on the beat, it engenders an exaggerated suspicion that reduces other people to the level of symbolic assailants.[4] In fact, this suspicion may be confirmed statistically because "the police are the only peacetime occupational group with a systematic record of death and injury from gunfire

---

[3] Barbara E. Webber, ed., *Handbook for Law Enforcement Wives* (Chicago: L E Publishers, 1974), p. 26. Webber is the wife of a police lieutenant attached to the police force in Urbana, Illinois.

[4] Jerome Skolnick, *Justice without Trial* (New York: Wiley, 1966), pp. 42-48.

and other weaponry."[5] It is this element of danger that "isolates the policeman socially from that segment of the citizenry which he regards as symbolically dangerous and also from the conventional citizenry with whom he identifies."[6] Thus, cut off from intimate interaction with civilian groups, the police officer falls back on his wife. Thrown together with few competing social relations, the connection becomes symbiotic and dramatically intense. The wife, already sensitized by her own apprehension, fatalistically identifies with her husband's perception of danger.

No matter how independent and resistant wives may be at first, eventually they are infected by anxiety concerning their husbands. A poignant illustration of this concern occurred at a lecture for policemen's wives by a high-ranking administrator commanding a new police department unit expressly established to provide a full range of services to the wives. The first question from a wife, "Who will notify me if my husband is killed or seriously injured on the job?" provoked a discussion that occupied the audience for more than 20 minutes.

Other wives have complained bitterly about the practice of the networks in broadcasting news of injured or slain police officers before formal notification is made to the family of the victim. Radio and television newscasts circulate the facts and then add that the name of the officer is being withheld pending notification of the next of kin. Many wives, hearing this, become frantic and bombard their husbands' precincts with desperate telephone calls.

Fear operates just as radically upon the wives, whether their husbands are members of large or small departments. How they verbalize their gut feelings is as varied as the wives themselves, and spans the spectrum from subdued frustration to overt pessimism. The wife of a former New York City police commissioner acknowledged that she shared her own sense of foreboding with other police wives:

I think most police wives have the same thoughts in the back of their minds—it's always there. You don't continually think about it but you're always happy to see him walk in after a 12-8 and you give a quiet Amen.[7]

Psychological sisters in the similarity of their response to the danger implicit in their husbands' work, other police wives have vocalized their subliminal alarm. This worry appears to be a ubiquitous syndrome of law enforcement wives around the globe. From the Midwest a spouse reflects:

I think what you're asking me is, "Will he come home again?" I never think about this, at least on the surface, but I know it's in the back of my mind. At such times, my philosophy is: What will be will be.[8]

[5] Ibid., p. 47.
[6] Ibid., p. 44.
[7] "Meet Mrs. Cawley," *Spring 3100* (September 1973):21.
[8] "Making a Police Marriage Work: The Policeman's Wife," *The Law Officer* (January-February 1977):8.

The wife of a constable in Toronto comments:

I'm really not sure that the factor of his coming home again sits that firmly in my mind. Some of the other police wives talk about it, but—from my standpoint—it's not something I dwell on, unless—of course—if a dangerous situation involving police and criminals gets a lot of publicity. Then, it would bother me, because the awareness would be there. But do you know what's odd about all this?

It's the fact that I seem to worry more now about Paul than I did in the beginning, even though he's been a constable [patrolman] for over 12 years.[9]

And an excerpt from a letter written by an Australian constable's wife reveals:

It is such a good feeling to hear the car pull into the garage at night, 2 hours overdue and to see one's husband get out of the car all in one piece, after lying in bed for hours imagining all sorts of danger that he could have confronted.[10]

Conceivably, because she is the wife of a police officer, she may face danger herself. In St. Anne, Illinois, the wife of the police chief often accompanied him on patrol in the squad car. While attempting to settle an altercation among three men, the chief was fatally shot and handed her his revolver as he died. Two of the assailants entered the police car and threatened to kill her. She picked up the revolver and killed the two of them.[11]

Sometimes even the home does not guarantee sanctuary to a member of the force, as this harrowing incident dramatizes. About 2:30 A.M. a Liberian diplomat and a professor from Rutgers University, while walking to their car in New York City, "were knocked down, pummeled, gouged, stomped and beaten" viciously by a gang of youths. The women in the group screamed for help.

One of those who came to a window was Officer John Crowe of the 30th Precinct. When he saw the beatings, he raced to the street in a white T-shirt and pants. The youths began beating him when he tried to break up the fight.

Officer Crowe's wife phoned in a 10-13—"policeman needs assistance"—call and soon patrol cars from the 50th Precinct in the Bronx converged on the intersection.

The police drove the two victims and the intervening policeman to the Montefiore Hospital for treatment.[12]

How can wives shunt intimations of tragedy from their thoughts when they are barraged so unrelentingly by the media? Headlines blazon crime and

[9] Ibid.

[10] Letter from Mrs. Monica M. Amos, "Views from Down Under," *FBI Law Enforcement Bulletin* (March 1976):15.

[11] *New York Times*, August 31, 1974, p. 45.

[12] Ibid., May 7, 1973, pp. 1, 10.

violence; perilous actions of law enforcement officers saturate front pages; television and novels sensationalize police work into gun-blasting adventure; police magazines and departmental newsletters feature news of ambushes and assaults upon the members of the force. But no matter how this morbid fascination of the media prepares the wife, when serious injury occurs to her husband, the anticipation never mitigates the personal horror of the episode.

After her husband, a 17-year veteran of the force, was nearly blinded by a mixture of lye and ammonia hurled at him by a barricaded ex-convict gone berserk, the shocked wife of the victim mused: "Even though you're married to a policeman, you're never prepared for this. The news didn't really sink in until this morning, waking up alone."[13]

Contributing to this disquietude, immediate and tangible omens of the ultimate disaster—a police officer slain in action—thrust their barbs at the morale of vulnerable wives:

An innocuous request from a police society to her husband to assist at an outing for children of officers killed on duty.

Immediate financial assistance from the Hundred Club to law enforcement families after a police officer's death or critical injury in the line of duty. (This private philanthropic organization of more than 60 clubs across the country provides scholarships to the children and pays off mortgages and other debts of the stricken family.)

Passage by Congress of the Public Officers Benefit Act of 1976, providing for a $50,000 award to survivors of officers killed in line of duty.

The utilization of a form letter of condolence from the President to the bereaved widow. (Because of the projected frequency of these deaths, the letters are programmed on magnetic tape selectric typewriters and signed mechanically by the automatic signature machine.)[14]

The funerals of police heroes where they are honored posthumously with the same ceremonial rituals accorded a slain inspector, replete with flag-draped coffin, muffled drumbeats, hundreds of uniformed fellow officers assembled in respectful tribute to a fallen comrade, and the final pathetic touch—the distraught widow supported by comforting relatives and friends.

Depressing confirmation of the wives' premonition of disaster is reinforced by the annual charts that tabulate macabre figures on the number of police officers killed and assaulted in the United States (see table 5-1). Would it not be natural then for a wife to react emotionally and interpret these impersonal computations into a grim statistic of one?

[13] Ibid., August 3, 1976, p. 33.
[14] Ibid., March 3, 1977, p. 33.

Table 5-1
Police Officers Killed and Assaulted in the United States, 1966-1976

Year	Number Killed	Number Assaulted	Rate per Hundred for Assaults
1966	99	23,851	10.6
1967	123	26,755	13.5
1968	123	33,604	15.8
1969	125	35,202	16.9
1970	146	43,171	18.7
1971	178	49,787	18.7
1972	153	31,763	15.1
1973	134	32,535	15.0
1974	132	29,511	15.1
1975	129	44,867	15.4
1976	111	49,079	16.8

Source: *FBI Uniform Crime Reports*, 1966-1976.

Overwhelmed by the mounting apprehension, some police wives have gone so far as to advise others, "Treat each day as if it were the last day of your husband's life," and to suggest that the casual kiss goodbye to a husband leaving for work might very well be a farewell embrace for eternity. And so with all this buildup of anxiety surfacing in our personal encounters with wives, articulated at meetings of police wives' associations corroborated by anecdotal evidence from other sources, we were reasonably certain that it would not require a sensitive seismic device to detect their tremors of concern for their spouses' welfare. Accordingly we predicted that their responses to our question, "When your husband is at work, do you worry about his safety?" would register high on this scale of worry. Instead, the wives reacted contrary to our inferences, as they also did to questions about adaptations to their spouses' around-the-clock work schedule. The majority, 116 (54 percent) worried a little, and 31 (15 percent) not at all, but only 63 (30 percent) of the wives admitted that they worried a lot.

What is the explanation for this discrepancy between their spoken words and their tallied responses? Dr. Bruce Danto of the Department of Psychiatry at Wayne State University suggests a rationale for these contradictory patterns.

Death expectation would appear to be important for the wife of a police officer for three reasons: she is aware of the danger inherent in her husband's work; she may see him through various kinds of injuries incurred through his work; and she is a member of the police family in the sense that she associates with other wives of officers and shares experience, loneliness, and doubt. It might be assumed that until such danger clues are present the police officer's wife deals with the prospect of injury and death through denial. She may unconsciously block fears of his dangerous tasks and the risks he takes. She may feel that such fate is for someone else, not for her and her husband.[15]

Solving this paradox and translating this sophisticated psychological analysis into language more appropriate for the police family, a cop's wife asserts:

Often I am asked, "Don't you worry about your husband's getting killed?" Of course I do, but if I worried about it constantly, I would not be able to function as a wife, parent or—as is so often necessary—as both parents to my children.[16]

Personnel of the employee relations section of the New York City Police Department become intimately acquainted with the fortitude of police wives, because this unit has the responsibility of notifying the next of kin when a police officer is killed or seriously injured while on duty. In an attempt to soften the shock, a team consisting of a captain from this division, a chaplain, and the police partners of the dead or stricken officer go at once to his home to inform the wife. A captain of this command told us that frequently the men in the team break down and have to lean on the grieving wife for support and consolation. Somehow, she finds the strength to bear the heartache.

In actuality, there is little choice for the police wife. Either she finds the psychological resources to bend resiliently under the crushing strains and stresses of the occupation and snap back or she will break under the pressure, with consequent disruption in family relationships. And many wives do possess this flexibility and insight:

It is not all honey and roses. We are truly a special breed. We must have the foreknowledge of twenty average wives, the stamina of ten men and the patience of a saint. The average wife can have a fight with her guy and let him go off to work without a second thought. We cannot do that, because he might not come home. We do not dwell on this thought, it will do neither one of us any good but it is a very real hard fact that we do live with.[17]

The manifest destiny of the policeman's wife is eventual submission to the job. Submission does not necessarily denote defeat, however. She copes by forging a new role—therapist to her husband—requiring her to be supportive, compassionate, and attentive. Since the impact of the job is funneled through

[15] Bruce L. Danto, "A Study: Bereavement and the Widows of Slain Officers," *The Police Chief* (February 1974):52.

[16] Lucille Gonzalez, "The Life of a Cop's Wife," letter to the *New York Times*, February 20, 1977, Long Island Section, p. 26.

[17] Newsletter of the New York City Policemen's Wives Association, Centereach, New York, December 1975.

her husband, her best defense is to nullify its adverse effect upon the marriage by fortifying him. To be consistent, her design is to convert the home into a haven, a buffer zone.

Typically, the wife pays a price for this successful adjustment. By assuming the traditional function of the homemaker subordinate to that of the male breadwinner, she may have to sacrifice many of her own aspirations and derive her sense of accomplishment vicariously through the exploits of her husband.

Two recent guidebooks written by police wives provide the blueprints for this lifestyle of self-help psychology, delegating responsibility to the loving helpmate at home for smoothing out the strains of law enforcement. These do-it-yourself handbooks on the power of positive thinking suggest that following their curriculum for adaptation will ensure domestic tranquility.

Girls, I hope this doesn't upset you, but I personally don't think that women's liberation has any place within a police department. You need to be a little happy homemaker. If your guy is happy, you'll be happy.[18]

Understand the man, find out what kind of a wife he wants. Then be that kind of a wife and you'll probably never have to worry too much about losing him.[19]

Sometimes a wife can best help a husband who's down by fixing him a good meal. She can help by being available to talk if he wants that, by steering his thoughts away from his hostilities, being considerate and sympathetic without encouraging self-pity, by understanding his silence during dinner and his unresponsiveness in bed and by just loving him. Understanding his need for status and a sense of personal worth and realizing he's in a game where all are losers, she can serve as an ego-builder when that's what he most needs. A psychologist says there's nothing like a judicious pat on the back to keep a man from getting ulcers.[20]

The candid answers of police wives to our open-ended question, "Do you have any advice that might be of help to other police families?" confirm that many of them have internalized these popular sentiments and have incorporated them into the family milieu. Curiously, the lower the rank and the shorter the time on the job, the more likely the wife was to give advice to other police couples. A sampling of typical responses to this item articulates this point of view.

The wife of police officer in New York City Police Department with 1 year on the job said:

[18] Donna Parker, "Be His Anchor," in Webber, *Handbook*, p. 55. Parker is the wife of a police officer in Champaign, Illinois.

[19] Marsha Wilson, "The Way We Are," in Webber, *Handbook*, p. 61. Wilson is married to an Urbana, Illinois, police officer.

[20] Pat James and Martha Nelson, *Police Wife: How to Live with the Law and Like It* (Springfield, Ill.: Charles C. Thomas, 1975), p. 52. James is the wife of a police officer in the Oklahoma City Police Department, and Nelson is her mother.

Never let your husband walk out that door angry with you. Apologize whether you're right or wrong. It may be the last time you get the chance.

The wife of a police officer in New York City Police Department with 5 years on the job said:

Give all the support, love and compassion you can. Smile, be cheerful and pray for him. Most of all, be proud of him.

The wife of a sergeant in the Hartford (Connecticut) Police Department with 13 years on the job said:

As a family stick together. Advice for a wife—be tolerant, try to understand and always be there when needed. Advice given to me many years ago by a policeman's wife. Don't ever send him off to work mad or with an empty stomach. Our lives are different and outsiders don't care. Just try to make the best of it.

The wife of a police officer in the Lansing (Michigan) Police Department with 8 months on the job said:

Patience. Understanding and as much objectiveness as possible in trying to understand the job and how it affects the man. Respect him, but don't expect him to be superman. Because of the tension involved in this kind of job I believe a pleasant home atmosphere is of the utmost importance. He has to react too quickly on the job to have unsettling thoughts of home following him throughout the day.

The wife of a patrolman in the Seaside Heights (New Jersey) Police Department with 4 years on the job said:

Well, I think the important thing for a wife is to work extra hard at loving her husband. Give him understanding and if he needs to blow steam off once in a while, let him do it. The only thing it hurts is your ears. My husband and I don't fight if he is in a bad mood. I let him blow off all the steam and when the fire is gone then we discuss.

The wife of a patrolman in the Beachwood (New Jersey) Police Department with 7 years on the job said:

To be as patient as humanly possible. To live each day to its fullest. Do things as a family unit (bicycle riding, bowling, etc.). Always communicate. A family not only shares good times, they should also share the hard times.

The wife of a rookie in the New York City Police Department with 1 year on the job said:

If a man goes on the job, and he really wants it, the woman (wife) has got to stick behind her husband all the way. If a man isn't happy with his job, this could cause marital problems. The wife of a patrolman must be strong. A patrolman's wife leads a very lonely life. Nite after nite I sit and restlessly wait for my husband to come thru the door and when he finally comes home I thank God for another day.

The wife of a police officer in the New York City Police Department with 7 years on the job said:

You must realize that when he becomes a cop he will make a definite change in attitude and personality. Sometimes he might go a little crazy for a while. Try to be patient and understanding. They will eventually come down to earth. Another thing I try to stress is trust. Learn to trust him and love him a lot because he's got a real tough job.

The wife of a patrolman in the New York City Police Department with 9 years on the job said:

Always make the most of the time you have together. The rotating shifts are especially difficult when children are in school and so the time spent as a family unit is valuable. Make your home as pleasant as possible, a place where he knows he is wanted, needed and loved very much. Don't nag about the hours and the social engagements you miss because of the shifts, remember he misses them too. Get yourself involved in other activities so time doesn't hang heavy when he is working. Most important of all, love him a lot—he has to put up with some pretty bad scenes in the course of his day—help him to enjoy his time away from the job.

The wife of a patrolman in the New York City Police Department with 12 years on the job:

Don't sit by and watch your man worry. Help him by listening to his problems. And then try to help him solve them. If your son or daughter comes home and tells you the P.T.A. needs cakes for their sale you're right there. If the local afternoon bridge club is short one player you can leave the dishes and let the housework go. These people and monetary things can all wait. Your husband has the toughest job of all so give him your all.

The wife of a detective in the New York City Police Department with 10 years on the job said:

Yes, I see the younger couples today leading really very separate lives. Don't try to plan just for your own immediate family outings, picnics, take the children to the park, visiting, etc. Love each other and be understanding of job-related problems. Be grateful and learn to be a self-content person. Be close to your children as their father will eventually see and appreciate all your efforts. Put your free time to good constructive use in whatever makes you as a person, well and happy.

On the surface, the marital philosophy of the police wives resembles the system expounded by Marabel Morgan, who conducts seminars to convert wives to the doctrine of the "Total Woman." She admonishes every wife to live through her husband and to "Accept Him! Admire Him! Adapt to Him! and Appreciate Him!" But Morgan administers an overdose of submission in her prescription for happiness in marriage. In our opinion, most police wives would consider it debasing to accept her formula of "total" immersion.

A Total Woman caters to her man's special quirks, whether it be in salads, sex, or sports. She makes his home his haven, a place to which he can run. She allows him that priceless luxury of unqualified acceptance.[21]

Love your husband and hold him in reverence, it says in the Bible. That means admire him. *Reverence* according to the dictionary, means "To respect, honor, esteem, adore, praise, enjoy, and admire."[22]

It is only when a woman surrenders her life to her husband, reveres and worships him, and is willing to serve him, that she becomes really beautiful to him. She becomes a priceless jewel, the glory of femininity, his queen![23]

The difference between the two groups seems to be that the Total Woman senses a threat of danger to her marriage, while the police wife senses a threat of danger to her husband. As a result, their tactical objectives reflect this contrasting motivation: for the Total Woman, an improvement in her inner security; for the police wife, an improvement in her husband's well-being. Nor would a policeman's wife endorse Morgan's placebo of contrived sexuality as typified by one of her personal anecdotes describing how she greets her husband at the door wrapped in "pink baby-doll pajamas and white boots after a bubble bath."[24] Nor would the ambience of the police work situation permit the wife of a policeman to copy Janet, one of Morgan's disciples, who telephoned her spouse to say, "Honey, I'm eagerly waiting for you to come home. I crave your body."[25]

Adaptation to the job by the police wife in no way connotes servility. Submission to the constraints and exigencies of police work cannot be avoided,

[21] Marabel Morgan, *The Total Woman* (New York: Pocket Books, 1975), p. 60.

[22] Ibid., pp. 64-65.

[23] Ibid., pp. 96-97.

[24] Ibid., p. 116.

[25] Ibid., pp. 145-146.

but this should not be misinterpreted as encompassing subservience. In many ways her mode of adjustment can be defined as an affirmation of her interpersonal competence. She is fulfilling the role of therapist, whose empathy provides equilibrium and contentment to another human being in need. She is convinced that the overtones of her regimen will resonate to absorb and soften the tensions of the occupation. And her own personal fulfillment will be derived through her loved one.

This talent for adaptation is the kind of self-actualization that Abraham Maslow and other behavioral psychologists advocate. It occurs customarily in healthy people who are realistic, problem-centered rather than self-centered, autonomous, and self-accepting.[26] How well a police wife functioning smoothly in a successful marriage fits this portrait.

The key word—*adaptability*—translates just as fluently into the sexual sphere. These women have managed to neutralize the shattering of the circadian rhythms and the fusion of job-related anxieties, the two factors that are offered as damning evidence that police marriages are riddled with emotional and sexual conflict. The wives showed a remarkably high degree of sexual compatibility. A convincing majority, 129 (60 percent) of the wives who answered our questionnaires, discounted sexual incompatibility. Very few—6 out of 127 married to patrolmen, 1 wife of the 57 married to superior officers, and none of the English and Australian wives—checked sexual incompatibility as a frequent problem in their marriages.

How can we explain this ostensibly blissful state of sexual contentment? Are the wives, as well as their mates, so responsive to the occupational mystique that police officers are supersexed and great lovers that it becomes a self-fulfilling prophecy? When we started this survey, we had intended to include data concerning the area of sexual behavior of police couples. But as we progressed in our research, we decided to minimize references to sex, for in our pilot study we noticed that the gears of interviews, rap sessions, and conversations with our respondents locked as soon as we tried to ferret out any sexual revelations. And as communicative as our police couples had been, they decisively drew a curtain of privacy around the intimacies of their sexual relationships. What this reticence discloses inadvertently about law enforcement couples, no doubt, could serve as the core of a separate report.

Assuming that we had managed to penetrate the reserve of our respondents, their intimate revelations, combined and processed into statistical averages and norms, would end as merely numerical abstractions. Knowledgeable marital counselors recognize that "each individual couple strikes a balance in sex that best satisfies the needs and desires of wife and husband alike, reconciling the differences between them in the best way they know how."[27]

[26] See Abraham Maslow, *Motivation and Personality* (New York: Harper, 1954).

[27] Robert J. Levin and Amy Levin, "Sexual Pleasure: The Surprising Preferences of 100,000 Women," *Redbook Magazine* (September 1975):57-58.

Despite this initial roadblock, we were able to chart the demographic characteristics of our 184 American wives by utilizing the information culled from our questionnaires (see table 5-2). We also anticipated that religion, ethnic background, and class might serve as important variables to explain the marital adjustment of policemen's wives.

The majority of the wives are young mothers, Irish or Italian, and Catholic, with roots in the working class. Even with a liberal interpretation of their fathers' occupations, only 29 patrolmen's wives and 12 superior officers' wives can be assigned to the middle class. Nevertheless, they can be described as upwardly mobile, since 80 percent of the police wives together with their husbands own their homes and 60 percent live in the suburbs.

In accordance with the latest work, we employed a definition of the term *ethnicity* "based upon the common experience of past nationhood, shared religious identity, and coincident arrival on American shores."[28] Since the composite of police wives—Irish Catholic or Italian Catholic—matches the criteria for ethnic groups, it could very well be that the standing of women in the traditional ethnic culture might have some bearing on the special roles of police wives.

The position of the married women in each of these two groups has been

Table 5-2
Description of the Sample of American Police Wives
(N = 184)

Characteristics	Wives of Patrolmen and Detectives *(N = 127)*	Wives of Superior Officers *(N = 57)*	Total *(N = 184)*
Average age	30	36	32
Number of children	2	3	2.3
Number working	42	23	65
College graduates	13	10	23
Religion			
Catholic	92	21	113
Protestant	15	8	23
Jewish	10	3	13
Ethnic background			
Irish	37	24	61
Italian	22	14	36
German	12	4	16
Black	3	1	4

[28] Andrew M. Greeley, *Ethnicity in the United States* (New York: Wiley, 1974), p. 188: a similar definition can be found in Nathan Glazer and Daniel P. Moynihan, eds., *Ethnicity: Theory and Experience* (Cambridge: Harvard Univ. Press, 1975), pp. 1-16.

rather acerbically analyzed. In a cynical description of the role of the wife in the southern Italian family, a male chauvinist defines her status:

Like a good weapon, she should be cared for properly; like a hat she should be kept straight; like a mule, should be given plenty of work and occasional beatings. Above all, she should be kept in her place as a subordinate, for there is no peace in the house where a woman leads her husband.[29]

Few deny that the father is dominant in the traditional Italian family, but the Italian mother still projects "a strong figure within her own world, the household."[30] The Italian wife might arouse sympathy as a victim of a cruel male domination; but in the traditional Irish Catholic family, the wife is portrayed as hypercritical and authoritarian in her control of the family.

We note that the Irish mother in the family simultaneously presents an attractive and repellent role model to her daughter. A mother competent in her tasks about the home (perhaps more than a daughter could ever hope to be), who at the same time dominates and humiliates her husband in a way that may well repel her daughter.[31]

Neither description is relevant to a police wife. She is not a "mule," not kept in her place as a subordinate by her husband, not a "repellent" model who dominates and humiliates her husband and sons. An acceptance of the implications of these cultural roles would lead us to predict that Italian wives would be more likely to disclose that their husbands made the important decisions. Our findings refuted this inference. When we asked the wives, "Who makes most of the important decisions in your family?" we observed that although there were one and two-thirds as many Irish wives as Italian wives (61 versus 36) in our sample, three times as many Irish wives (19 versus 6) reported that their husbands made the important decisions. And not one of the 127 wives of patrolmen and detectives traced the locus of decisionmaking power to herself, although 26 of this group allocated this power to their husbands.

Once interest centers around questions of marital dominance or submission, Robert Winch's theory of complementary needs comes to mind. He proposed that among otherwise eligible candidates, "persons whose need patterns provide mutual gratification will tend to choose each other as marriage partners."[32] His

[29] Greeley, *Ethnicity,* p. 160.

[30] Ibid., p. 161.

[31] Ibid., pp. 164-165. See also Andrew M. Greeley, *That Most Distressful Nation: The Taming of the American Irish* (Chicago: Quadrangle Books, 1972), p. 110, in which he states, "It is my impression that there is a tendency for Irish women to have far more power in the family life than do women in some other ethnic cultures."

[32] Robert F. Winch, *The Modern Family*, rev. ed. (New York: Holt, Rinehart and Winston, 1963), p. 607.

type II pattern is exemplified by one partner with a high need to dominate who satisfies this need by marrying a person with a high need to be submissive.[33] Unfortunately, this one-to-one explanation has lost a good part of its credibility because of the substantial criticism of its underlying assumptions. Udry, one of the researchers in family sociology who has failed to confirm Winch's results, offers a powerful critique that exposes the pitfalls of the theory:

Many criticisms have been leveled at the idea of complementary needs. Several seem especially hard to answer. First, no study shows that the spouses themselves were aware of the complementary traits or that the existence of the traits had anything to do with the selection. There is abundant evidence to indicate that there is considerable discrepancy between what people perceive as the traits of others and what the others are really like. People have sung for centuries of the blindness of love. Second, there is something implausible about the idea that when whichever sex has whichever trait, it will be equally satisfying to both spouses.[34]

In addition, fully half the wives married their husbands before the men joined the police force. Some sociologists maintain that the police occupation inculcates traits of power and authoritarianism in police officers whether or not these qualities were present before.[35] In that case, it would be impossible for a wife to perceive characteristics that did not develop for years afterwards.

Our feeling is that the wife develops her role as a response to the challenge posed by her husband's occupation. The husband enjoys the benefits and encourages her. And as we have previously pointed out, this group of wives is upwardly mobile, climbing from working-class toward middle-class status. Thus they are divesting themselves of the traditional working-class wives' role as subordinate to the husband and are assuming an egalitarian model that is the hallmark of the middle-class wife.[36] Experts on marriage and the family reiterate this theme: "In the United States at present, women in all classes, except the most economically deprived, place companionship above economic support, sexual gratification, or the possibility of having children, as the prime value in marriage."[37]

Perhaps it is a combination of nostalgia and reaching for the unattainable

[33] Ibid., p. 586.

[34] J. Richard Udry, *The Social Context of Marriage*, 2d ed. (Philadelphia: J.B. Lippincott, 1971), pp. 207-208.

[35] For example, see Arthur Niederhoffer, *Behind the Shield* (Garden City, N.Y.: Doubleday, 1967), pp. 103-151. Skolnick, *Justice Without Trial*, pp. 42-70; Richard Bennett and Theodore Greenstein, "The Police Personality: A Test of the Predispositional Model," *Journal of Police Science and Administration* 3 (1975):439-445; and Larry Tifft, "The 'Cop Personality' Reconsidered," *Journal of Police Science and Administration* 2 (1974):266-278.

[36] For an analysis of the difference in the role of the middle-class and working-class wife, see Lillian B. Rubin, *World of Pain: Life in the Working Class Family* (New York: Basic Books, 1976).

[37] Betty Yorburg, *The Changing Family* (New York: Columbia Univ. Press, 1973), p. 127.

that explains why these women, evidently so dedicated to a role in which family and home are of central concern, should inconsistently still feel a sense of rapport with the modern feminist movement. Paradoxically, despite having reached a decision that definitively deflates their dreams of self-actualization, these wives view the feminist movement rather positively. In answer to our question, "How do you feel about the women's liberation movement?" 42 percent reported that they favored it, 31 percent opposed it, and 26 percent expressed indifference to it.

The majority of wives predictably cluster closer to the midpoint of the continuum, coping and adjusting to an unusual and difficult pattern of life. Not having committed themselves to the same extent as their sisters at the ends, these wives are ambivalent. They feel drawn toward liberation but realize that once committed to self-actualization, they might be less supportive of their husbands. Again, when faced with a decision, the wife decides in favor of the husband to the detriment and even the destruction of her own aspirations toward independence and fulfillment. It is almost a forced choice determined by the weight of the job acting on and through her husband.

These wives share the same dilemma that currently plagues other women across the nation concerning support for the pending equal rights amendment. Intellectually they endorse it, but subjectively they fear the consequences, not only for themselves, but also for their children. Having strived for and having finally entered the middle class, they vacillate as to whether they should vote for an amendment that has the potential of agitating traditional arrangements in business, the professions, and the home. They ponder whether it would be fair to their children if their own mothers engender the conditions for a chaotic new world. For their daughters, they still prefer the time-honored feminine occupations; for their sons, they desire entry into the professional world.

When we asked these women what their reaction would be if their daughters wanted to become police officers, 52 percent of those responding to the question vetoed this choice of career; only 26 percent found it acceptable (the rest were neutral). Among those who would reject this selection were many who vehemently dissented: "I would literally have a heart attack"; "Think her a jerk"; "No way"; "Dismay"; "Sad"; "Hysterical." The same question pertaining to their sons stirred a mental conflict for these mothers. If they opposed their sons' ambition to become a police officer, they would be indirectly criticizing or derogating their husbands' occupation. Approximately 29 percent of the wives answering this question would reject this choice by their sons; 43 percent indicated that they would be favorably disposed.

A final opportunity to clarify their true feelings presented itself when we asked, "What career would you prefer for your daughter?" and "What career would you prefer for your son?" Given the opportunity on this open-ended question to route the career path for their sons, the individual responses of the police officer husbands and the wives demonstrated that they would detour their offspring from a choice of law enforcement as a profession. And in common with the aspirations of most parents who wish that their children will surpass them, these mothers and fathers longed for professional careers for their boys. Their expectations for their daughters, however, conformed to conventional norms for feminine pursuits: teacher, nurse, and housewife (see tables 5-3 and 5-4).

If wives disapprove of law enforcement as a career for their children, how pleased are they with their husbands' job? On our questionnaire fewer than half the wives (44 percent) expressed happiness with their husbands' work, and a majority (51 percent) said they were "resigned to it." Consequently, it is reasonable to assume that most police wives have made an uneasy peace with the occupation.

But they are by no means brainwashed; they comprehend all the short-comings and injustices, and they gripe: "My mother always told me never to marry a salesman or a policeman. She said he'd never be home when I needed him. So, of course, I did what she told me not to do."[38] Almost 50 percent of the wives whose patrolman and detective husbands rank at the bottom of the hierarchy complained about low salaries, low public prestige, and the biased promotion and disciplinary system. In culmination of their simmering discontent, 80 percent of the wives wanted their mates to retire from police work when they became eligible to do so, although it would be an economic hardship because of the inadequate pensions.

Some wives resent the job from the beginning and only reluctantly come to terms with it. And when discontent brews, it may not mellow, even after many department promotions. In a published interview, Assistant Chief Inspector Simon Eisdorfer of the New York City Police Department describes the persistent opposition of the women in his family from the moment that he made

Table 5-3
Parents' Choice of Career for Their Sons

Police Officers (N = 182)			Wives (N = 184)		
Rank Order	Career	Number Choosing	Rank Order	Career	Number Choosing
1	Lawyer	51	1	Son's choice	70
2	Son's choice	44	2	Lawyer	41
3	Doctor	37	3	Doctor	35
4	A profession	19	4	A profession	15
5	Business	13	5	Business	12
6	Law enforcement	9	6	Law enforcement	6

[38] *New York Times*, January 21, 1977, p. A16.

Table 5-4
Parents' Choice of Career for Their Daughters

Rank Order	Career	Number of Choices	Rank Order	Career	Number of Choices
	Police Officers (N = 182)			Wives (N = 184)	
1.	Teacher	38	1.	Daughter's choice	54
2.	Daughter's choice	31	2.	Nurse	39
	Nurse	31	3.	Teacher	32
3.	Housewife	26	4.	Housewife	15
4.	Lawyer	15		Office work	15
5.	Office work	14	5.	Doctor	11
6.	Doctor	13	6.	Lawyer	10
7.	A profession	4	7.	A profession	7

Note: Many respondents listed more than one occupational choice (doctor *and* lawyer for example). Miscellaneous occupations that received no more than two choices were omitted from the table.

the police list in 1938: "His wife, Beatrice, like his mother long ago, did not like his becoming a policeman. 'For thirty years she kept after me to get into something else,' he said, 'She finally gave up.' "[39]

Ever sensitive to the pressure points of police work, most of the wives have compromised and repressed their resentment, opting for a peaceful coexistence as aides-de-camp in a buffer zone. This ambience of compliance diverges from the tenets of the emerging feminist climate of contemporary middle-class America, which so disparages the archetype of the traditional female role in the family.

For the police officer husband, it is equally rewarding to contemplate a daily ego massage and to be the center about which family life orbits. And by his tacit approval he stamps in this mode of behavior.

The police job intrudes as a grey eminence, a shadowy partner in this merger. When everything is going smoothly, she's OK, he's OK, the job's OK. And elastically, the wife flexes with the tension of law enforcement. She has learned to "cool it" and maintain her equanimity when confronting the erratic jumps of the work schedule and the gloomy threat of danger.

The formidable responsibility of safeguarding the police revolver was accepted with nonchalance by nearly 50 percent of our sample of American wives to whom it presented no problem at all; to another 20 percent, it caused only minor inconvenience. Police wives routinely carry a large handbag on trips to the beach, etc., to store the weapon safely when, obviously, it would be impossible for their husbands to comply with the regulation requiring them to have the firearm in their possession at all times.

[39] Ibid., June 16, 1974, BQLI Section, p. 15.

In a police marriage already in trouble, however, these tangential occupational obligations often aggravate conditions. Contrast the remarks of this disgruntled police wife, staying married for the sake of the three children, who perceives her husband's police revolver as a horrible excrescence: "There's that gun. I hate it. It's with him, part of him, 24 hours a day, attached to his body. It's like a cancer, a large tumor, sticking out of his body."[40]

Interpersonal relations thrive on communication. And certainly, free-flowing lines are a prerequisite for the success of a marital partnership. Because the police wife has invested so heavily in the marriage by assuming a vicarious role in relation to her husband, she ends by becoming dependent on her spouse for the infusion of thrills and adventures as he recounts his experience on the job. She can relieve humdrum domestic routines by enjoying at second hand the excitement of police work. Her psychological stance cries out for open and full communication to prove intimacy and trust. One authority on the sociology of the family proposes that "the assumption in back of these beliefs is that many, if not most, problems exist because people do not communicate and therefore do not understand one another."[41]

But the police officer operates on his own wavelength. He finds it expedient not to reveal much about his work. Formulating his own concept, based on the secret society nature of the police force, he learns or is conditioned to be closemouthed about his job. Much of his work is too confidential; much of it is too revealing about conditions within the department or on the beat. Even in an intimate relationship a policeman senses that it would be discreet to keep these matters concealed from his wife. His code of silence may also be prompted by a chivalrous desire to protect his family from exposure to the real depths of society's violence, brutality, and personal agony. Without knowing it, the husband by a combination of occupational conventional wisdom and personal reticence has moved beyond the simplistic rule of full disclosure that is widely advocated but often proves a cause of dissension. He has reached a more sophisticated level that calls for a high degree of interpersonal competence in which the partners accept the principle that "probably selective communication is the key to the successful marriage. There are some thoughts and desires and attitudes which are destructive when communicated."[42]

The flaw in this arrangement is that both partners must accept the contract on communication. We found in our interviews with police wives that many of them resented and deplored the withholding of information and news. One wife wistfully contrasted the reticence of her police officer husband with the relaxed free flow of citizen-band communication.

We suspect a similar note of complaint underlies the answers to our query,

[40] Micki Siegel, "Don't Think About the Bad," *New York Sunday News Magazine*, February 23, 1975, p. 30.

[41] J. Richard Udry, *The Social Context of Marriage*, 2d ed. (Philadelphia: J.B. Lippincott, 1971), p. 250.

[42] Ibid., p. 251.

"How much does your husband tell you about the police job?" because 114 wives (54 percent) answered that their husbands told them a little; and 18 others added that their husbands told them nothing. Only 67 (31 percent) indicated that they were told a lot; and a mere 11 wives said that they were told everything by their husbands. A police widow nostalgically admitted that she was so accustomed to being her late husband's confidante that her life had become empty because she could no longer share his daily adventures.

No matter how intensely interested and involved they would like to be, most police wives are decisively locked out of their husbands' work world. Department fiat and the police officers' shared views of protocol preclude any significant or even potential intervention on her part. A psychological barrier, compounding her feeling of being an outsider, prevents her from entering the physical field of her husband's police duty: the beat he patrols.

Most police wives decry the obstacles placed between them and the job. For this reason, we were surprised that the popular and long-lived television police series "McMillan and Wife," depicting a police commissioner's wife as deeply involved in the activities of the department, was not included among the favorite programs of the police wives. Table 5-5 lists their television preferences. It is likely that this group of wives reacted so negatively to "McMillan and Wife" because they could see the artificiality of the contrived situation. They found it impossible to identify with a commissioner's wife who assisted him as an aide-de-camp. A former deputy police commissioner who, as an insider, would be highly qualified to comment on the authenticity of this network drama, spotted the false note and justified the rejection of the program by the wives.

I suggest that hardly anybody in this country knows what a police commissioner does. One thing he does not do is move through the police world accompanied by his wife as McMillan does. The police world is an all-male world. Even a good many of the police department's social functions—communion breakfasts and

Table 5-5
Wives' Ranking of Television Police Programs
(N = 213)

Rank	Program	Number of Choices
1	Kojak	62
2	Police Story	43
3	Columbo	16
4	Rookies	13
5	Streets of San Francisco	13
6	Adam 12	12
7	Toma	8
8	Policewoman	4

the like—are stag. It is true that most police departments contain a few policewomen. In New York the number is about 300 out of a force of 30,000. The sight of a luscious dish such as Mrs. McMillan hanging about all the time would distract the cops. No work would get done while she was around, and eventually her presence would become downright annoying.[43]

For once the male chauvinistic ideology cannot be blamed for the police protocol that discourages the presence of the wives in locations where their spouses are on patrol. The wife of an office worker can visit her husband's place of business occasionally and chat casually with his fellow employees while the children explore the copier, the calculator, and the switchboard. At most the visit causes a few minutes of delay in the office routine, but it is usually considered a pleasant interlude by everyone. But the policeman's office is in the street where theoretically he may be at any moment encountering emergency, disaster, or crime. This constant threat of danger would justifiably deter a conscientious officer from encouraging his family to visit him on post. Even on those occasions when he is assigned to relatively peaceful and enjoyable duty at a parade or sporting event, the crowds and congestion prevent a close view of a police officer husband.

Presumably, it would require an unusual degree of self-confidence or perhaps naiveté for a police wife to violate this unwritten code in order to observe her husband in action. One wife who did so learned at firsthand that the initiation of new police officers into the intricacies of law enforcement may prove embarrassing. She recounted this anecdote with wry humor:

His very first day out of the Academy, my parents and I went to his precinct and observed him giving out his very first ticket. All the other rookies gathered round to watch. When it was all finished, the man drove off; everyone patted my husband on the back and then he realized he forgot to get the man's name.

Statistical affirmation of the gulf separating the work space and the living space, with the attendant avoidance syndrome, appeared in our questionnaire. In our sample of wives, the majority (54 percent) had never observed their husbands on duty, fewer than 4 percent had observed them frequently, and the remaining group had observed them only seldom.

And while a police wife may not have actually pounded a beat with her spouse, she can tread the transparently thin line between on patrol and off duty. How the occupation erects a gangplank between work and leisure time has been outlined to us by law enforcement families in these scenes of thwarted recreational activity:

[43]Robert Daley, "Police Report on the TV Cop Shows," *New York Times Magazine*, November 19, 1972, p. 96.

A police officer aborts his family's long-awaited vacation trip because on the congested highway he stops to arrest a drunken driver who had been endangering other motorists.

A police officer intercepts a holdup in progress while routinely sharing the marketing chores with his wife at the local supermarket.

A police officer spoils an evening out on the town with his wife by jumping off a crosstown bus to apprehend a teen-age hoodlum in the act of mugging an old man.

Some departments, breaking with the conservative policy of keeping wives away, have taken an opposite and innovative direction by going out of their way to acquaint wives with a sense of what the occupation is about. They are permitting and encouraging police wives to accompany their spouses on radio car patrol once or twice. Modeling his program closely after a plan instituted on the West Coast, the chief of the Lockport, New York, 50-man police force introduced this type of ride-along project.[44] On an experimental basis and for only a two-month period, he invited wives to accompany their husbands on patrol for three hours from 7 P.M. to 10 P.M. on weekday nights (usually quieter than the weekends). By sensitizing wives to the pressures of the job, he hoped that they might develop an empathy to their husbands' work situation; and thus they might achieve the chief's long-range goal, which was to shore up the floundering marriages in his department in which the divorce rate stood at a menacing 20 percent.

If they can understand why their husbands just can't come home at night and be the typical husband or father after dealing with the kind of people they do for eight hours, that they just can't turn it off, then it might help their marriages.[45]

But even when urged to join their husbands in the field, more than half the wives eligible to do so did not participate. Evidently once they had compartmentalized these disparate zones, they did not wish to trespass. This reaction is consistent with our finding that more than half the wives in our survey had never observed their husbands at work. Judging from the evaluation by some of the wives who did ride as radio car partners, the program was only partially successful. Several wives felt too frightened by the imminent danger; others thought that they were too shielded from serious calls. But as a result of these mobile sensitivity training sessions, a few did develop an insight into the reasons for their husbands' moodiness and taciturnity when they finished their tours of duty.

Whether she is consumed with eagerness to participate or overwhelmed by apprehension, a police wife feels like an alien in the police world. Law

---

[44] *New York Times*, January 21, 1977, p. A16.

[45] Ibid.

enforcement news of any import is censored, filtered through the dark prism of her husband's guarded revelations. If she tries to break through the wall of resistance by so much as a telephone call to her husband's precinct station house, she is made to feel that she is doing the wrong thing:

We as police wives, need to be extra careful of everything we do and say because at times our motives are not completely understood. It is not a good policy to call your husband at the station unless it is essential.[46]

The police wife who wrote that advice to others cautioned that wives who demand a share of their husbands work life "are sometimes called 'bitch' behind our backs by other officers."[47]

You can't call him. If you do, the other cops will think he's henpecked. They'll make his life miserable. The only time you can call is if something really, really serious comes up.[48]

And when there is an emergency at home, police wives may have to dial 911 like everyone else. They know that to get a message through to their husband will take too long.

A harrowing moment for one Canadian police wife occurred when she called radio headquarters with a message for her husband who was on night patrol because she was certain that some "maniac" was trying to break down her door. She shrieked, "Come home immediately, if not sooner." When the radio car raced to her home to investigate, the maniac turned out to be "a slightly drunk little old grandmother who wanted to report to the police that her husband had locked her out of the house."[49]

Motivated by the psychology of the outsider, a police wife compensates by reaching out for a sense of community into her immediate neighborhood. And like other subjects involved in experimental situations, she often endures a series of aversive shocks. Already on the defensive as the wife of a police officer striving for acceptance as a middle-class suburbanite, she may have to contend with an additional burden—a covert form of social segregation. On display as the spouse of an officer, she must behave circumspectly, keep her social distance, restrict her speech in company, and become a model of deportment. Because everybody watches the police wife, it does not take long for her to realize that she is special. As one wife expressed it:

[46] Webber, *Handbook*, p. 14.

[47] Barbara E. Webber, "The Police Wife," *The Police Chief* (January 1976):48.

[48] *New York Sunday News Magazine*, February 23, 1975, p. 16.

[49] B.F. Newell, "Salute to the Wives," *RCMP* (Royal Canadian Mounted Police) *Quarterly* 40 (October 1975):13.

Whenever I go downtown shopping I feel like I'm wearing Bill's uniform. When people do special things for you, you're not sure if it's because they like you, or because you're a policeman's wife. It works the other way, too. If I park in the wrong place some people will talk about it.[50]

If a cartoonist were commissioned to capture the essence of police familial life, he might well draw a caricature of a police officer, his wife, and their children swimming in a goldfish tank surrounded by a group of spectators watching every movement. The invasion of privacy is recognized and accepted as a condition of police life. A police lieutenant in Santa Ana, California, tells us in his book on law enforcement that a policeman's private life cannot be private because "he's a cop":

And everyone watches the policeman to see how he behaves. If he scolds or punishes his children, he's mean. If he argues with his wife, he's cruel and probably a wife-beater. If he drinks, he's a drunk, or at least approaching alcoholism.[51]

Fully aware of their high visibility and the tendency of the public to scrutinize and denigrate their police image, law enforcement families must behave discreetly. They avoid ostentation. Many officers have told us that they did not buy the luxurious big car they so wanted but settled for a less conspicuous model because they were afraid that the neighbors might write a letter to the department urging an investigation of their finances. Yet the anomaly is that our respondents could compartmentalize these reflections from the goldfish tank and maintain, as nearly two-thirds of them did, that police families behaved like other families, neither more nor less carefully. However, a majority of the English and Australian police families asserted that they did behave in a more guarded manner.

A police wife soon learns that "community has a surveillance function"[52] and that in modern society gemeinschaft intimate relations are the stuff of dreams because "people can be sociable only when they have some protection from each other; without barriers, boundaries, without the mutual distance which is the essence of impersonality, people are destructive."[53] It may be the snide remark of an acquaintance encountered at the supermarket, "What are you doing here standing on line? I thought your husband gets everything free!" that conditions her to avoid openness. Or when an investigation of graft in the police department hits the front page, the wife of a police officer may feel the anxiety

[50] Jack J. Preiss and Howard J. Ehrlich, *An Examination of Role Theory: The Case of the State Police* (Lincoln, Nebraska: Univ. of Nebraska Press, 1966), p. 34.
[51] Thomas F. Adams, *Law Enforcement: An Introduction to the Police Role in the Community* (Englewood Cliffs, N.J.: Prentice-Hall, 1968), p. 227.
[52] Richard Sennett, *The Fall of Public Man* (New York: Knopf, 1976), p. 300.
[53] Ibid., p. 311.

of guilt by association and interpret her neighbor's smiles or quiet conversations as condemnation.

Warm ties with neighbors are inhibited because of her apprehension that she is not accepted as a person with her own identity but rather as an extension of her husband, the cop. In fact, in the informal conversations of her friends she may be herself dubbed "the cop." Acquaintances on the block consider her husband to be the policeman in residence and will ask him to make house calls at inconvenient times to settle disputes, ticket an automobile blocking a driveway, quiet noisy children at play, and so forth. As one wife puts it, "My neighbors feel that our street is being patrolled by my husband."

An extreme illustration of stoicism is the experience of a British police wife who tried to maintain her composure while contending with hostile neighbors who urinated on her steps and rubbed excreta into her doormat because her husband was a police officer.[54]

How 70 percent of the police wives can inform us that members of the community treat their families in a normal fashion seems at first glance to present an irreconcilable paradox. But it is these same wives who have accepted the troublesome facts of police life, coping with the danger and the schedule, who also manage to adapt to this irksome aspect of police social relations. Wives, too, become cynical, probably through contagion from their police officer husbands, whose cynicism has been well documented. They reach a point where they assume it is normal for the public to treat them in an overbearing manner. And it is with resignation that they conclude that it is the price they must pay for being married to police officers.

Acutely sensitive to the barometer of public opinion, the wives look beyond the immediate community to those powerful molders of ideas, the mass media, to detect signals of approval or criticism. We asked our sample of wives to indicate whether each type of media was favorable, objective, or unfavorable in its delineation of police and police work. Table 5-6 sums up the results.

Television received the highest marks of the media, with more wives, 76 (36 percent), evaluating the television presentation of the police as favorable. But according to their scoring, the media do not deliver the proper police message. For straight down the list, these wives recorded their disillusionment with the media's projection of the police image, expressing their strongest displeasure with the newspapers.

No possible change in the wife's personal behavior would affect the news media policy, but she ordinarily will conform to protocol to placate the civilian guardians who watch her family lifestyle. And she must remain equally astute not to cause her husband embarrassment on the job. One wife had to change her daily culinary routine after her husband received a promotion to undercover

---

[54] For a description of this and other tribulations of police wives in Great Britain, see Sheila Mitchell, "The Policeman's Wife—Urban and Rural," *The Police Journal* 48 (January 1975):79-88.

Table 5-6
Police Wives' Rating of Mass Media Portrayal of the Police
(N = 213)

Type of Media	Favorable	Objective	Unfavorable
Television	76	69	56
Movies	40	70	76
Books	36	102	53
Radio	24	118	48
Magazines	16	108	63
Newspapers	5	77	114

officer and sometimes came home unexpectedly for lunch with his superior officer. In her customary pattern she would relax for a few minutes before lunch with a cocktail. But she now thought it wise to abstain because she was afraid that the supervisor might smell the liquor on her breath and, with typical police suspicion, classify her as a secret alcoholic.

An experienced police wife grows accustomed to the pace. If it is not the discomfiting, it is the unexpected. But at 3 A.M. it requires a special talent to be gracious. When one wife's spouse called to tell her that he wanted to bring home an adorable fifteen-month-old child whose mother had been arrested for intoxication and child abuse, this wife, undaunted, dressed, dropped her own still sleeping little daughter at her sister's home, and rushed to the station house to pick up the new addition to her household. Subsequently, when a welfare department representative appeared to take the baby to a shelter, the officer's wife and her five-year-old daughter expressed disappointment that they could not keep the child.[55]

When a wife manages to unravel the tangled logistics of the duty chart to attend a party, she may still not be able to unwind. Invariably, if her husband is identified as a policeman, he becomes the conversation piece. Each guest takes a turn to relate an invidious anecdote about his personal encounter with a police officer. No wonder that four out of five police officers and two out three wives in our survey try to avoid this hostile reception by seldom or never mentioning their affiliation with law enforcement.

A police couple ruefully confessed to us that they did not expect to be invited anymore to their friends' parties. At the last gathering, the pair noticed immediately the loss of spontaneity as soon as they arrived. Later, their harried host admitted that the guests had been experimenting with pot and were afraid that the policeman would become a "party pooper."

An equally awkward incident described to us by a police wife reinforces the supposition that a police officer may actually be weighted down by his shield

[55] *New York Post*, May 3, 1973, p. 30.

and gun 24 hours a day, even on festive occasions. Invited to an engagement celebration, she entered first while her husband circled the block searching for a parking space. Soon after, she heard a commotion at the door and saw her spouse still in his overcoat, with gun drawn, forcing one of the guests to lean against the wall while he frisked him for weapons. The overly observant husband suspected that he had found a wanted person and detected a suspicious bulge in the man's pocket. Mistaken, he apologized, but his wife burst into tears and left at once, too humiliated to face her friends.

With so many of these wives' painful memories peppering our interviews, we were certain that our findings would disclose that police couples withdrew into a more friendly circle of their own kind for their social activities. But disputing our logic, nearly 60 percent of the wives reported that they seldom or never socialized with other police couples.

There are many reasons for this anomalous phenomenon—of avoiding close friendships with colleagues despite the empathy of shared experiences. Some wives told us that it was too difficult to match convenient times for socializing with police couples when their husbands' schedules did not dovetail. Others complained that they grew tired of listening to "cop talk" all the time when they did get together. A pervading pressure against regular interaction with other police associates was the fear of some husbands that their wives would learn too much about what really went on within the police department.

The law enforcement caste system adds another barrier to close friendship among police families. Officers, good friends when of equal rank, discover that promotion infects the relationship. Wives, too, respect the pecking order of the law enforcement hierarchy and unconsciously respond to the unspoken vibration that "my husband is superior to yours," and they begin to feel uncomfortable socializing with one another. If patrolman and superior officer manage to sustain their friendship, it can become station house gossip. The man in the lower rank may be accused by the backroom cynics of "brown nosing."

But it is this same cynical view, one that is nearly universal within the police occupation, contaminating the wife as well, that prepares the police couple to discount the noticeable provocations of their civilian friends, impelling them to define the contours of their acquaintances' behavior as natural and normal reactions to authority figures. Thus, fortified by this insight, police couples can rationalize the social peccadilloes of these outsiders and endure them without excessive strain on their relationships.

In Great Britain, police couples seek the comfort of closer ties with their immediate family and enjoy the security of old friendships dating back to premarital times.[56] Conceivably, wives know that they are cynosures who are never allowed to get away with anything in public. Or perhaps they have a strong sense of propriety. In any case, when we asked how they would expect to be treated if an officer stopped them for a traffic violation, 60 percent of the 178

---

[56] Mitchell, 'The Policeman's Wife," p. 88.

American wives who responded said they expected to be treated like any other driver and given a summons; 40 percent expected professional courtesy after they identified themselves to the officer. By contrast, 24 (83 percent) of the 29 English and Australian wives expected to be treated like any other driver and given a summons.

Of the 179 American policemen who replied to this question, 148 (80 percent) expected the officer to extend professional courtesy and let the wife go with a warning. But the English and Australian policemen followed the pattern of their wives; almost two out of three thought that their wives would (or should) be treated like any other drivers and given summonses.

The ideal of abstract justice may be more powerful in Great Britain. In the United States, the American police officers may be attuned to the broad discretionary powers delegated to the police, permitting them to adopt a more subjective mode of law enforcement. Perhaps the American wives were content to answer according to a higher principle because they know that it is hardly likely that a policeman in the United States would give another officer's wife a traffic ticket unless the violation was so serious that he could not avoid doing it. And notwithstanding the protestations of the wives expressed in the questionnaires, the truth of the matter is that no one really wants to receive a traffic summons.

Sometimes an officer is forced to appear to go through the motions of issuing a summons to a colleague's wife, although he adheres to the unwritten code of professional courtesy. Upset by the prospect of actually receiving a personal traffic summons, one distressed police wife nearly talked her way into it by refusing to keep quiet and to follow the policeman's cues. After he stopped her car and asked to see her license, she immediately informed him that she was the wife of a sergeant in the police department. But to her consternation the police officer imperturbably took out his black memorandum book containing the sheaf of summonses and started to write. She grew excited at the thought of getting a ticket and started to expostulate. Suddenly, the exasperated policeman exclaimed, "For God's sake, keep still! Can't you see I'm writing this on a piece of scrap paper? Too many people are watching and they know that you are a policeman's wife. If they think that I'm letting you go, they'll complain."

Occasionally, a strict commanding officer may insist that a member of his command give his own wife a ticket. When a new legalistic police chief was appointed to reform a rather "sloppy and undisciplined" police department, he chose to tighten up his administration by rooting out nepotism.

Soon after the new chief arrived, he called his men into his office and asked them, "What would you do if you were patrolling the downtown area and you caught your wife making a U-turn?" Anyone who did not immediately say, "Give her a ticket," was sharply rebuked. Though it would be absurd to assume that he ever got his men to ticket their wives. . . .[57]

---

[57] James Q. Wilson, *Varieties of Police Behavior* (Cambridge: Harvard Univ. Press, 1968), p. 219.

When you are a backstage wife, incommunicado in the wings, rarely venturing out to observe the police officer playing his part, it makes little difference if your husband walks, rides, or covers a fixed post in the living theater of police action. Wives understand and accept the implications of the police mystique that—because their nattily costumed spouses perform in the limelight and symbolize authority—other women are attracted to their husband's strength, virility, and good looks. Often the service role of hero calls for the husband to protect, carry, or succor female clientele. Most wives have acknowledged and come to terms with this irritating and sometimes titillating scene in the drama of police work, although in every precinct there are authenticated reports of wives who followed their husbands on patrol for weeks and months to prevent them from succumbing to temptation.

The wives realize that wherever men work, they maintain contact with women in the organization. In law enforcement until 1972, less than 5 percent of the force consisted of females, and most of these executed special tasks: clerical work, youth work, guarding female prisoners, and a narrow range of duties in the control of vice. But there were always a few policewomen assigned to the detective division to act as decoys to trap rapists and muggers, who would then be arrested by a backup team of male detectives. One such policewoman, fittingly dubbed "Muggable Mary," has been honored "as one of the ten most outstanding officers in the country" because she has been primarily responsible for the arrest of 300 felons.[58]

Police wives react to the presence of policewomen in such limited aspects of police work in much the same way that wives of men in other occupations accommodate themselves to the reality of females supplementing or assisting their marital partners. It was entirely consistent with this attitude that 142 (70 percent) of the wives in our survey disclosed that they were not at all concerned about their husbands' contact with women in the course of their work; only 3 percent said that they were deeply concerned; and 41 (20 percent) were somewhat concerned.

In 1972, the Title VII amendments to the Civil Rights Act of 1964 extended the provisions of the act to police departments. After brief resistance, police administrators bowed to court orders, new laws, and the pressure of the Law Enforcement Assistance Administration, which insisted that all institutions receiving LEAA's generous grants observe the act and demonstrate that they were equal opportunity employers. Female applicants besieged police departments, and as a result of two years of campaigning for equality in their assignments as well as in their appointments, by 1974 more than 1000 females were actively serving on police patrol throughout the country.[59]

Policewomen who had been barred from the regular civil service promotional channels vociferously demanded their rights, winning permission to compete with male officers on the tests for promotion. Soon there were female superior

[58] *New York Times*, October 7, 1975, p. 37.

[59] Peggy E. Triplett, "Women in Policing," *The Police Chief* (December 1976):46.

officers. Next policewomen campaigned for parity in status and work assignments, including the license to enter the last bastion of male supremacy—the radio patrol car. With the assignment of policewomen as partners with policemen in radio cars, placid police wives exploded.

All the smoldering resentment on the part of the wives, sublimated or throttled up to this point, burst forth in outrage at what they considered an attack upon the integrity of family life. In our conversations with wives, many remarked sardonically that their husbands felt closer to their radio car partners than to their mates. But when the partner changed gender, the humor drained from their truism. The wives imagined their husbands rubbing elbows and knees with a policewoman in the front seat of the radio car for eight or more hours—a longer and more intimate waking period of the day than the husbands spent with their wives. Even the least sophisticated wife could contemplate the warm bond enmeshing two partners of the opposite sex who worked together, faced danger together, ate together, cooped together, and possibly played together. They knew instinctively that the younger, more active, and probably more attractive policewomen would be assigned to the radio cars. And it unnerved them to contemplate that this intimacy would flourish within the automobile, whose phallic symbolism has become a logo of the American culture.

The introduction of policewomen into radio car patrol aroused an even more intense emotion than jealousy: fear for their husbands' lives. Wives expressed apprehension that because of the intrinsic physical limitations of policewomen, in a dangerous confrontation they could not back up their partners as effectively as male counterparts could. Placing women in radio cars would be tantamount to exposing their husbands to double jeopardy. Wives were fearful of the higher potential for danger because the subtle interplay between the sexes might stimulate a police officer to flaunt his bravery unnecessarily or to protect his female partner out of a misguided sense of chivalry. Thus it would not be a matched team sharing risks equally as men riding in tandem.

As police departments from coast to coast became equal opportunity employers, police wives vehemently protested this sexual parity and set up barriers to male-female radio car groupings. Now converted to frontstage wives, reading from a new script punctuated with positive thinking and assertive action, they linked arms to overcome this threat to their conjugal equanimity.

In New York City, a group of these wives recruited their children to dramatize the urgency of the issue and together picketed police precincts and headquarters, marching steadfastly while waving banners proclaiming, "Roses Are Red, Violets Are Blue, If Your Daddy Wore Blue, You'd Worry Too!"[60] From California to New York, this rash of indignation erupted into an upsurge of a new type of militant police wives' associations. Although in the past, many police departments had sponsored clubs and associations for wives of their members, these functioned predominantly as social groups or ladies' auxiliaries

[60]*New York Times*, June 21, 1974, p. 41.

without political goals or clout. But now with their consciousness raised by the feminist movement, their hackles raised by the example of the policewomen, these wives appeared ripe for radicalization.

Some of these burgeoning associations discreetly disguised their goals and zoomed in to a public relations focus, insisting that basically they aimed to create a better image of the police officer in the public's eye, to counteract the public's and the department's abuse of the police officer, to speak up when the police officer could not do so, and to inform the public of the views of police officers' families. The Long Island Police Wives' Association not only openly admitted its credo in the name of the organization, COP (an acronym for Cops' Other Partners), but also unabashedly underscored its primary function: to oppose co-ed patrol cars for professional and personal reasons.[61]

At the meetings of the police wives' associations that we attended during the nascent period of their development, members consistently articulated familiar objections emphasizing the policewoman's physical limitations, which would prevent her from providing sufficient protection and backup strength for her male partner in their shared duties. Other wives pointed out female inadequacies, dredging up stereotypes such as the purported lack of familiarity with cars. One member cited an incident in which her husband was embarrassed and ridiculed by his colleagues as a result of a policewoman's inefficiency. After responding to the scene of a radio run, his female partner accidentally locked the doors of the car with the only set of keys still in the ignition, immobilizing the car for half an hour while he tried unsuccessfully to catch the interior door lock with a wire coat hanger, to the great amusement of a crowd of spectators.

Many of the police officer husbands, undermined psychologically at the prospect of being supervised and superseded by policewomen, supported their spouses' protest, even to the extent of supplying them with additional case histories that denigrated the ability of policewomen. Despite their intrinsic agreement with their wives' position, few husbands attended the meetings because they were afraid that they might get in trouble with the department for public opposition to departmental policy. Both husbands and wives cautiously skirted any intimations of sexual attraction between partners in the cars.

Unexpectedly, these associations gained support from a number of male police officers, who for their own reasons publicly resisted the equalization of the sexes in law enforcement. Whether the arguments they advanced were couched in logical, philosophical, physiological, or psychological terms, the major premise asserted women's inferiority to men and contended that placing females in radio cars would create serious problems. A top administrator of a large law enforcement agency in California marshalled his knowledge of female biology to imply that hormonal cycles would impede performance of police-women in predictable periods. He remarked in no subtle terms that "in the

[61] Personal communication from Lowell Thomas, November 6, 1973, in which he reported to us the background of a brief announcement on his radio news program.

history of my wife and two daughters there were certain times during the month when they did not function as effectively as they did at other times of the month."[62]

Dressed up in more academic verbiage, a sophisticated *argumentum ad mulierem* illuminates the stance of a police officer-psychologist who explains why he is "100 percent against placing women in that part of police work where they had to face violence or indulge in it":

Not only was there a psychological difference between men and women, but there was a physiological basis for an emotional difference. Women had different glandular systems from men's, and their physical reactions were bound to differ.

Also, I believe a woman had to give up too much of her femininity when she faced or inflicted violence. It was too high a price for her to pay. She was used to getting what she wanted from a man by being seductive, not by threatening him or drawing a gun on him. Possession of a gun unconsciously turned her into a man.[63]

The ultimate putdown, albeit a euphemistic cover-up for male chauvinism, involves the rejection of a young woman applicant in Long Island who placed first on a civil service list for police officers. She alleged that the police chief refused to appoint her on the ground that "she was too pretty to be a cop."[64] She filed suit with the New York State Human Rights Division officer charging the chief of the 76-member all male force with sex discrimination (the case is still pending).

These fulminations against women sought to prove anatomically that female Karma could never be fulfilled in a radio car. But they bypassed the true core of the dissent: a realization of the extraordinary emotion—attachment or repulsion—that could be generated between two partners of different gender sharing the same radio car.

The newspapers fueled the controversy by reporting several sensational cases that far exceeded the issue of female inadequacy. One account of an affair between two radio car partners of opposite sex (both married, although not to each other) exposed a squalid tangle of assault, harassment, alcoholism, and some ugly aberrant sexual overtones. The short-lived liaison was terminated by dismissal of the pair from the force.[65]

An equally bizarre situation arose in the Midwest in a bloody dispute over the right to drive the patrol car. The news story disclosed a tale of violence. When a black policewoman who had just completed her probationary period of one year sat down behind the wheel and prepared to drive, her male partner, a white police officer with eight years of service, attempted to remove her. After

---

[62] See *New York Times*, June 6, 1972, p. 32.

[63] Schlossberg and Freeman, *Psychologist with a Gun*, p. 205.

[64] *New York Times*, March 24, 1977, p. B2.

[65] Ibid., July 23, 1974, p. 74.

swinging at each other with nightsticks, they drew their revolvers and shot each other. Both were taken to the hospital for treatment of their gunshot wounds. It would be a gullible wife, indeed, who could accept the police department communiqué that "race and sex did not appear to be a factor in the shooting."[66]

Because police wives have been so heavily bombarded by innuendoes about policewomen, we projected that the wives in our survey would erect a wall of resistance against the infiltration. When we asked the wives, "What would your reaction be if your husband were assigned to radio car patrol with a police-woman as his steady partner?" we expected that 9 out of 10 would oppose the assignment. Fewer than anticipated—a majority, 122 (57 percent)—opposed, although a rather large minority, 81 (38 percent), indicated that they occupied a neutral zone. It turned out to be fortuitous that we asked the wives to elaborate on the reasons for their answers to this question. Even those who were neutral qualified their replies, revealing that their neutrality was tainted by anxiety and clouded by jealousy. Their admissions fell into three slots: danger to the husband, possible sexual involvement between the partners, and inadequacies of the policewoman.

Avowing their neutrality, two wives of police officers in Great Britain nonetheless demonstrated that hedging on lack of concern is a cross-cultural female marital ploy.[67] The wife of a constable in the Cumbria Constabulary added this explanation for her neutrality: "I would be neutral about the assignment providing the woman in question was 75 and looked like King Kong." The wife of an inspector in the Metropolitan London Police Department commented: "I would be neutral about the assignment. After all my husband trusts me with the milkman and baker, so I'm sure that he's safe with a policewoman." The wives who opposed the assignment for reasons of jealousy intimated that their husbands might succumb to temptation.

The wife of a patrolman in the New York City Police Department with 1 year on the job said:

Contact too close in radio car. More hours with her than me. I know that my husband would go too far if he really liked her.

The wife of a superior officer in the Hartford (Connecticut) Police Department with 28 years on the job said:

I don't want him fooling around.

The wife of a captain in the New York City Police Department with 13 years on the job said:

66 *New York Post*, December 29, 1975, p. 12.

67 For a good review of the status of policewomen in Great Britain, see Jennifer Hilton, "Women in the Police Service," *The Police Journal* 49 (April-June 1976):93-103.

Steady partners are at times closer than blood relatives. Why look for trouble?

The wife of a detective-investigator in the Seaside Heights (New Jersey) Police Department with 5 years on the job said:

I'm jealous of his brotherhood with fellow police officers, no less it be female. Forget it.

The wife of a sergeant in the New York City Police Department with 10 years on the job said:

He wouldn't be able to do his job properly. If she was pretty, he would be too busy making an impression. If she was a plain Jane, he'd be grumbling all the time.

The wife of a patrolman in the New York-New Jersey Port Authority with 4 years on the job said:

My husband has sticky fingers.

Many wives expressed their opposition in terms of the danger to their husbands, emphasizing once again that the physical limitations of women made them inadequate partners. The wife of a patrolman in the New York City Police Department with 1 year on the job said:

Danger is an integral part of an officer's life. Unnecessary risk is foolish. Not only are most policewomen incapable of fulfilling physical aspects of the job, but I feel my husband would feel more responsibility for her safety.

The wife of a patrolman in the New York City Police Department with 7 years on the job said:

Because in time of danger the natural thing to do would be to protect the policewoman. Also because I am very possessive and jealous.

The wife of a patrolman in the New York City Police Department with 5 years on the job said:

My husband is 6 foot 2 inches, weight 215 pounds and has been knocked around on a few occasions. He works in a high crime area and a woman is not typically equipped to back him up.

The wife of a patrolman in the New York City Police Department with 10 years on the job said:

I too am a woman. In no possible fashion could I be as strong physically in performing a "man size" job. With the short training requirement the police-woman is ill-equipped physically for a Harlem street.

The wife of a patrolman in the Harrison (New York) Police Department with 3 years on the job said:

He has too much respect for women and would always be worried about her safety and his actions (language, etc.).

Police wives could certainly recruit sympathetic and enthusiastic support from firemen's wives in their crusade against feminine integration. Not only does this latter group endorse the same plank of grievances against the female firefighters' lack of strength and stamina, but also they complain about an even more intimate frustration. One wife of a 15-year veteran of the fire service stated boldly:

How am I going to explain to my six children why their daddy goes to work and sleeps next to another woman? I'm the only woman who has a right to shower with my husband.[68]

An officer of the Concerned Wives of Firemen, a newly formed association in San Diego, elaborated:

Our families and homes will be threatened if they bring women into the firehouses where they will share dormitories and bathing facilities with the men during their 24-hour shifts.[69]

How do those policewomen actually patrolling in the radio cars with male partners feel about this controversy about compatibility? Are they content to have been displaced from their secure niche in law enforcement and set down in the whirring public display of the radio car? Based upon her experience in working with a male partner, one policewoman in New York City asserted that a mixed team has the edge on any other combination in handling the broad spectrum of police incidents in a metropolis. After pondering the possibility of patrol car romances, she concluded: "Well, if you really wanted to, I guess you could find the time. There are probably some people who do."[70] Several enthusiastic New York City policewomen, when interviewed by a reporter, expressed their eagerness to patrol with male officers, but they clearly sensed the resistance of their co-workers' wives and ascribed its source to jealousy. As one of the policewomen put it:

[68] *New York Times*, July 28, 1974, p. 46.
[69] Ibid.
[70] Alice Fleming, *New on the Beat: Woman Power in the Police Force* (New York: Coward, McCann and Geoghegan, 1975), pp. 213-214.

Wives don't usually fuss about men and women on foot patrol—It's the radio car that bugs them.

Being in a car on Times Square is like a fishbowl. But people figure that if a cop's in a car with a pretty girl, something's got to be happening. Men in offices have affairs, but cops are supposed to be more lecherous than other men. And we're supposed to be better than other women.[71]

Just 2 from our sample of 27 policewomen objected to assignment to radio car patrol with a policeman as a steady partner. A slight majority (14) were neutral, and 10 acknowledged their support of the assignment. With one exception (the policewoman who referred to mutual trust between her and her husband), these respondents refused to dignify critiques of joint occupancy of radio cars that implied biological inferiority, endangerment to their partners, or innuendo of sexual liaison. Here are some typical observations. A policewoman in the New York City Police Department for about 1 year said:

We are both police officers and there are certain situations when a male is needed.

A policewoman in the New York City Police Department for almost 2 years said:

I know my husband trusts me enough that it wouldn't bother him and I also love my husband enough not to get involved with other men.

Another policewoman in the New York City Police Department for almost 2 years said:

If they can do the job, I'm in favor of them.

A policewoman in the New York City Police Department for 8 years said:

It would depend on the character of the person—whether man or female. If he was dependable, fair and unprejudiced toward having a woman partner, I don't think my reaction would be any different than if my partner were a female.

In a study of policewomen's attitudes, Solomon Gross asked a group of 127 college-educated policewomen what their reaction would be if they were married to police officers who were assigned with policewomen partners in radio cars. More than two-thirds (68 percent) of those answering the question stated that they would not object, and one-fifth (19 percent) indicated that they would; the others were uncertain of their reaction.[72]

---

[71] *New York Times*, November 2, 1974, p. 34.

[72] See Solomon Gross, "Perceptions of the Role of Women in Policing by Police Educators, Policemen and Policewomen Attending College" (Master's thesis, John Jay College of Criminal Justice, 1974). We are indebted to Professor Gross for permitting us to review the original data sheets from which this material was obtained. For these items, the sample size was reduced from the original 127 to 98 policewomen.

The policewomen's response pattern is understandable. If they are striving for complete equality with male officers in law enforcement, and that must include assignments to the radio car, then they must be consistent. They cannot press for that assignment for themselves but object to other policewomen riding with their husbands. They are in a position where the role of policewoman supersedes the role of wife. Furthermore, policewomen's responses demonstrated even more conclusively the primacy of this role, for more than 90 percent agreed with the following statement: "I wish to be thought of as a police officer rather than as someone who belongs to the homemaker role."[73]

The responses of the 21 husbands of policewomen in our sample veered noticeably from those of the wives of policemen. In our culture, a male breadwinner (the spouse of a policewoman) generates more power than a housewife (the spouse of a policeman), even when she may also work outside the home. And although the policewoman has authority in her job, the occupational prestige of a policewoman is not high enough to clothe her with a status superior to that of her husband within the ambit of the family.

Exchanging her police uniform, which symbolizes command, for her homemaker uniform (the apron), which symbolizes service to her husband and family, constitutes a covert acknowledgment that the husband is still the master. To wear an apron instead of the police uniform may challenge her adaptability, but it lightens the weight of the shield in the home, making it easier for a husband to cope with his career-oriented wife. At the same time, its ritual significance facilitates her daily transition to the role of a housewife. As yet the currents of the feminist movement have not perceptibly weakened the structure of the patriarchal family system in the modern world.

In general, this divergence in status may explain several of the observable differences in response patterns between the wives of policemen and their opposite numbers, the husbands of policewomen. The majority of police wives disclosed that their husbands told them little or nothing about the job; conversely, more than half the husbands of policewomen reported that the wives told them a lot or everything about the job.

Another discrepancy in response, this time gender related, appeared in the answers to the question, "What would your reaction be if your wife were assigned to radio car patrol with a policeman as her steady partner?" Only 24 percent of the policewomen's husbands opposed the possibility compared to nearly 60 percent of the wives who vetoed the assignment of policewomen as their husbands' partners. Conceivably, the three-quarters of the husbands who were in favor of, or neutral to, this position may have been motivated by the thought of the greater protection from danger that a male partner almost guarantees. And this concern probably influenced the husbands' preference for youth work as the choice of assignment for their wives. Here are the remarks of the husbands in favor of, or neutral about, the assignment of mixed teams to radio cars. A husband of a policewoman in the New York City Police Department for 2 years said:

[73] Ibid.

She has in fact been assigned to a steady partner. I find that I can live with it comfortably.

The husband of another policewoman in the New York City Police Department for 2 years said:

Because I trust my wife and if this question is meant do I feel my wife and her partner would screw around I do not think that she would have to go into a patrol car to do that.

The husband of a policewoman in the New York City Police Department for 8 years said:

She has virtue enough to cope with it.

The husband of a policewoman in the New York City Police Department for 7 years said:

If my wife was going to fool around with another man (which I don't believe she would), I am sure she would pick a time and place other than a car in public view.

The husband of a policewoman in the New York City Police Department for 1 year said:

If the question is one of trust, that applies to any job or situation. So it makes no difference as to the assignment. Any problems in this area would be due to our own relationship.

The husband of a policewoman in the New York City Police Department for 1 year said:

If I can't trust my wife, who can you trust?

Husbands of policewomen who disapproved justified their stand in much the same terms as the wives of policemen. The men complained: too close a relationship; the job of patrol is too dangerous for my wife; women are not suited for patrol duties.

At the moment, the ripples of controversy spread by the issue of policewomen sharing radio car patrol have been smoothed over by pressing economic crises. Unprecedented layoffs of police officers (including many of the recently hired policewomen) and the contractual impasses over the demands for higher salaries and improved working conditions, counterbalanced by management's proposals for higher productivity and one-man radio car patrol, have combined to make equal opportunity for women within law enforcement a moot issue.

But once aroused by the stirrings of power, police wives have not reverted to their former, passive lifestyle. Strengthened by their kinship of shared experience and feelings and newly cognizant of their leverage as a group, they have branched out, even enlisting their children to carry placards and blow piercing shrieks on police whistles to attract attention to the police family's plight. When one wife was asked why she kept her school-age children out of classes in order to join a demonstration, she countered: "I consider this an educational venture. Some kids take a day off from school to go on field trips. These kids are out of school to fight for their daddy."[74]

Accompanied by their families, the wives march in support of police officers on trial, or picket to protest the administration's refusal to grant union demands. Although their off-duty husbands diffidently join them in protest, adding false noses and eyeglasses to conceal their identity for fear of department reprisals, their outspoken spouses can, with impunity, resort to chants, catcalls, and stomping to make their point.[75]

An impassioned letter dispatched to the wife of the New York City police commissioner rationalized the wives' platform of militant dissent, reflecting their involvement in a situation where several policemen were suspended for taking part in a disorderly protest against the introduction of a more onerous work schedule.

Our husbands would prefer us to stay home with our children since they themselves do not get to be with their children that often. But I feel that if we stop now, what is to become of the suspended officers and also how many families will break apart because of the work charts. It is very hard to live with a man who is unhappy in his work, the work that he once loved so much. There is just not enough time for him to unwind and get into step with his family life with one day off between tours.[76]

To their chagrin, police departments that previously ignored wives have now discovered that the contemporary feminist variety of collective bargaining is dramatic and effective. Actually the former indifference of law enforcement administration to the wives and families of their members had never been motivated by the laudable intention of respecting the right of privacy of the family: a department rarely hesitated to call an officer at 3 or 4 A.M. and order him to report immediately for emergency duty. The lack of concern was a product of the belief that wives and families were not important enough as spheres of influence to justify serious attention.

[74] *New York Times*, October 2, 1976, p. 49.

[75] Ibid. See also, ibid., September 14, 1976, p. 36.

[76] See the newsletter of the New York City Patrolmen's Benevolent Association, *Front and Center* (December 1976):6.

128

This limited view of the police family had not been confined to the United States. In Great Britain, a survey that explored the role of the police family concluded that "the family was irrelevant to the work situation" for the city police.[77] In the county police force, possibly because of the peculiar insularity of rural police, the British wives exerted more influence. But the peer group of police colleagues dominated as the most forceful shaper of police attitudes and behavior—understandably so in a quasi-military male organization bound together by restrictive regulations and ideological codes.

Furthermore, the policy of the police administrators specifically minimized and discouraged family intervention. The official statement of the Association of Chief Police Officers to the Royal Commission on the Police in Great Britain underscored this tenet of police administration:

A police constable does not merely take a job, he embarks upon a new way of life . . . the first claim on him must be made by his duty, and the convenience of his wife and family must be a secondary consideration.[78]

Occasionally in the United States, a minority dissent widened this perspective and assessed police wives as a potent force regulating the performance of husbands:

Although wives were not formally part of the department, their influence was recognized as powerful, and to some policymakers ominous. For a recruit in training, his wife was frequently a source of encouragement and incentive. At times she was also a producer of doubt and worry as she pondered a future as a policeman's wife.[79]

But this exception to the general rule seemed to be applicable only to the midwestern state police force, the subject of that investigation. The state police are much closer to the armed forces than to the urban police departments in their discipline and their culture, and it may very well be that barracks life accentuates the importance of the wife.

It would be no exaggeration to say that the wives have been the forgotten women in police administration. They are accorded a place of honor only when attending the funeral or unveiling a plaque in memory of a husband killed in action. In most departments, policemen's wives are generally relegated to ladies' auxiliary associations, which meet once every month or two and concentrate on social, charitable, religious, and funereal objectives. The wives rarely intervene in

---

[77] Maureen E. Cain, *Society and the Policeman's Role* (London: Routledge and Kegan Paul, 1973), p. 232.

[78] Ibid., p. 7. See also, Royal Commission on the Police (1960) Interim Report, Cmnd. 1222, London: HMSO.

[79] J.J. Preiss and Howard J. Ehrlich, *An Examination of Role Theory: The Case of the State Police* (Lincoln, Neb.: Univ. of Nebraska Press, 1966), p. 33.

department affairs or make waves that may annoy the brass. Police officer organizations reinforce this syndrome, discouraging wives from attending meetings, except for the annual gala party. And then the wives are no more than decorations—a mere pastel background for the contacts and the "contracts" (police officers' wheeling and dealing) in a male-dominated jamboree.

Until the current consciousness raising induced by the women's liberation movement, the typical city force for the most part continued to ignore policemen's wives. Police academy instructors occasionally injected some humorous comments about the wives to spice up a lecture. Then in a more serious vein, they might advise the rookies to be careful about choosing the right type of woman to marry because she was going to be subjected to many pressures and limitations. A very few departments, more innovative than the rest, developed short orientation programs for the wives of recruits.

This persistent neglect of the wives' interests by law enforcement agencies might be interpreted as another manifestation of a chauvinistic occupation exhibiting its habitual indifference or resistance to the emotional effects of the vocation on women. A more political and sociological explanation might suggest that given the well-substantiated inertia of bureaucracy and its unyielding opposition to experimentation, the wives' lack of power and absence of militance never generated enough momentum to budge the administrators of the old school to change. But the climate of the 1970s has thrust police wives into a more aggressive position. The air is charged with talk of sensitivity training, encounter groups, feminist movement, and equal rights. And these wives, responding to the cultural vibes, do not hesitate to ventilate their feelings and views, as one group did in this memo to their husbands:

Let us not forget, That WE the Wives, are people too! We do have questions, to be answered, and we do have anxiety about your job. We are NOT in any way trying to emasculate you. Being a POLICE OFFICER is your PROFESSION. You take the risks you take abuse and the harassment from the public and the Department. BUT, we listen to it from John Q. everyday. We are also tired of the discontent, and the frustration you portray when you come home.[80]

The wives have finally made an impact on the leadership. They have been assisted by latent forces working in the same direction. Law enforcement territory has been penetrated, surveyed, polled, probed, and investigated by an army of researchers. A result of all this study is that the top administrators have absorbed a new perspective on the occupation, marking a turning point in their thinking about family life. Productivity studies point to the possible connection between poor work performance and poor marital conditions.

It does not require much imagination to envision that a policeman who goes on duty after an explosive argument with his wife will be "on a short fuse" when

---

[80] See Newsletter of the New York City Policemen's Wives Association, Centereach, New York, October 1974.

he is on the beat. And the corollary follows that a patrolman who finds it difficult to turn off "the flashing red lights and the screaming sirens" of the job will carry home the danger and the tension. This undercurrent of anxiety can activate subtle tugs-of-war between husband and wife over police matters, for instance, an impasse over the officer's specific assignment within the department. A policeman's wife may plead with her husband to avoid hazardous duty for the sake of his family, while her mate may relish the excitement of a dangerous detail.

A common refrain running through our informal interviews and conversations with police wives has been their eagerness to share their thoughts and ideas about police work. Call it catharsis, empathy, or just a listening, sympathetic ear. Whatever the reason, they enthusiastically communicated, and many expressed an interest in family guidance and counseling services initiated by the department as an aid in dealing with their individual problems. In fact, wives tell us that they want much more than a lecture by a veteran police academy instructor, who from his position of authority talks down to them. Many would prefer to participate in panel discussions with older police wives, who from their years of experience in coping with the job could communicate their strategies of adjustment and disseminate their practical guide for survival as a police wife.

The wives acknowledged this need and desire for such services in answering our open-ended question, "What type of services do you think the police department should provide for families of police officers?" At first, it was difficult to reconcile the majority view tabulated in table 5-7 with the rather

Table 5-7
Police Department Services Desired by Police Wives
(N = 213)

Service	Number of Requests
Family or marital counseling	58
Orientation for wives	31
None	21
Social activities	15
Financial assistance	11
Medical services	11
Information services (such as: notifications about emergencies and injuries)	7
Services for children (such as: day care, jobs, education)	7
Miscellaneous	5

substantial number of wives who wanted no services at all. But in their comments this latter group made it clear that the fear of departmental intrusion into their private lives overrode their desire for help.

Support for the position of the wives on the subject of department-provided services comes from John Stratton, staff psychologist of the Los Angeles County Sheriff's Police Department. After reviewing the array of pressures on law enforcement marriages that cannot be avoided—the change in the husband, the displaced anger, the lack of communication, and the unspoken fears, his recommendation to ameliorate the situation is to develop a sound program for the families of police officers.

It would be worthwhile for an agency to have regular orientation workshops for the wives of entering policemen, as well as having an additional workshop every six months to a year for spouses who have married within that time period. This workshop can be conducted by older wives who've been confronting the pressures and pitfalls of law enforcement life for some time. In addition, regular open workshops for husbands and wives separately and together, both at the time of entrance into the agency academy and throughout the law enforcement career, can increase the possibility for open communication and awareness.[81]

The logical step for police departments would be to establish well-rounded service programs to assure better relations and fuller understanding vis-à-vis police families. In an attempt to define the extent of this involvement in family-oriented services, we wrote to the 150 largest police departments in the United States asking them for information about their programs for the wives of the members of the force. Of the 94 departments that replied, 60 percent offered no program at all, and more than half the others provided only a brief orientation of a few hours during the recruit training period. Even when they do have programs of this nature, many police departments are lax in promoting and publicizing them to their potential clientele. Asked point-blank "Does the police department provide any orientation, counseling, or other types of services for families of police officers?" only one-fifth of the 184 American wives in our sample answered "yes," two-thirds "no," and the remainder indicated that they did not know of the existence of any department programs for police families. It is ironic that many of the husbands worked as colleagues in the same police forces, yet their wives had divergent perceptions of what the department offered. The clustering of the responses at the positive and negative poles spotlights the failure of these agencies to develop strong service programs and/or to communicate this vital information to their constituents.

Sporadically, within the United States, enlightened law enforcement agencies have made breakthroughs in this area. An early leader, the Los Angeles

[81] John Stratton, "Pressures in Law Enforcement Marriages: Some Considerations," *The Police Chief* (November 1975):44-47.

County Sheriff's Department in California, the fifth largest police department in the nation, has consistently recognized the negative pressures on the police family and attempted to alleviate them. It has signaled its concern by initiating such services as bereavement counseling after a death of an officer, family orientation for regular and reserve forces, and crisis counseling for family, marital, emotional, and alcohol-related problems. Most innovative of all, a spouses' training program—eight seminars held at weekly intervals plus an annual all-day workshop—has improved familial communication and understanding by providing the wives of new recruits and recently married wives with a passkey to the locked gates of the police arena. Wives thus become familiar with the routines and procedures of their law enforcement spouses as a result of the detailed explanations and intimate glimpses into academy instruction, ranging from the physical training of the cadets to the vivid descriptions of the myriad job divisions within the occupation, such as helicopter pilot, patrol deputy, or vice officer. Moreover, wives learn to identify with and develop an intense awareness of the visceral tensions of police work as they simulate their husbands' job experience by riding in squad cars, touring station houses, visiting custodial facilities, and even trying to qualify at the same firing range where their husbands have learned to shoot.[82]

In the Harrisburg, Pennsylvania, region, a well-conceived orientation, "The Officer's Lady," welcomes wives, fiancées, and mothers of new police officers and aims to make law enforcement a veritable family occupation by involving the women behind the men. The utilization of the police recruits in the design of the program and the incorporation of personal case histories—for example, the dean of the training institute (a former Arizona police sergeant) invited his son to tell what it was like to grow up as a "policeman's little boy"—added depth and poignancy to the presentation. Titled "The Police Occupation and Family Relations Program," and originally organized into a nine-hour curriculum of three sessions, it covered police organization and administration, off-duty activities, emotional pressures of the officer, and family relationships and pressures.[83] As a result of its initial success it has now been expanded to 21 hours, with the new curriculum including a session led by a psychologist on the subject of mental health and the police family and another devoted to a husband-and-wife forum.[84] This series ends with a bang as the wives try their skill on the firearms range.

The response of the participating wives has been uniformly enthusiastic to the model program for police wives developed by the Washington State Criminal Justice Training Center. With the unique advantage of being directed by two

[82] John Stratton, "The Law Enforcement Family: Programs for Spouses," *FBI Law Enforcement Bulletin* (March 1976):16-22.

[83] John S. Megerson, "The Officer's Lady," *The Police Chief* (October 1973):34-38.

[84] John S. Megerson, "The Officer's Lady: A Follow-Up," *The Police Chief* (January 1976):50-52.

women, one of whom has been the wife of a police officer for 20 years, its goals encompass more than mere orientation for wives and a review of anticipated marital problems. Ten weekly sessions of four hours each covered the following areas of stress: "husband's change of attitude toward people, husband's complete involvement in his work, reaction and change of attitude of friends and neighbors, minority status, lack of communication, irregular shifts and odd days off, and very little social life because of hours."[85]

The key to the success of the project seems to be the improvement of communication, encouraging the free flow of ideas between husband and wife. Nothing is omitted. The wives tour station houses, ride in the radio cars, enjoy field trips to other components of the criminal justice system, visit the firing range, share discussions with a panel of experienced police wives, participate in frequent small-group sections, learn police jargon, offer suggestions for improvement, and finally, evaluate the program.[86]

The objectives of the Indianapolis (Indiana) Police Department Seminar for Wives and Fiancées of Recruits are equally ambitious, since the program is designed primarily to familiarize wives with the awesome responsibilities and problems of police work, to disseminate information about the services available to the wives, and to analyze the potential conflict situations to which police families are vulnerable. Ultimately, it tries to inculcate leadership qualities in the wives so that some of them may become group directors for the next cycle.

In almost every one of the nine sessions, which meet once a week for three hours, a portion is devoted to recreating vicariously the police husband's street experience. For example, the simulation in the fifth week is fittingly labeled "Keep Your Cool." The plan is to shock the wives, exposing them to the drama and violence of the police officer's encounters on the beat by describing the

brutal rape of a three year old girl by her own father; the death of a young child as the result of a drag race; physical abuse and neglect of a baby which he finds abandoned in a clothes closet; the accidental shooting and death of a young boy while playing with a loaded gun; a crippled 75 year old store merchant whose head had been pistol whipped because he did not move fast enough to satisfy demands of a drug-crazed hold up man.[87]

Searching to involve the wives more deeply, the directors of the seminar advocate encounter group techniques. The wife who draws a marked card assumes her position in the "hot seat" and the other members of her group question her about areas that are certain to be sensitive:

[85] Claudia Baker and Peggy Rhodes, "Final Evaluation: Seminar for New Officers' Wives," Washington State Criminal Justice Training Center, Providence Heights, Washington, July 19, 1971, p. 1.

[86] Ibid., attachments A, C.

[87] Revised Seminar Program for Wives and Fiancées of Recruits, Police Department, City of Indianapolis, Indiana, 1972, p. 23.

her housekeeping, her dress and general appearance, her husband and his current occupation along with his current social status. . . . What have been your family's accomplishments? What activities are your children currently engaged in and what are their grade school accomplishments and successes?[88]

The thrust of the Indianapolis seminar, at first, appears laudable: to promote empathy between husband and wife by suggesting parallels between the scorn and ridicule the police officer must contend with and the wife's personalized problems of family life. This may contribute to the wife's self-awareness, but it remains questionable whether her ordeal of defending her personal life under cross-examination will transfer her insight from introspection to a sympathetic understanding of the husband's situation. If the department is willing to undertake an experiment in sensitivity training that in some ways resembles an EST marathon, then it may be morally obligated to provide some follow-up counseling for wives who may be upset by such unexpected confrontation.

Telescoping its guidance services into one session of three hours the Omaha, Nebraska, police force patterns its format after more elaborate systems. Within this pared-down structure, it formulates the reasons for undertaking the project even more explicitly, calling attention to police cynicism, the high divorce rate among police personnel, and the correlation between poor work performance and poor marital relations.[89] A long-range study might analyze the effects of this one-time intensive orientation as compared to more extensive programs, using the frequency of marital problems and the rate of divorce as variables. Perhaps a project of this type might be able to determine statistically the optimum length of time in which domestic equilibrium can be most economically achieved.

To supplement its already smoothly functioning counseling services provided by chaplains, psychologists, and honorary psychiatrists, the New York City Police Department added a comprehensive family orientation program to the police academy curriculum. And in a progressive step, it established the employee relations section, a small unit with wide-ranging powers and discretion, which has assumed the role of ombudsman for police families, breaking through bureaucratic bottlenecks to find solutions to problems quietly, speedily, and effectively. In addition, the department sponsored "Family Days" at the police academy twice a year for the wives and families of its personnel, enabling the wives of the recruits to thrash out their questions about the job with the wives of veteran police officers. But when austerity hit the city—with thousands of police officers laid off and no appointments of recruits made for three years—this program understandably became quiescent.

---

[88] Ibid., p. 25.

[89] Police Officers' Wives Orientation Program, Omaha Police Division, Department of Public Safety, Omaha, Nebraska, 1975.

Through the years, a specialized type of counseling service has been consistently, although unobtrusively, provided by police chaplains to troubled law enforcement families. As awareness of the emotional impact of the job becomes increasingly prominent, it is logical that the role of the chaplain in controlling or mitigating this stress would become a challenging subject for discussion.

At the conference of the National Association of Police Chaplains, 50 chaplains representing all parts of continental United States joined with behavioral scientists and police officers to scrutinize facets of stress on the police officer and his family.[90] We participated in this seminar, and it proved to be of particular value to us as a balance wheel to orient our frame of reference concerning the causes of police familial conflict. Our data have derived principally from fairly well-adjusted families, while the chaplains have observed families in distress.

At the conference, 20 Protestant, 11 Catholic, and 2 chaplains of undisclosed religious persuasion gave us their views in a brief questionnaire (see table 5-8). Based upon their cumulative experience, the chaplains ranked lack of communication, infidelity, and the work schedule as the three most serious problems that police families faced.

When we juxtaposed these conclusions with those obtained from our sample of police wives, it turned out that the wives acknowledged many of the same problems. But the difference is that while 60 percent of our wives agreed that police families faced more problems than the average family, they had developed a positive attitude toward life, the family, and the job. They had learned to cope, sometimes even taking overt action to gain limited objectives. But realizing the power of the job, their opposition had to be intelligent and strategic. Tactics varied. When they were frustrated by lack of communication, they demanded orientation sessions; when they were threatened by the possibility of their husbands' infidelity (policewomen in the radio car), they rallied with other wives in aggressive protest; when they were inconvenienced by the inflexible schedule, they reset their tempo to a different rhythm. The one eventuality they knew instinctively they had to avoid was a long war of attrition against the job, which would ultimately degenerate into a desperate confrontation with their police officer husbands, forcing the men time and again to choose between job and family.

Other bothersome concerns for the police wife necessitated less assertive methods of adaptation. Nevertheless, our findings on the effect of finances and alcoholism on police family life differ from those of the chaplains. The majority of our wives considered the salary adequate, and only 28 (13 percent) indicated that financial troubles caused difficulty. Not one wife of the many we talked to

[90] "Controlling Stress: The Role of the Chaplain," a conference and workshop sponsored by the John Jay College of Criminal Justice, Law Enforcement News, and the National Association of Police Chaplains, New York City, May 4-5, 1977.

Table 5-8
Police Chaplains' Views of the Police Family
(N = 33)

Question	Response	
1. In comparison to other families you have known, would you rate the average police family as A. Happier; B. About as happy; C. Less happy?	A. Happier	0
	B. About as happy	28
	C. Less happy	5
2. In comparison to other families you have known, would you rate the average police marriage as A. More stable; B. About as stable; C. Less stable?	A. More stable	0
	B. About as stable	16
	C. Less stable	17
3. In comparison with other children you have known, would you rate the average child of a police officer as A. Better adjusted; B. About the same as other children in adjustment; C. Less well adjusted?	A. Better adjusted	1
	B. The same in adjustment	31
	C. Less well adjusted	1
4. In comparison with other wives you have known, would you rate the average wife of a police officer as A. More content; B. About as content; C. Less content?	A. More content	1
	B. About as content	16
	C. Less content	16

5. In your experience what are the three problems that police families encounter most frequently?	Rank	Frequent Problems	Number of Choices
	1.	Work schedule and time	25
	2.	Money-finances	16
	3.	Lack of communication	8
	4.	Alcohol	7
	5.	Infidelity	5
	6.	Children	4

6. In your experience what are the three most serious problems occurring in police marriages?	Rank	Most Serious Problems	Number of Choices
	1.	Lack of communication	12
		Infidelity	12
	2.	Work schedule and time	10
	3.	Money-finances	8
	4.	Alcohol	7
	5.	Lack of understanding of the police job by the wife	5
	6.	Job stress	4

mentioned alcoholism as a distressing issue. And even in our cross-reference to the subject, which asked the forked question if they might cope with a bad day by drinking, only 10 husbands and 5 wives admitted that they drank frequently under those circumstances.

The chaplains listed lack of understanding of police work by the wife and job stress as contributing factors to unrest in marriage. Our opinion is that these two grievances are views of the same phenomenon seen from a different perspective. It hardly can be lack of understanding, for it does not take any length of time for a wife to comprehend what the job entails. Rather it is the lack of willingness or the lack of ability to adapt flexibly to its encroachments on family life. If this attitude persists, job stress traps the couple and everything becomes a problem. Unable to work out a solution themselves, they seek help from the chaplain.

That the complaints of these anguished couples parallel those listed by already divorced couples in other fields of work suggests that their marital interaction has also reached an impasse. Marriage counselors are quick to point out and sociological studies confirm the principle that when a divorce is imminent, couples complain about almost every area of their relationship.[91] It appears to us that police couples confronted with serious difficulties in married life are using the police job as a scapegoat to mask deep-seated disturbances.

By contrast, our sample of wives, well adjusted to marriage and the job, reduced most problems to manageable proportions. Serious problems demanded extra effort to contain, but the smaller ones became normal conditions of life that hardly upset the daily routine. This familiar reprise recapitulates the dominant motif recurring in this chapter: police wives contending with the pressures of the job grow to be indomitable.

---

[91] See, for example, William J. Goode, "Family Disorganization," in Robert K. Merton and Robert Nisbet, eds., *Contemporary Social Problems*, 3d ed. (New York: Harcourt, Brace, Jovanovich, 1971), pp. 504-505.

Children of the Force

Against a backdrop of rolling hills and verdant lawns, the pastoral playground scenes unfolding resembled an up-to-date version of a Breughel canvas. The tableau of children frolicking, tossing balls, rolling in the grass, balancing on skateboards, and cavorting at the water's edge animated the sun-drenched landscape of a summer's afternoon at a mountainside resort. At the moment, most of the adults were otherwise engaged, either at a softball game or at the cocktail hour. Located at the entrance to the grounds a larger-than-life heroic statue of a police officer standing tall with his arm entwined protectively about a child offered possibly the only visible clue that the youngsters at play might be the offspring of police parents.

Of course, we wanted to include observations about children to round out the police family constellation. And the Police Recreation Center, located in an idyllic vacation setting in the Catskill Mountains and planned exclusively for the leisure-time enjoyment of New York City Police Department personnel and their families, seemed the perfect place to meet them.

Asking permission first from their parents, we interviewed a group of police officers' children ranging in age from four to thirty-one, clustered in the nine to fourteen category. In these relaxed surroundings the boys and girls communicated freely and uninhibitedly, for as it turned out, this al fresco approach breezed a ripple of fresh air into their comments and did not set limits to their responses, as would have a formalized "fill-in-the-blanks" questionnaire. In this informal atmosphere their parents too seemed less suspicious and guarded and much more willing to grant permission for their children to cooperate in our research than did their police counterparts in the city. Because we had suggested that parents might wish to audit the interviews, frequently a mother or father listened in, interjecting personal reminiscences of the job.

Convinced from our observations of police conjugal relationships that the job dominates family lifestyles, we hypothesized that children in police families would also fall into orbit around the occupation and that feeling the weight of the shield in their early years, police offspring would generate a sense of unique identity. Instead, we discovered from our interviews with these youngsters that at least until they reach their teens, their concept of police work markedly resembles that held by their peers whose parents earn their living in other fields. Elaine was able to note this parallel, because during her years of experience as a nursery and elementary school teacher, she had observed the development of attitudes about the police in countless children from prekindergarten through sixth grade.

As a control, we asked the 25 students in a fourth-grade class to write an essay about the police. A content analysis disclosed that their views of the police matched quite closely the descriptions given by our sample of police children of about the same age. The fourth-graders had a fairly accurate idea of what police officers do, as their ingenuous observations reveal:

I also feel that policemen that help children cross streets are as important as policemen that catch robbers.

Most policemen are very nice and they protect you so you don't get robbed or anything like that.

I think that policeman are grate [sic] but I would not want to be a policeman because I don't want to get my head shot off.

Some policemen direct traffic and some give out tickets but my real opinion is that policemen try to do their jobs and a lot do their jobs well.

I really think policemen are very good to have around to risk their lives to try and save our lives.

The policemen that control traffic have a easy job. But the policemen that catch crooks and robbers have a hard job.

To draw an analogy: just as in the silk screening process, each stage of design adds another color and overlay to the production, so we learned from police children that the concept that their parent is also a police officer changes its pattern with every stage of chronological development. For the very youngest, for whom the home defines the main boundaries of the world, the image of a loving, nurturing father figure is dissociated from the occupation. Until about the age of three, when a finer sense of visual discrimination maturates, seeing a parent in uniform through a child's eyes projects a rather confusing and dazzling picture. Our own children would invariably shout a warm greeting of "Daddy!" to any policeman in blue they met, to the embarrassment of their mother and the amusement of the police officer.

Depending on his assignment, a father's job may have been associated with a bit of fun for preschoolers, for the children often related with delight the happy occasion when he may have treated them to a ride in a police scooter, boat, patrol car, or even a police helicopter. Some kids recalled with nostalgia, as a highlight of their childhood, an excursion to an amusement park or a pass to a baseball game when their dads worked that detail.

Civic-minded nursery school teachers give their pupils a headstart in social studies by encouraging the children to "play policeman." The children construct police hats and in their paper regalia pretend to direct traffic, find lost kids, help classmates cross the street, and catch robbers. When preschoolers are asked what they want to be when they grow up, invariably, the police career ranks high in popularity.

In some elementary schools, enterprising instructors develop units on community helpers and occasionally invite a patrolman to discuss with the group aspects of police work geared to the children's level of comprehension. One youngster who at first felt proud that her father, a police officer, had been invited to her class for this public relations stint, afterward lamented to him, "I couldn't laugh along with my friends when you told a joke because I've heard all of your stories before."

The children's rooms in public libraries are stockpiled with informative books about the work of the police, for most young readers whether or not their parent is a real-life police officer, find this subject fascinating.[1] One book in particular, *My Daddy Is a Policeman*, carries realism to its tragic conclusion.[2] With a photo-essay format aimed to appeal to children from about four to eight, a little girl describes in her own words how her policeman father earns his living and how they have fun together when he is at home. On one side of each double-page layout, a large photograph illustrates these activities. On the opposite page is a one-sentence comment by the daughter. Her opening words are, "My Daddy is a policeman." And after a sequence depicting the officer shot down while on duty, the story ends movingly with the little girl sitting disconsolately by herself as she sobs, "My Daddy was a policeman."

Our younger son, Roy, enjoyed playing cops and robbers with Arthur's old police hat, long after Arthur had retired from the force. And to this day, Roy's friends frequently borrow this prop to lend authenticity to Boy Scout skits and school plays.

Children are naturally quite curious about "what daddies do," although when they are small, they can be quite disconcerting with the naiveté of their questions when they learn that a classmate's parent is a police officer. "Why is your daddy home during the day?" "How come your daddy is a policeman?" "Does he shoot any robbers?" "Can he help us if a robber robs our house?" "How come he has a gun?"

The majority of our 62 police children respondents did not hesitate to tell their friends how their parents made a living; only 6 (10 percent) preferred to remain close-mouthed about it. That they could expose the police roots in the family tree so openly attests to a level of social sophistication that belies their years, since they were able to maintain their good humor and accept with nonchalance the outspoken comments of their peers. Quite often their acquaint-

[1] For example, Laura Sootin, *Let's Go to a Police Station* (New York: Putnam's and Sons, 1957); Louis Slobodkin, *Read About the Policeman* (New York: Franklin Watts, 1966); Richard Erdoes, *Policemen Around the World* (New York: McGraw-Hill, 1967); Barry Robinson and Martin Dain, *On the Beat* (New York: Harcourt, Brace and World, 1968); Walter Arm, *The Policeman* (New York: Dutton, 1969); and Robert Coles, *Saving Face* (Boston: Little, Brown, 1972).

[2] Elizabeth A. Doll, *My Daddy Is a Policeman* (Englewood Cliffs, N.J.: Prentice-Hall, 1973).

ances' remarks were tinged with disbelief, teasing, or malice: "You must be kidding. I can't believe your father is a pig!" "He doesn't look like a cop." "He must give you a bad time." "I'd better be good. Your father is fuzz." "I'm not going to your house." "How could a woman be a policeman?" Others blatantly displayed their avid curiosity about the nature of police work: "Did he ever shoot anyone?" "Did he ever arrest a member of the mafia?" "Where does he work?" "What is his rank?"

Until puberty, boys and girls feel secure and comfortable, regulated by set rules of behavior within the snug sanctuary of the home. The police parent acts as a paternal but firm protector and reinforces the umbilical cord attaching the youngster to the family. A number of children told us that they benefited from their parent's status: "He can teach me the law." "I feel safe." "Bad kids stay away from you."

The children seem to flourish in this nurturing family ambience. Fully 75 percent of our sample said that they acted the same as other children did, and 85 percent of them rated their fathers as easygoing in discipline. The sources of conflict are minor domestic crises easily contained within the limits of the home: not doing household chores and homework, watching too much television, going to bed too late.

The family group encourages intergenerational activities such as Little League and Boy or Girl Scouts, and the children reported that they enjoyed doing things with their fathers—playing ball, fishing, going places. One daughter, more anxious than the others, said introspectively, "I just like to sit and look at him because when he goes to work, I think that I will never see him again."

Most of the children whom we interviewed did not seem to be bothered excessively when a police officer parent had to miss a family celebration or a school play because of the work schedule. Although they may have felt sad, they accepted the frustration philosophically, recognizing that, "There are 24 hours in a day to sing 'Happy Birthday' or to go bowling."

At adolescence, the social antennas of the children of police personnel become particularly sensitized to flak from their peers, and they may feel hurt by their friends' negative reaction to what their parents do for a living. In our off-the-record conversations with older sons and daughters of police parents, some of them told us that they tried to avoid this criticism by rarely volunteering information of their parent's affiliation or by not telling anyone unless asked. And when an intimate did respond in a noncommittal manner to the disclosure, a "So what!" was especially appreciated.

Unlike the preteeners whose attitudes toward the police are generally favorable, adolescent groups exhibit a wide diversity of opinion. For those not related to law-enforcement families, gut feelings about the police are internalized as part of a broader ideological position, more dependent on variables such as class, education, and ethnic and racial background than on facts. For a large group hypnotized by television, opinions fluctuate according to the networks' latest presentations of police heroism or corruption and brutality. In the inner-city neighborhoods, a significant proportion of the adolescent population writes off the police as the enemy.

In the late 1960s, college youth and the police struggled against one another in violent confrontations. It is still unclear whether those hostile attitudes have been mitigated or are merely lying dormant on academic campuses. It may be a sign of improvement that many middle-class youngsters are now willing to assume a flippant but neutral demeanor toward police officers, symbolized by the currently standard greeting, "Hi Kojak!" (a reference to the popular video detective lieutenant).

A burgeoning social consciousness coincides with an intense peer pressure for conformity. At this age, teenagers are motivated by an overwhelming desire to be accepted and liked. A seventeen-year-old girl perceptively analyzed the nuances of this sensitivity in a written postscript to her questionnaire:

When I first came to High School, no one knew my father was a cop. I had two friends who knew but that was it. The next time I turned around, everyone knew. It didn't bother me. But it bothered some people. I would tell them not to act so strange. Be for real; carry on friendship as if they never knew. People don't hassle me because they see I don't try to act so high class because my father is a cop.

Typically in the mid-teens, a sense of their special identity as children of police parents crystallizes. As they move in ever-widening arcs away from the hub of the home, they experience and assimilate controversial concepts of the police image. At this time, the adolescent peer group competes with and sometimes displaces the family as the purveyor of norms and standards, and the role of the parent imperceptibly changes from benevolent protector to restrictive guardian. But for the police child of this age there is a unique blue dimension arising from his personal contact with law enforcement that colors his personality and values, that gradually solidifies as a result of family interaction and loyalty to the police parent. At times this special sense of identity intersecting with the long arm of the job can work to his advantage.

Several teenagers we talked to admitted that they had sometimes received preferential treatment from traffic officers when they were stopped for driving violations. Occasionally the officer yielded to the blandishments of professional courtesy and instead of issuing a summons let the young offender proceed after mildly reprimanding him or her, "You should know better." Our oldest respondent (thirty-one) revealed that she talked herself into her first job as a security guard in a large department store, although totally inexperienced, on the strength of her disclosure to the personnel director that her father was a policeman.

A college student at an ivy league school recounted how the traditionally cool and even hostile relation between "town and gown" was replaced by a friendly, almost intimate connection in his personal encounter with the police. At about 3 A.M. he was parked in an out-of-bounds lovers' lane with a young lady, when a radio car pulled up. The officer began to question him in a stern manner and then tersely ordered him to step out of the car. Before the situation could deteriorate further, the collegian whispered to the Boston police officer that his father was a police lieutenant in the New York City Police Department. After a brief set of questions to make sure that the young man was not lying, the patrol officer's attitude changed completely. Nudging the lieutenant's son conspiratorially, he congratulated him on the attractiveness of his female companion, commented, "Aren't Boston girls great?" and advised him not to stay in the lovers' lane too long.

A co-ed majoring in the behavioral sciences explained how she was able to exploit her father's police affiliation. His police colleagues, by graciously consenting to be interviewed by the daughter, provided her with a rich source of primary research material for her term reports. Her police family background continued to be an advantage in her professional duties as a marriage counselor. Confronted by a difficult case involving a police couple who were at first uncooperative, she gained instant rapport when she confided to the police officer husband that she was the daughter of a retired police officer.

Once marked as sons and daughters of police officers, these children must also contend with subtle pressure from external figures of authority, especially in the schools. In our discussions we heard youngsters complain, "I'm tired of hearing teachers say to me, 'You should know better. Your father is a policeman. You should set an example.' "

Like other loving and solicitous fathers and mothers, law enforcement parents want their adolescent children to be good and to live according to a high standard of conduct. However, police officers major in adolescent psychology on the street, not in college, and their laboratory studies and internships take place in prisons, hospital emergency rooms, and the morgue. Because they have seen so much disaster, they tend to be overcautious, overprotective, and oversuspicious with their own children, and intolerant of their misconduct.

Teenagers eager for emancipation no longer appreciate a hovering parent whose loving care they had welcomed just a few years before. Now they reject this kind of solicitude. The conflict situation is built into the relationship: the police parent cannot change. When he gives his son the keys to the car, he recalls the mangled bodies in speedway accidents. As his daughter leaves the house on her big date, he visualizes the horror of the rape case or the overdose victim he handled not long before. Although all adolescents do not react to this surveillance in the same way, most resent it, and they become increasingly aware that the parent's job imposes certain regulations and limitations on their lives that others do not have to face. Some seem to submit but simmer. The apparently happy, well-adjusted daughter in one police family vented her resentment: "My father always had a kind of string on the kids. He's suspicious of everybody. He'll give my boyfriends the third degree. I felt trapped."[3]

---

[3] The George Family, "Six American Families," WNET Channel 13, April 25, 1977.

Others respond with humorous tolerance and may tease the parent about being the voice of doom. But when the discipline becomes more forceful and the confrontation between the generations comes to an impasse, a police parent may be shocked by this emotional barrage: "Go ahead and hit me with your nightstick! You're not a father. You're nothing but a cop!"

A final group is openly belligerent, fomenting a dangerous challenge to parental authority. A colleague at John Jay College of Criminal Justice who has several police officers of high rank in his family told us that one son bided his time until he was eighteen and strong enough to tackle his police officer father. He then thrashed his parent in a fist fight in order to get revenge for the years of punishment and humiliation from a despot who figuratively wore his uniform even at home. Is the police parent the composite visualized by this type of adolescent? Is the father figure just a facade for the police officer underneath—suspicious, cynical, and authoritarian?[4]

The police parent would summarily dismiss this description. From his point of view, he is still wearing essentially the same parental mantle of benevolent protector with which he sheltered his children when they were small. Now the dangers and problems facing the adolescent have multiplied, and reflexively, the parent wants to draw his offspring closer.

A college-graduate police sergeant with 20 years of service in the New York City Police Department, father of seven children, describes his efforts to shield his wife and children. Well qualified as a spokesman, he articulates the familial philosophy of many of his police colleagues:

Police are protective of their families and rightfully so. Most struggle to purchase one family homes, and usually in suburbia. . . . We protect our children educationally. Most policemen still residing in the city send their children to parochial grammar and high schools. The expense is enormous, but we feel the results are worth it. We would like our children to grow up "soft," as free as possible of the worldly wise-guy mouthings of the youths we meet on the "job." We also want them taught the tenets of our religion. . . . We are willing to accept the added expense of private schooling to teach discipline, that trait which is most necessary for any successful person.[5]

His statement does not reflect a regional ideology; it is characteristic of other sections of the nation as well. For example, in this excerpt from an interview with a veteran police sergeant attached to a Midwestern force, the officer comes across powerfully, asserting his respect for his co-workers and their pattern of child rearing.

I'll tell you who the police are. They're men from plain, ordinary families. . . . They go to church. They try to bring up their kids to respect older people and obey the law. They send their sons into the army, so the country will be the

---

[4] These three traits figure most frequently as characteristics of the police officers in the research literature.

[5] Excerpt from a term paper submitted in a graduate sociology course, John Jay College of Criminal Justice, 1976.

strongest on the earth, and they teach their daughters to be good wives and good mothers.[6]

But what parent is so infallible that he can bring up his children to be models for others? Of course, no one has yet broken the code that will reveal the best way to raise children. If there is one point of agreement among most researchers on the family, it is that the presence of children places a strain on a marriage. Most certainly, in police work, the logistics of the rotating schedule complicate family life even further. After a late tour, it requires nerve-wracking effort to fall asleep with several preschoolers running noisily about the house. When a police couple has planned a night out by plotting the schedule for two months in advance, it is a psychological catastrophe when the babysitter reneges at the last moment.

For police couples without young children, the occupational hazard of safeguarding the service revolver in the home appears to be minimal. The burden of the gun can be oppressive, however, when there are inquisitive youngsters underfoot. Because boys and girls are often fascinated by firearms, shocking fatalities can occur when they manage to ferret out the hiding place, experiment with the revolver, and possibly end up shooting themselves or friends.

When Arthur was a police officer, he meticulously followed police department regulations. He unloaded the gun as soon as he entered the house; he stored the bullets in a separate location; then he secreted the revolver in the rafters of the basement. Years later, our married daughter, Diane, confessed to us that when her friends had visited our home, they invariably had asked about her father's gun, and obligingly, she had led them to the supposed hiding place.

One tragedy developed from a seemingly innocuous situation. A police father who was shaving before going to work wore his revolver in the holster attached to his belt. Because each time he turned to see better in the mirror, the gun struck the ceramic sink over which he was leaning, he removed the pistol from the holster and placed it on the adjacent counter. When his three-year-old son wandered in to watch, the boy's attention was immediately caught by the sight of the weapon lying at his eye level. The father, unaware of the child's presence, suddenly was transfixed by the sound of the shot that exploded a bullet through the cheeks and mouth of his little boy.

A New York City police sergeant was puzzled by reports of three- and four-year-old children shooting themselves accidentally with their parents' service revolvers. He did not believe that youngsters of that age could have the necessary strength in their fingers to discharge the weapon when the hammer was not cocked. As an experiment, he carefully unloaded his revolver and gave it to his own three-year-old son to play with. The youngster did a surprising thing. Holding the gun with two hands, he reversed it so that the barrel pointed directly at himself. Then he placed both thumbs around the trigger and straining

[6] Robert Coles, *The Middle Americans* (Boston: Little, Brown, 1971), p. 52.

with all his might, he was able to snap the trigger. Had the pistol been loaded, the bullet would have torn right through his head.

Individual variations in adaptation are mandated when there are youngsters about, as this wife of a police officer advised in her addendum to an item on our questionnaire:

Anyone whose husband is a police officer sort of has to make their own adjustments. Much depends on if children are involved versus those that don't have children. The way I arrange my life around his job and my children may not be the ideal situation to someone else.

But in the more important child-rearing practices, a consensus emerges that fortifies the police marriage. If we accept the premise that the arrival of children places a strain on a marriage, then the danger signal for marital stability would be a serious disagreement in methods of raising the children. In our sample, harmony in styles and goals of child rearing predominated, which translates into a positive prognosis for these marriages.

About 75 percent of our respondent police officers and spouses who were parents classified their method of raising their children as flexible, as opposed to strict or permissive. And only 5 percent of them reported children's misbehavior or the lack of communication between parents and children as problems that occurred frequently. These self-evaluations of child-rearing practices are subjective interpretations. For instance, underlying this divorced traffic cop's account of his method of disciplining his sons, aged twelve and fifteen, is the implication that he is merely firm in laying down the law. In our opinion, he comes across as a rigid and harsh disciplinarian.

My sons adore me. My wife can't understand this. If they do something wrong in my presence—even though I don't live in that house—they get punished. My wife said, "You're so hard with them at times, yet they worship the ground you walk on." When I used the belt on them I'd always tell them why. They understood and they accept it. My oldest boy is now on the honor rolls at Notre Dame High School.

He gets a little stubborn. He'd confront me with things: "I want to wear my hair long." "You want to wear your hair long, get out of my house. You know what it represents to me. Till the day you are twenty-one and you will leave my jurisdiction, you will do as I tell you. You understand?" "Okay Dad, you're the boss." That's all there is to it. There's no resentment. No animosity. It's just an understanding that I lay the law down. There are rules and regulations.[7]

How can we reconcile the police self-image as flexible parents when we have analyzed their intense concern and control of the children and their deep allegiance to enforcing discipline and obedience? We believe that the police occupation potently but so immutably influences these latent areas of family life

<hr>

[7] Studs Terkel, *Working* (New York: Pantheon Books, 1972), p. 136.

that unconsciously the typical police couple marches to the cadences and directives of the job. And yet they can insist that they themselves are calling the tune, especially for their children's future.

Back in 1958, social psychologists Daniel Miller and Guy Swanson moved into a more sociological framework when they hypothesized that the father's occupation significantly determined child-rearing practices. Recognizing the dominance of the bureaucratic form of occupational organization over the entrepreneurial, they theorized that the entrepreneurial family, already an anachronism, would yield to the bureaucratic family type.[8] The police family dovetails into their definition of the bureaucratic family because the police officer works for somebody else, in an organization with three or more supervisory levels, and his income is primarily in the form of wages or salary.

When we asked the police parents in our sample to choose the qualities they considered most important for their children, their choices clustered about bureaucratic qualities: honesty, respect for authority, obedience to parents, and dependability. (Table 6-1 lists these traits in rank order.) According to Miller and Swanson, it would be expected that submission to the security and routine of the occupation would strip the officer of his ambition and his potential for striking out on his own.[9] This mechanism would also explain the desire of police officers to inculcate bureaucratic traits in their children.

Paradoxically, though, most of them want their sons to be professionals. Success in these demanding pursuits often requires the entrepreneurial qualities of perseverance, independence, high achievement in school, and thrift, all

Table 6-1
Children's Qualities Ranked by Parents

Quality	Ranked in Order of Importance by Policemen (N = 182)		Ranked in Order of Importance by Police Wives (N = 184)	
Honesty	1	(90%)	3	(71%)
Respect for authority	2	(74%)	1	(80%)
Obedience to parents	3½	(73%)	2	(73%)
Dependability	3½	(73%)	4	(70%)
Perseverance	5	(60%)	6	(55%)
Independence	6	(55%)	5	(57%)
High achievement in school	7	(33%)	7	(33%)
Thrift	8	(30%)	8	(30%)
Popularity	9	(12%)	9	(12%)

[8] Daniel R. Miller and Guy E. Swanson, *The Changing American Parent* (New York: Wiley, 1958), p. 193.

[9] Ibid., p. 102.

characteristics that constitute a throwback to the Protestant ethic. Yet these police parents ranked them much lower in importance compared to the bureaucratic virtues. Popularity, the quality that trailed the rest, proved to be the only exception where a possibly bureaucratic trait was calibrated at the bottom of the scale.[10]

The police occupation interlocks so neatly with the bureaucratic pattern of organization that it is no wonder that police officers are classified as bureaucrats. The search for security, the dream of the pension, the fixed rules, the rigidity, and the submission to hierarchical authority are all classic attributes of the bureaucratic personality. On patrol, however, the successful police officer must be authoritative and independent; most of the tour he works alone; he is permitted wide powers of discretion; often he makes instantaneous and critical decisions that may mean life or death; and he must be willing to take risks. Obviously, this cluster of traits is more characteristic of entrepreneurs than of bureaucrats.

This contradiction between the bureaucratic form of the occupation and the entrepreneurial aspect of the policeman's actual role clarifies the apparent anomaly that permits police parents to opt for professional careers in law and medicine for their children while at the same time prizing the bureaucratic virtues of obedience and dependability.

This explanation of the process is too simplistic, however. The average parent does not formulate a clear-cut blueprint for raising his children. He does not say to himself, "I want my child to be a bureaucrat or a professional; therefore, I will try to inculcate those qualities that are most appropriate for that career." In most cases, styles of child rearing are more a product of psychological, sociological, and interactive processes, most of them existing at the unconscious level rather than as a specifically rational plan of action.

Because the police officer on the job assumes the role of authority and independence, this becomes his customary approach to interpersonal relations. Can he switch off this role when he travels from station house to ranch house? Very few are able to accomplish this transition smoothly; generally, the police identity spills over into the father figure. For instance, most of the police in our sample rated themselves as flexible in child rearing, yet the police authority neutralizing that flexibility was apparent in their consistent choice of obedience and respect for authority as the prime qualities they wished to foster in their children.

It is unrealistic to expect police parents to deviate from this concept of

[10] In a replication of Miller and Swanson's work, Franklin and Scott hypothesized that bureaucratic families would want their children to be popular. See Jack L. Franklin and Joseph E. Scott, "Parental Values: An Inquiry into Occupational Setting," *Journal of Marriage and the Family* 32 (August 1970):407. Their rationale probably was that popularity was to a large extent determined by others and was somewhat beyond the control of the individual. In our questionnaire only 12 percent of the men and women listed popularity as very important for their children.

control and authority within the family. Based on equal shares of experience and ideology, the majority of police officers are certain that strong parental supervision is the one necessary ingredient to prevent trouble in or out of the home. To them, the rampant delinquency they see on the job is a problem located largely among the lower-class and minority communities. And they blame juvenile crime on parental neglect. (Through the years, Arthur has taught thousands of law enforcement officers in courses in criminal justice and criminology. Although they discuss dozens of competing explanations for crime and delinquency, the students hold tenaciously to the idea that the real cause is lack of proper supervision by parents.) Therefore, police parents continue to instill a code of obedience, dependability, honesty, and religious instruction. And police occupational ideology coalesces with this pattern of child rearing.

Buttressed by this belief in delinquency causation, the police parent must prove to himself and others that he is not guilty of the same type of neglect. Every moment that he can spend with his children becomes a precious commodity.

A patrolman, demonstrating at city hall to protest a departmental revision that would increase the workload of the members of the force brought his three children—the oldest eleven years of age—to join him on the picket line. His statement exemplifies the credo of his colleagues.

Being a street cop, I know that to bring children up properly you have to give them time. You have to have someone there. I see what happens to kids when they don't have fathers around—thev run wild on the streets day and night.[11]

The fact that the intricacies of his work schedule may force the police officer to juggle the time he spends with his family agitates him. By a process of psychological generalization or displacement, the chart becomes the barrier between him and the children. Similarly, his first defense against any proposed change in schedule is to proclaim that the new timetable will disrupt family life by robbing his already deprived children of the little time that he can devote to them.

In reality, this is fallacious logic, although it will infuriate the average police officer to hear this. Certainly, a knowledgeable law enforcement worker is aware that in the larger cities, police department hours of work, time off, and vacations compare quite favorably with those of other civil service workers and most of the working force in the private sector as well. What is really provoking his anxiety is the realization that because he is a police officer, he is on call for possible emergency duty 24 hours a day, and he feels uncertain that he will really have enough time to spend with his family. Nevertheless, by judiciously manipulating his periods of sleep, a police officer on rotating shifts can enjoy far more of the day with his children than does the average working father with

[11] *New York Times*, October 2, 1976, p. 49.

regular hours. He can also see his children at different times during the day, an especially rewarding benefit when the children are small and have early bedtimes. Compared to a busy professional or the harried middle-class executive who brings his work home with him almost every night, the police officer enjoys a great advantage.

It is a dreadful blow to any family when a son or daughter gets in trouble with the law. However, to a police family it is far more devastating. Not only does the adolescent's transgression violate the family's moral code, but also it undermines the police parent's position as an upholder of the laws of society. Immersed in the belief that mothers and fathers by their neglect or failure to enforce discipline are responsible for their children's wrongdoing, police parents are inundated by a cascade of guilt feelings if their child is arrested. Of what use were the constant warnings and admonitions? The police parent oscillates from sympathetic concern to fury at the offspring who has brought this disaster upon the house. The anguished mother pleads, "You're a policeman. Do something!" For an outsider to come to the precinct to intercede for a prisoner would probably end up in a charge of obstructing governmental administration, or possibly, bribery—a felony. It is hardly less criminal for a police officer to do so, but in his desperation, he tries it.

In agony, he forces himself to enter the precinct station house where his arrested child is being held. What disgrace burns him as he searches for a key to stop the implacable process of justice. Fighting his humiliation, he diffidently approaches the arresting officer or the detective assigned to the case, ostensibly to find out the charges, but really to plead for mercy. He will be permitted to speak to his arrested child. Often this interview is a frustrating confrontation. Having heard the child's side of the case, he may once more attempt to convince the arresting officer to forget the arrest or possibly to reduce the charge to a lower degree of crime. He does this although he knows that if he talks to the wrong person, he may jeopardize his own police career and may at the same time compromise the other officer as well.

Sometimes he knows the commanding officer or the lieutenant in the precinct and will appeal in guarded language, hoping that they will understand and acquiesce to his veiled plea to permit irregularities in the reporting and processing of the case. As a last resort he will appear in court to influence the district attorney to be sympathetic, and he may even request an audience with the judge in his chambers trying to find a loophole.

One police officer, now retired from the New York City Police Department and living in another state, attempted to help his son by appearing in court with him to answer a summons for a traffic violation. When the son's case was called, the retired officer went forward with him, and the son informed the court that he was the defendant. The judge, perhaps assuming that the father was the attorney representing his client, asked the father to identify himself. Unable to forget his past prestige and authority, the veteran officer held up the gold shield his police colleagues had given him as a retirement gift and said proudly, "Your honor, this is my son and I am a retired New York City police sergeant." The judge sardonically replied, "That's all right. We won't hold that against you." The sergeant was crushed. Later, he complained to us that the judge should not have humiliated him that way in front of his son.

Among our acquaintances are several police families whose sons became chronic delinquents, and the policemen fathers went through these ordeals several times a year. One parent suffered a massive heart attack. The other endured two concomitant tragedies: a prolonged depression and a stormy divorce.

One perverse aspect of these tragic situations is that some people experience a vindictive pleasure when a police officer's child gets in trouble. The realization that a son or daughter in a law enforcement family can become a lawbreaker often represents the public's vicarious vengeance against the police who symbolically serve as society's superego. Even the 1974 national teacher of the year was not immune from this snide denigration of the police. In the course of an interview, the reporter asked the educator about streaking (the term applied to the fad of running nude in public). As the award-winning pedagogue recounted it, the student body in her high school raised about $30 to be won by the first student(s) brave enough to streak through the halls. Vying for the prize, several youths streaked, then dressed rapidly, and ran out of school. They were quickly identified:

The school called their parents to let them know . . . and one of the mothers, upon hearing that her son was a streaker, said that her husband was a policeman. And, lo and behold, he the policeman father was in front of the school trying to get a carload of mooners who had been going by the school. Do you know what a mooner is? These are kids who are nude in a car and the car goes by and they're leaning out of the window. Yes, they were nude. I don't know if it's new, but anyway this is what it was. And this kid's father was out there to see if he could catch these guys who were mooning, and here his son was being picked up for streaking inside. Oh, we had such a laugh over that![12]

To the police family, anecdotes and jokes in which the punch line derives its kick from the put-down of the occupation or its personnel are a malicious brand of sick humor. Parents and children alike might ruefully ponder whether the distress to a mother and the imminent shame to a police father, which caused the teacher of the year to display such merriment, would have been such a laughing matter if it did not concern a police family.

For any parent, the process of rearing a child successfully in today's kaleidoscopic society is more a mystery than an art or science. Compounding the difficulty for police parents is their own ambivalence about their proper

[12] *American Teacher: Official Publication of the American Federation of Teachers AFL-CIO* (May 1974):18.

function and responsibility toward their children. The police occupational ideology, shared by a majority of the force, proclaims that our society is at the point of disintegration because of excessive permissiveness, loss of respect for law and order, and the continuing erosion of parental authority. There is a definite conflict between the police parents' desires to maintain authority and control within the family and the push toward egalitarianism, which is more appropriate to newly acquired middle-class status.

Like all adolescents, the teenager in a police family struggles to attain self-expression and independence from parental control. Having traversed a comfortable and secure childhood in the glow of the father's power as a figure of authority, just a few years later, the young person finds that same aura of power converted into a tenacious restriction of his or her freedom of action. During this same period, the adolescent becomes more aware of status and class distinctions, and the luster of the police job dims when it is compared with the professions of the parents of middle-class friends.

In the face of such potential for tension between parent and child, the adolescents who discussed their problems with us rarely voiced frustration or resentment toward their parents. Instead, they expressed an appreciation of the police officer parent as an anchor of stability during the turbulent years of coming-of-age.

7 Divorce: Police Style

In 1975, financial experts cheered when the Dow Jones average shattered the 1000 barrier. Simultaneously, marital counselors groaned when the annual number of divorces in the United States broke through the one million mark, skyrocketing to an astronomical 50 percent of the more than two million marriages occurring in the same period. How many police marriages penetrated that losers' circle? You don't have to be a statistician to hypothesize that divorce rates will soar in an occupation where a married police officer works around the clock and where he is inevitably thrust into situations providing intimate contact with members of the opposite sex.

Our personal experience with police-couple friends, our in-depth interviews with members of the force and their spouses, and our preliminary review of the available literature reinforced our expectation that police divorce rates would be among the very highest. After all, the manifold problems of the average marriage—challenge and response, compromise and readjustment—are augmented by the heavy stress of police work.

It was disheartening to observe our police acquaintances' marriages disintegrate under the pressure of the job. For one couple the work schedule cut them apart. Afraid to sleep alone, the wife could never adjust to her husband's late tours (midnight to 8 A.M.). Before every late tour, they reenacted the same traumatic domestic tableau. She insisted that he drive her and their young child to her mother's house across town where they would spend the night. In the morning, the arduous safari reversed itself. This upheaval every third week eroded their relationship until finally, the distraught husband made one last exodus to his mother-in-law's home, depositing his young family there permanently.

A strange twist ruptured still another marital partnership of our police friends. The diurnal rhythms of the couple beat in contrapuntal tempo. Their lifestyles contradicted each other. A day person, the policeman's personality and energy waxed and waned with the sun. By contrast, the wife, a night person, responded to the moon's influence. In an ordinary existence they might have been able to adjust to each other, but the shifting hours of police work made time of the essence. After a 4 P.M. to midnight tour of duty, he would return home exhausted, ready to collapse into bed. His wife, attuned to the beat of her own nocturnal drum, was just getting lively. Or he would have some reserve energy after a late tour, but she would be sleeping soundly. And on the 8 A.M. to 4 P.M. schedule, by the time he returned home it was dinner time. During the evening hours he was rapidly running down while she was gathering steam. It just did not work; they are still friends, although divorced, their circadian rhythms still worlds apart.

Other divorces battered our already fragmented social circle. One friend employed his police expertise to trap his wife in flagrante. The scenario of another breakup unraveled like a contemporary television detergent drama. Supportive of his brilliant young bride's ambitions to continue her education, the police officer solicitously assumed domestic chores and later took on the obligations of child care. Barely able to scrape together her tuition costs, they could not afford a housekeeper on his detective's salary. Consequently, when he had to appear in court as an arresting officer, he brought their young child along and would have to leave her with a clerk or attendant until he finished his court attendance. With pride and concern he would explain to his surrogate baby sitters that his wife could not miss her college classes. But as his spouse climbed the ladder toward her Ph.D., she left her husband on a lower rung. The final clout to this shaky marriage was delivered when she fell in love with a classmate.

And thus traumatized by the conjugal vicissitudes of our close friends, we inferred that divorce was an occupational hazard of the police job. Somehow it is human nature to exaggerate the impact and swathe of a disaster when one can identify and empathize with the victim. But as we probed more deeply, substituting objective data for intuition and popular opinion, our research disputed our original observations: there was evidence that police divorce rates were not as high as we had been led to believe.

When we broached the subject of divorce in our interviews with police officers, we found that our own preconceived stereotype about high police divorce rates was the prevailing view among them as well. We started out in low gear by mentioning that some reports disseminated by police departments indicated average and even low divorce rates. Unimpressed by our research, many of those we interviewed reacted with disbelief and derided our statistics. They echoed the same refrain: "How could you be so gullible as to believe those figures? The police have a very high divorce rate." Each substantiated his conviction by describing case histories of police divorces.

One zealous and self-assured officer offered to survey his precinct for us. "I'm certain that a tally would disclose that almost one-half are divorced," he expostulated, citing an informal count that he had conducted. "Today I had lunch with six fellow officers from my command. Among the seven of us we account for 14 wives. And we're not bigamists." A few weeks later that policeman was a little less certain of his position. He was planning to incorporate his research on divorce into a master's thesis that would test his hypothesis.

The media also resort to shock tactics. In the opening minutes of a training film on police marriage, the portentous voice of the narrator declaims the alarming statistic that as many as "75 percent of working officers will divorce in the first three years on the job."[1] It is quite likely that this is a garbled

[1] George Kirkham et al., "The Police Marriage: Three Films on Personal, Social and Family Issues" (New York: Harper and Row Media, 1976).

restatement of the tentative findings in some preliminary studies. Probably the correct statement, albeit less dramatic, should be that 75 percent of police officers who obtain a divorce will do so within the first three years on the job. But the same allegation as that contained in the film is repeated in the brochure describing the training package.

Since this series was prepared by George Kirkham (a professor of criminal justice who became a cop) in association with three police psychologists, the powerful auspices almost guarantee the authenticity. And the verisimilitude of the tension-producing situations, in which real police officers are the principal actors, reinforces the credibility. What viewer could doubt the accuracy of the pronouncement on police divorce? Moreover, the series with its discussion outline is used by many police departments for orientation, thus spreading this misleading premise.

Police wives are prominent among those who spread the rumor of high police divorce rates. Eager to aid other police wives in surmounting the difficulties of marriage, Barbara Webber's "how-to" book, instead, succeeds in agitating them with this unverified and pessimistic statement:

The police profession's ranking first in divorce, second in actual suicides, and high in mental breakdowns makes it increasingly important that the wife function in her capacity to provide a good home environment for her husband.[2]

Updating her ranking of the police profession, the same author in a later publication cites a figure of "well over 50 percent" for police divorce, once more failing to list a source.[3] Another police wife reiterates the same dismal diagnosis and gratuitously lays the blame for the dissolution of the marriage on the wife, not on the husband or the job: "Policemen have the highest divorce rate in the United States. In too many cases this divorce is caused by a wife who cannot accept and understand her husband's job."[4]

A cursory review of the chapter headings in another guide for police wives, written by a police wife and her mother, conveys its message: "Love Me Love My Work," "He's Going to Need Your Tender Loving Care," and "Make Your Home a Haven." These conjugal sermons imply that the home must be the sanctuary to provide catharsis from the oppressive demands of the occupation. And subliminally, the finger once more points to the unfortunate wife who fails in this supportive role. She is identified as the scapegoat responsible for a catalog of police plagues:

Divorce, ulcers, alcoholism and suicide take a frightening toll in police families these days, and these are often triggered by unhappy wives unable to cope with the very real stresses the law enforcement task brings to the officer's family.[5]

[2] Barbara E. Webber, "The Police Life," in Barbara E. Webber, ed., *Handbook for Law Enforcement Wives* (Chicago: L E Publishers, 1974), p. 20.

[3] Barbara E. Webber, "The Police Wife," *The Police Chief* (January 1976):48.

[4] Joanne Beegan, "Letter to a Rookie's Wife," in Webber, *Handbook*, p. 93.

[5] Pat James and Martha Nelson, *Police Wife* (Springfield, Ill.: Charles C. Thomas, 1975), p. 108.

158

When psychologists who are consultants in mental health to police departments claim high police divorce rates, they generate even more credibility than do police wives. And once again the wives are assigned the responsibility for the family pathology:

The [police] officer's wife probably had no understanding of her husband's job demands when she married him. She also did not bargain for the insecurity, the danger to her husband, or the antipolice feeling she herself may encounter in some social settings. It is not surprising that indices of social alienation are high within police ranks; divorce and alcoholism often reach serious proportions.[6]

A consultant and counselor for several medium-sized police departments, Henry Singer, forcefully and convincingly repeated the same theme:

Policemen have the highest divorce rate of any group in the country, some claim as much as 40 percent. In talks with police officers it becomes clear that their life has very little privacy. If they live in a neighborhood where it is known they are policemen, they often receive verbal abuse in a constant stream of phone calls.[7]

Catherine Milton conducted an exhaustive study of women in policing for the Police Foundation, which was established by the Ford Foundation to help American police realize their fullest potential. She reported that wives of male officers opposed the expansion of the role of policewomen and concluded that the wives' apprehensions were justified because:

the divorce rate among police officers is extraordinarily high. As one former policewoman wrote, "A police officer is a police officer 24 hours a day and he can be (and sometimes is) called at any time. The high divorce rates . . . reflect many of the strains that the work situation puts on the family.[8]

To gain practical experience in criminology, a professor of sociology, David Rafky, joined the police force of the St. Charles Parish Sheriff's Office in Louisiana near Loyola University where he had been teaching. His first day at the police academy alerted him to the threat of divorce. The lieutenant instructor, a former homicide detective with the New Orleans Police Department, opened his lecture to the recruit class by asking, "How many here are married?" As a great many hands shot up, he frowned.

The reason for his chagrin, we quickly learned, was that typically one-third of the married cadets are divorced within their first two years on the force, and

---

[6] Jeffrey A. Schwartz and Donald A. Liebman, "Mental Health Consultation in Law Enforcement," in John R. Snibbe and Homa M. Snibbe, eds., *The Urban Policeman in Transition: A Psychological and Sociological Review* (Springfield, Ill.: Charles C. Thomas, 1973), p. 560.

[7] *New York Times*, August 13, 1973, p. 29.

[8] Catherine Milton, *Women in Policing* (Washington, D.C.: The Police Foundation, 1972), p. 26.

that some marriages do not even survive the three months of training. In response to this problem, Lt. D. devised a "wives' night" as part of the training program where spouses view a movie describing the duties of a police officer, question the instructors, share their feelings with other wives, and discuss job-related problems in a helping atmosphere. I recall feeling that the department's concern was silly, if not meddling, and I decided that I would not invite my wife to visit the academy for "her" night.

After five months as a deputy sheriff in neighboring St. Charles Parish, however, I was indeed sorry that I did not heed Lt. D.'s advice to share my police experience with my wife. She, like other spouses, was disturbed when there were floods in our area and I had to leave her to protect someone else's family; she, like other wives was not happy to hear the telephone ring during the middle of the night when a juvenile detective was needed to interrogate a runaway; she, like other police wives, did not greet me lovingly when I returned home after investigating a "ripe" (decomposing) death—I smelled so offensively that my clothes had to be burned. And sadly, like an increasing number of women, my wife was "worried sick" by a radio bulletin she heard when home alone which reported sketchy details of the killing of a St. Charles deputy.[9]

In some cases police personnel, themselves alerted to the rumors of divorce, have joined together in informal surveys of different departments to gauge the magnitude of the problem. The authors of one such report, convinced that there are a great number of failing and unsuccessful police marriages, insinuate that divorce may only be the visible portion of the iceberg of marital dissatisfaction.[10] From their findings it would seem more like a frozen continent rather than an iceberg. Their limited and informal research in three departments generated the following figures on divorce: Baltimore, Maryland, 17 percent; Santa Ana, California, 27 percent; and Chicago, Illinois, an incredible 33.3 percent. Because of self-professed limitations in their study, however, the authors caution that these high rates "cannot be considered a true indication of the problem."[11]

The most frightening figures on police divorce were casually exposed by a former police officer, now a professor of criminal justice, who did not adduce any evidence to support his conclusion:

It should come as no surprise, then, when estimates of the divorce rate among police range from a low of sixty percent to a high of eighty-four percent. . . . Incidents of ulcers, hemorrhoids, hives, migraine, and other physical anomalies associated with tension and anxiety are also reportedly high.[12]

But personal experiences, empathy with acquaintances' marital upsets, subjective inferences of professional observers, and informal explorations of the

[9] David Rafky, "My Husband the Cop," *The Police Chief* (August 1974):62.

[10] James A. Durner et al., "Divorce—Another Occupational Hazard," *The Police Chief* 42 (November 1975):49.

[11] Ibid.

[12] John S. Megerson, "The Officer's Lady," *The Police Chief* (October 1973):34.

160

subject lack the authenticity to justify scientifically conclusions about an occupation numbering some 500,000. Although we cannot deny its persuasive impact, it is our obligation to assess this public opinion by utilizing studies of the police that meet more rigorous standards in methodology, as well as in the source of the data.

Is divorce an occupational hazard of police work? Admittedly, police work precipitates strains in the marital relationship. But this hypothesis of hazard and strain does not categorically imply that there necessarily will be high divorce rates. The great majority of marriages endure distress, frustration, and bitter confrontations. The truth is that divorce is a contingency in every marriage. And the overwhelming number of marriages do survive. At most, one can draw a rebuttable presumption that police divorce levels will be high.

Without doubt, the factors in the police job that are often cited as the causes of high divorce rates—the schedule, the tension, the shock of police experience, the low status and salary—have been ameliorated in the last decade. Compared to the last 10 years, occupational conditions were much worse in 1960 and wretched in 1900. Therefore, the same reasoning that leads so many observers to expect high divorce rates today should operate to support the conclusion that police divorce rates in the past were probably equally as high relative to average rates. But there is some evidence that police divorce rates were lower than average in those periods. Using data from the census of 1900, James Lichtenberger ranked occupations according to their divorce rates, from 1 (the highest) to 39 (the lowest). The police placed near the low end, number 30 out of the 39 occupations. Doctors, lawyers, and professors were higher on the scale.[13]

In a thorough review of the marital problems facing police officers, Jack E. Whitehouse reports that he was successful in obtaining data on police and detective divorce compiled in the 1960 census by the Bureau of the Census and the Bureau of Vital Statistics of the Department of Health, Education and Welfare. Those figures revealed that police and detectives in the United States had a low divorce rate of 1.7 percent compared to a national average of 2.4 percent for males in the same age distribution.[14] Like us, he discovered the same ubiquitous refusal to believe his statement that police were not high in divorce: "[He] has never talked to another law enforcement officer who did not feel police officers had a higher divorce rate than the community average."[15]

Considered a classic in law enforcement literature, Jerome Skolnick's study of the Oakland, California, Police Department surveyed the 616 members of the force. A most representative sample—285 (46 percent)—responded to the

[13] James Lichtenberger, *Divorce: A Study in Social Causation* (New York: AMS Press, 1968), pp. 95-96. This study was also cited in Durner et al., "Divorce."

[14] Jack E. Whitehouse, "A Preliminary Inquiry into the Occupational Disadvantages of Law Enforcement Officers," *Police* (May-June 1965):31.

[15] Ibid.

questionnaire. In this population 90 percent were married, 3 percent were single, and 7 percent were separated or divorced.[16] It is a fair assumption that 2 percent of this last group were separated, leaving a figure of 5 percent divorced, which is higher than the national average but not by much.

Bayley and Mendelsohn concentrated on the police force of Denver, Colorado. Utilizing rigorous standards of research methodology, they conducted personal interviews with 100 officers from the total complement of 813. From this randomly selected 12 percent sample, the researchers discerned a high degree of family stability and propounded a rationale for it:

Policemen are family men. In our sample of Denver policemen, not one was single . . . Moreover, policemen seem to have more stable marriages than are to be found in the community as a whole. *Only 2% of the officers had been divorced* against 5% generally. Policemen are also parents. A mere 3% of them had no children. . . . This is an important point to bear in mind. Policemen represent family men, men who value family stability highly and who may rely on their families for support against a populace which they often regard as hostile. [Italics added.][17]

In his official capacity as departmental psychologist for the Los Angeles Police Department, Martin Reiser was not only cognizant of the rumors circulating about police divorce, but also deeply disturbed by specific allegations of an extremely high incidence of divorce endemic to the Los Angeles force. The culminating event, a newspaper article alleging that in an informal tally of the Seattle, Washington, force 60 percent of the newly appointed officers joined the ranks of the divorced within three years, impelled him to conduct his own research within his department to establish the facts. Distributing questionnaires to a stratified population of 800 officers (a 10 percent sample of the total force) and focusing on that critical three-year period after appointment, he tabulated only 39 divorces for a percentage of 4.9, markedly lower than that of Seattle.[18]

Departing from this method of computation as he expanded his aim, he calculated the sample's total divorce rate by comparing the number of divorces to the number of marriages rather than to the number of individuals in the sample. He derived an index of 21 percent, which he interpreted as a "comparatively low" figure "in contrast to a national divorce rate of approximately 30 percent and a California divorce rate of approximately 45 percent." Reiser determined that nearly 5 percent of the total number of divorces had occurred before the men joined the force. During the first three years of police work, the most vulnerable period, divorces surged. Interestingly, in the ranks of captain and above, divorce rates were one-half those in the lower echelons.[19]

[16] Jerome H. Skolnick, *Justice Without Trial* (New York: Wiley, 1966), p. 266.

[17] David H. Bayley and Harold Mendelsohn, *Minorities and the Police: Confrontation in America* (New York: The Free Press, 1969), pp. 4-5.

[18] Martin Reiser, *The Police Department Psychologist* (Springfield, Ill.: Charles C. Thomas, 1972), pp. 101-105.

[19] Ibid., pp. 101, 102-103.

A national police survey reported by Watson and Sterling was carefully planned, meticulously executed, and comprehensive in scope.[20] Because of the availability of the unique resources of the International Association of Chiefs of Police that penetrated into every corner of the police world, a project of that magnitude could be expedited and accomplished. The survey encompassed 294 police departments, and returns from 246 of them represented every state but Vermont. From the 7099 questionnaires distributed, they received more than 4900 usable returns. Table 7-1 compares the Watson and Sterling data with the national figures compiled by the Bureau of the Census for the same year.

The low 2 percent divorce rate for policemen, well under the national average for men, constitutes an irrefutable challenge that cannot be overthrown by rumor, subjective estimates, or informal surveys. Although the Watson and Sterling project accumulated wide-ranging coverage for policemen, only 94 policewomen responded to the questions pertaining to marital status.[21] In contrast to the low divorce results for the males, however, the policewomen traced an erratic marital pattern; 16 percent divorced, a startling eight times the rate of their male counterparts.

Another researcher amassed a sample of 150 policewomen as part of an

Table 7-1
A Comparison of the Marital Status of the Police and the General Population, 1968

	Percent Married	Percent Divorced	Percent Separated	Percent Single	Percent Widowed
Policemen (Watson and Sterling)	93	2.0	1.0	3.7	0.5
Adult men in U.S. (Census)	75.6	2.6	1.6	18.2	3.6
Policewomen (Watson and Sterling)	49	16	2.0	28	5.0
Adult women in U.S. (Census)	69.2	3.6	2.4	13.4	13.9

Source: Nelson A. Watson and James W. Sterling, *Police and Their Opinions* (Gaithersburg, Md.: International Association of Chiefs of Police, 1969); U.S. Bureau of the Census, *Current Population Reports,* series P-20.

[20] Nelson A. Watson and James W. Sterling, *Police and Their Opinions* (Gaithersburg, Md.: International Association of Chiefs of Police, 1969).

[21] An earlier study by the IACP covering 6,267 police officers from 609 departments in all states but Alaska and Hawaii reported a low divorce rate of 2.6 percent. But they cautioned that the study might not be representative since it contained a higher proportion of juvenile officers, policewomen, and chiefs but no officers attending recruit school. For this reason, we did not include it in table 7-1. See George W. O'Connor and Nelson A. Watson, *Juvenile Delinquency and Youth Crime: The Police Role* (Washington, D.C.: International Association of Chiefs of Police, 1964), pp. 75-76.

inquiry into their characteristics. Eager to learn about themselves, 138 respondents representing well-known police departments in 14 states contributed information on their marital status. Seemingly reinforcing the Watson and Sterling findings, this group revealed a divorce rate of 15 percent with 65 percent married.[22]

As part of an exploration into the attitudes toward the role of women in police work, still another investigator gathered a sample of 127 policewomen who were attending college. This, too, closely mirrored the two previous studies, with 23 percent divorced and 37 percent married among the 98 policewomen who completed the questionnaires.[23] Table 7-2 summarizes the data of these studies.

Even a superficial review of the disparity in the patterns of divorce between the sexes stirs speculation. Where does the locus of responsibility lie to account for the instability of the policewomen's marriages? Does the cause reside in the policewoman, her spouse, or police work itself?

The policewoman steps into a work world of preselected men—virile, strong,

Table 7-2
Marital Status of Policewomen

Name and Date of Study	Number in Sample	Percent Married	Percent Divorced	Percent Single
Watson and Sterling	94	51[a]	16	33[b]
Perlstein (1971)	138	65	15	20
Gross (1974)	98	37	23	40
Totals and averages	330	49	18	29
National rates for adult women (Bureau of the Census, 1972)		68.5	4.3	28

Source: Nelson A. Watson and James W. Sterling, *Police and Their Opinions* (Gaithersburg, Md.: International Association of Chiefs of Police, 1969); Gary Perlstein, "An Exploratory Analysis of Certain Characteristics of Policewomen" (Ph.D. diss., Florida State University, 1971); Solomon Gross, "Perceptions of the Role of Women in Policing by Police Educators" (Master's thesis, John Jay College of Criminal Justice, 1974); U.S.: Bureau of the Census, *Current Population Reports,* series P-20.

[a]Includes 2 percent separated.

[b]Includes 5 percent widowed.

[22]Gary Perlstein, "An Exploratory Analysis of Certain Characteristics of Policewomen" (Ph.D. diss., Florida State University, 1971), p. 72.

[23]We thank Professor Solomon Gross for making available to us his data sheets containing the marital information we cited. For a fuller treatment of his research, see Solomon Gross, "Perceptions of the Role of Women in Policing by Police Educators, Policemen and Policewomen Attending College" (Master's thesis, John Jay College of Criminal Justice, 1974).

and vigorous—whose physical attributes are heightened by daily acts of courage and selflessness in the performance of their duties. Any husband's image might diminish when compared to these paragons. The aura of glamour and excitement surrounding her male colleagues contrasts starkly with the frequent banality and trivia of domestic routines shared with her husband. And a policewoman who sees her husband as less attractive may unconsciously become less resilient and less conciliatory in conjugal controversies.

The reciprocal of this process entails the gradual disillusionment of her husband as his policewoman wife matures into a powerful authority figure. A married man who has internalized the conventional view of the marriage relation may well envision his wife as a sex object, compliant and dependent. This reversal of roles, a contemporary scenario, reenacts the classic theme immortalized in Ibsen's *Doll's House*. Threatened by the transformation of his wife, Nora, from a flighty bird into a competent woman who has secretly maneuvered him successfully through a financial crisis, Nora's husband reacts with irrational frenzy, and the marriage falls apart. How much more traumatic for a present-day husband of a policewoman to observe his wife emerge from the chrysalis, metamorphosized into a self-sufficient woman.

Although plausible, this rationale for the finding of marital instability among policewomen would obviously apply only to divorces that occurred after they joined the force. In Perlstein's study, the 138 policewomen averaged 35.3 years in age with a mean length of service of 7.6 years, and 90 of them were married, 27 single, and 21 divorced. Since the women were clearly not rookies, it would be logical to assume a causal connection between the stress of the police job and the propensity to divorce. But Perlstein's questionnaire contained this pair of perceptive questions: "What was your marital status at the time of entry into police work?" and then as a check, "What is your marital status now?" From his respondents Perlstein determined that all the 21 divorces actually had occurred before the women joined the force, and not one divorce took place during the years of police service of the 90 policewomen who were married at the time they entered the occupation.

If entry into the police career acts as a cutoff point for divorce, it effectively dichotomizes the research on police divorce into time slots, before and after, adding a new dimension. The innuendo that police service may be the preserver, not the destroyer, of marriage is beguiling. That premise can be applied equally well to divorces of male police officers. The strong likelihood that a proportion of their divorces, like those of policewomen, occurred before they joined the force points to an even lower rate of job-related divorce among policemen than we have already determined.

The three studies cited in table 7-2 corroborate that the rate of divorce for policewomen is far higher than the national average for women in general. But in view of Perlstein's research, it would be fallacious to assume that the policewomen's divorces were for the most part job related.

Is there some intrinsic characteristic in the nature of a woman who chooses a police career that propels her toward divorce? Is she more susceptible to the lure of the feminist movement? Has the driving force that steered her in the direction of a heavily male-dominated occupation activated currents of personality that are inimical to stable marriage? (Contrast this attitude with the remark of a police officer's daughter. When interviewed, she initially had expressed interest in joining the force. As she reflected, however, her enthusiasm plummeted and she plaintively wailed, "But who will walk me home at night?")

Predictably, it is a fact of life that a high proportion of divorced young women seek a career that maximizes their opportunities for meeting eligible men. Their intuition about the availability of policemen for marriage is confirmed by the 93 percent rate of marriage among policemen, almost 17 percent higher than the national figures for all adult males (see table 7-1). However, policewomen show a 49 percent rate of marriage, 20 percent lower than that of the national adult female population (table 7-1). Is this discrepancy a reflection of the policewoman's reluctance to marry or of her difficulties because of the repugnance of men toward the idea of marrying a policewoman? An even more self-serving reason that lures women to the occupation is job security, though in our present economy, this is a spurious expectation.

Activated by the possibility that policewomen might account for a much higher percentage of divorce than the national average for women and still uncertain of the data we had unearthed on the male officers, we planned to secure further information on police divorce. We decided to send questionnaires to a national sample of police departments and to update Whitehouse's study of police divorce, which was based on the 1960 census data. Unfortunately, in response to our letters of inquiry, the Bureau of the Census and the Division of Vital Statistics of the Department of Health, Education and Welfare informed us that they had not compiled statistics relating marriage and divorce rates to type of occupation. Of necessity, we had to limit our research to questionnaires requesting divorce figures from the police departments in the 150 largest cities, as well as from the major state and county forces.

To be candid, we did not expect many replies. As liberated as the United States of America has become, divorce still projects a pejorative image. Moreover, police administrators are notoriously closemouthed and wary about volunteering any information about departmental personnel. But to our surprise, 30 departments mailed us the figures we had requested, supplying returns with specific information in all the categories, and another 10 contributed a partial breakdown. The spirit of cooperation manifested by the respondents—who ranged from civilian aides and administrative assistants up to captains, inspectors, and chiefs—did not preclude inaccuracies of underreporting and imprecise definitions of terms. The innate distaste of the subject of inquiry undeniably generated a degree of reticence, which, consciously or unconsciously, may have motivated the representatives of the various departments to lower the number of those divorced. And it would be expected that many agencies with high divorce rates would be reluctant to send us the report.

Moreover, when a person has been divorced and later remarries, the record of his or her present marital status may only indicate "married." That specific divorce never appears on the personnel card. Others who have been divorced several times may merely check the box indicating "divorced." That entry is counted as a single instance of divorce, instead of two or three.

Table 7-3 reports the marriage and divorce statistics of the 30 departments who provided us with the information we had requested. An additional 10 agencies complied partially, but they did not send the complete breakdown. They tended to stop at "number married" and "number single," or they estimated the "number divorced" as a percentage of the force. We decided not to use these estimates or to compute the omitted numbers, restricting ourselves to returns that gave us firm numbers in all the categories. Even then it is obvious that the total number on the force sometimes does not exactly equal the "number married, single, and divorced." We believe that this discrepancy exists because the department may have had other categories in addition to those we listed (such as, widowed or separated). Not only did we eliminate returns that submitted estimates, but we also excluded two sets of figures from police departments that did not report any divorce.

Acting as an anchor to hold down the divorce rates, which were higher among the small departments, the three largest police forces on the list—New York City, Washington, D.C., and New York State—noticeably dominated. Nevertheless, the complete listing represents numerically nearly 50,000 police officers, a 10 percent sample of the total sworn police complement in the United States. According to our calculations, the average divorce rate for the departments represented in the table is 2.5 percent, a figure well below the national divorce rate of 3.7 percent for males eighteen and above in 1975. And in the tabulations for rates of marriage, these same departments score 83 percent, which is substantially higher than the national average of 72.8 percent for all men in the same year.[24]

Perhaps a more balanced view of the table would note that 17 police forces were higher than the national average for divorce, and only 13 were lower. But even if we disregard the skewing effect of the New York City Police Department statistics because their numbers outweigh all the other departments added together, the divorce rate for the remaining 29 departments is slightly below an average of 4.5 percent, which may be somewhat high, but nowhere as elevated as those who cry havoc would lead us to believe. And some of the police were divorced before they entered the law enforcement occupation.

We have adopted a well-established figure for divorce: the percentage of

[24] *Statistical Abstract of the United States: 1976,* p. 68.

Table 7-3
Police Marriage and Divorce, 1975

Police Department	Total Number of Personnel	Number Married	Number Single	Number Divorced
Canton, Ohio	211	188	11	12
Charlotte, N.C.	540	463	32	45
Cincinnati, Ohio	1,148	928	77	38
Dearborn Heights, Mich.	101	79	13	9
Duluth, Minn.	130	118	9	3
Elizabeth, N.J.	337	212	98	26
Flint, Mich.	478	325	93	60
Fremont, Calif.	185	159	22	4
Grand Rapids, Mich.	304	264	8	32
Hammond, Ind.	216	191	14	11
Hampton, Va.	194	143	10	11
Hollywood, Fla.	225	176	20	28
Knoxville, Tenn.	320	285	15	20
Lincoln, Neb.	300	247	45	8
Newark, N.J.	1,551	1,323	161	56
New Haven, Conn.	420	375	25	20
New York, N.Y.	31,196	26,233	4,040	480
New York State Police	3,234	2,970	157	107
Parma, Ohio	94	84	1	9
Portsmouth, Va.	210	196	10	4
Riverside, Calif.	275	241	24	10
Savannah, Ga.	227	205	11	11
Scranton, Pa.	171	131	20	20
South Bend, Ind.	264	241	18	5
Stamford, Conn.	268	244	10	12
Topeka, Kans.	217	176	21	20
Torrance, Calif.	204	159	27	18
Trenton, N.J.	392	255	133	4
Washington, D.C.	4,583	3,222	1,039	111
Yonkers, N.Y.	491	390	73	11
Total	48,486	40,223	6,237	1,205
Average rate		83%	13%	2.5%
National average for adult males[a]		72.8%	23.5%	3.7%

Note: Most of the reports were received at the end of 1974, but some came in during 1975 and a few as late as 1977. We chose 1975 as the median year for the rates.

[a]*Statistical Abstract of the United States: 1976*, p. 68.

168

males eighteen and over who are divorced. This measure seems particularly applicable here since police officers are predominantly male and eighteen or over. But the Bureau of the Census commonly employs another statistic of divorce: the rate of divorced males per 1000 married. For the United States in 1975, that rate was 54 for males.[25] In our sample of some 50,000 police officers, the rate per 1000 married was just under 30, a very low divorce figure.

Our hopes of learning more about divorce among policewomen were smashed when in 1975 austerity hit the large cities, and the policewomen who had been hired in substantial numbers under affirmative action programs were laid off. Their story deserves a book of its own.

Considering that a conservative estimate for the number of separate police agencies in the United States is slightly under 20,000, presumably there must be hundreds of police forces with high rates of divorce. And certainly, these departments will reflect the rates of the regions and cities in which their personnel live and work: Pacific and Mountain states are high in divorce rates, whereas Northeast and Middle Atlantic states are generally lower.

No one would dispute that the same forces that are inflating divorce rates all over America are affecting police marriages as well. Since police marriages are afflicted with a range of peculiar problems endemic to the occupation, one might predict that police families would have even higher divorce rates. But that was not what we found.

Our problem was to corroborate our data covering 50,000 police officers that pointed to an average, or possibly lower-than-average, divorce rate. The only support for our position that we could find came in an evaluation of the police family by Monsignor Joseph A. Dunne, the Catholic chaplain of the New York City Police Department for more than 20 years. During the past decade he has been director of the department's alcoholic rehabilitation program. This unit has been ghoulishly dubbed "The Body Snatcher Squad" because it is responsible for transporting alcoholic members of the force to the rehabilitation center. Monsignor Dunne states authoritatively:

The question as to why police officers leave their wives and seek divorce and remarriage might also be asked in regard to other areas of human ills, e.g., why so many alcoholics, mentally ill, heart victims, etc.? Obviously, the answer is because police are people and have their share of personality problems. No one can say with certainty whether police have a higher incidence of marriage problems, without proper investigation and evaluation.

I would venture to say that there is nothing in police-work which of necessity contributes to the destruction of marriage. We have thousands of happily married officers who will validate this.[26]

However, at one of the sessions of the conference of the National Association of Police Chaplains, some of the police chaplain discussants

[25] Ibid.

[26] Joseph A. Dunne, "Marriage and the Police Officer," *Spring 3100* (July 1976):10.

indirectly disputed Monsignor Dunne's hypothesis.[27] Pooling their experience, they disclosed divorce rates in their respective police departments, ranging from a low of 30 percent to a peak of 75 percent. We realized that they too had done some soul-searching about police marital stability when we analyzed their responses to a questionnaire they had so graciously consented to answer for us. (See table 5-8.)

Tabulating their replies, we noticed that the opinions of the 33 chaplains maintain an almost perfect equilibrium, for their views balance at opposite sides of the scale. For example, 16 rated police marriage as stable as other marriages; 17 neutralized this position by asserting that police marriages were less stable; 16 felt that police wives were about as content as other wives, and the same number thought that police wives were less content than other wives. It is an interesting sidelight that the chaplains' list of serious problems that undermine police marriages coincided precisely with the chart of reasons submitted by couples outside of law enforcement who were already divorced.[28]

A police psychiatrist cautioned us that our questionnaire sample of police officers and wives of police officers did not take into account troubled marriages. He reminded us that in his practice he treated many police couples with pathologically disturbed marriages. In his opinion, these couples were at the brink of emotional divorce, if not yet ready to take the final legal step.

We do not discount his observations or those of the chaplains. But couples who go to a psychiatrist or chaplain for help are already in an agitated condition and not at all typical of the great majority of police marriages. Thus these counselors are presented with one dimension of a multifaceted structure.

In defense of our sampling procedure, we must point out that our only criteria were that the respondent be either married and a member of a police force, and/or married to a police officer. Therefore, all police marriages, whether happy or unhappy, had an equal probability of inclusion. And while it is true that distressed couples with serious marital difficulties would hardly be in the mood to answer our rather detailed questionnaire, this did not negate the possibility that they might decide to ventilate their feelings by answering our questionnaire. Most significantly of all, the statistics from which we have derived our conclusions on police marriage and divorce were based on the official records of many police departments whose members constitute a 10 percent sample of the total police complement in the United States.

Viewing the panorama of police divorce through an objective lens, we gain a sharper image of the critical elements. The experts are divided; the data are not conclusive; the issue is fogged in a cloud of propaganda. At the same time, the

[27] "Controlling Stress: The Role of the Chaplain," Conference and workshop sponsored by the John Jay College of Criminal Justice, Law Enforcement News, and the National Association of Police Chaplains, New York City, May 4-5, 1977.

[28] William J. Goode, "Family Disorganization," in Robert K. Merton and Robert Nisbet, eds., *Contemporary Social Problems*, 3d ed. (New York: Harcourt, Brace, Jovanovich, 1971), pp. 504-505.

prevailing pessimistic attitude based on reports of numerous divorces in many medium-sized and small departments has been congealed by repetition rather than validated by research. Grafted onto law enforcement ideology as a defense mechanism to explain the charges of an extraordinarily high divorce rate, this widely held opinion popularizes the hypothesis that police work with its corroding stress is ultimately destructive to the marital relation.

But our analysis, based on a review of the available research on police divorce and the results of our own survey of police departments representing 50,000 law enforcement personnel, contravenes the prevalent assumption that divorce is an occupational hazard of police work. Weighing the evidence, we conclude that the rate of divorce for the police occupation as a whole rises no higher than the average level of divorce in the United States. And in the face of an ever surging national incidence of divorce flooding past one million, police marriages have managed to maintain a fair degree of stability. Divorce, police style, may well be lower than divorce, American style.

Appendixes

Appendix A
The Survey

The Survey

From our own personal experience, supplemented by informal conversations, preliminary interviews, and rap sessions with police officers and their wives, we could trace a definite pattern of issues, interests, and problems relevant to police family life. Combining this with our research into the literature on families and occupations, we prepared a questionnaire embodying the salient points. Assisted by several college students in Arthur's seminar, we interviewed about forty police couples using this experimental form as a guide. After this pilot study, we eliminated questions that aroused resistance (for example, we encountered resentment of items that probed sexual behavior), and we added other areas of interest that flowed from the interviews. Eventually, we arrived at a basic form of 78 items, which we modified slightly to use with our four categories of respondents: policemen, wives of policemen, policewomen, and husbands of policewomen. Later in our research, we prepared a questionnaire for children of police officers. And fortuitously, a representative group of police chaplains agreed to answer a brief list of questions concerning their views of the police family.

Graduate students, police friends in the United States, Great Britain and Australia, and professors of police science and criminal justice all generously assisted us in the distribution of our questionnaires. But disappointingly, a hoped-for distribution among Israeli police officers failed to materialize because of insurmountable difficulties in translation. Table A-1 charts the distribution of the questionnaires.

To determine the class affiliation of the sample, we focused on the type of work performed by the individual officers before they joined the force. In most cases, they were too young at the age of entrance to have obtained occupational stability, so we turned to the occupations of their fathers for a clue to their class membership.

Using this criterion, about two-thirds of the American contingent could be classified as of working-class origin when they became police officers. In 13 instances, their fathers had been policemen themselves, and the sons stepped into their shoes. For 88 other patrolmen, some other member of the family had been on the force. Only 29 individuals in the sample fit into middle-class occupations before having become police officers, and 37 fathers could also be placed in this category, with some overlap of fathers and sons. For this purpose we used a most liberal interpretation of the designation *middle-class occupation,* stretching it to include such positions as salesmen, printers, draftsmen, and store managers.

174

Table A-1
Distribution of Questionnaires

Type of Questionnaire	Number Distributed	Number Returned	Percent Returned
Male police officers	400	211	53
Wives of police officers	400	213	53
Policewomen	100	27	27
Husbands of policewomen	100	21	21
Children of police officers	100	62	62
Police chaplains	50	33	66

Class position of our respondents had definitely improved at the time the questionnaire was administered. There were 35 college graduates, and a resounding majority of 126 were striving for middle-class status by working toward baccalaureate or graduate degrees, with 107 still in college and the remaining group of 19, all superior officers, in graduate schools.

Sample

Our final sample consisted of 211 male police officers, 213 wives of police officers, 27 policewomen, 21 husbands of policewomen, 62 children of police officers, and 33 police chaplains. About half the sample was concentrated in the New York City metropolitan region, although six other states, as well as England and Australia, were represented. Because of this overrepresentation in New York City, we decided not to perform any statistical tests of significance. In Appendix C, the demographic characteristics of the sample are presented in detail.

We were eager to obtain a large sample of policewomen, but economic crises in many municipalities dictated austerity in hiring, or layoffs of recently appointed policewomen. At most, there are no more than 3 percent of policewomen in law enforcement today. Our low rate of return for policewomen's questionnaires reflects this recession.

We did not merge the responses of policemen, policewomen, wives of policemen, and husbands of policewomen because the factor of gender is too important a variable to ignore. But wherever pertinent within the text, we commented on and compared the views of the various groups. Consequently, since almost 90 percent of our police sample was male, we decided to use the conventional term *police officer* and the pronouns *he* and *his* even when we stated generalizations that applied to officers of both sexes. We avoided the use of the unisex designation *policeperson* because it sounded awkward to our ears.

Appendix B
The Questionnaires

The Questionnaire for Policemen[1]

To the Person Filling Out This Questionnaire

This questionnaire is part of a study of the police family being conducted by a retired police officer and his wife. We believe that this project will help police families across the country. Undoubtedly, you are the real experts on this subject, and we request your cooperation in sharing your insights and knowledge with us.

Most of the items in this questionnaire can be completed by the addition of one word or number, or by placing a check or a circle in the appropriate place. All questionnaires and responses will be strictly anonymous. No names or other identification are required.

When you have completed the questionnaire, please return it to the person who gave it to you. Or if you prefer, mail it directly to:

Professor Arthur Niederhoffer
Department of Sociology
John Jay College of Criminal Justice
445 West 59th Street
New York City, New York 10019

We thank you for your assistance.

Arthur Niederhoffer
Elaine Niederhoffer

Part 1

Instructions: Please write in your answers to each of the questions in Part 1.

1. Name of your police agency _____

2. State in which it is located _____

3. Approximate number of police officers in the agency _____

---

[1] A modified form of this questionnaire was used for wives of policemen.

4. How many years have you been a police officer? _____

5. What is your present rank? _____

6. To what type of police duty are you assigned? _____

7. Do you work around the clock? _____ Or work a steady shift? _____

8. Which tour of duty do you like most? _____
   Which do you like least? _____

9. Which of your tours of duty does your wife like most? _____
   And which does she like least? _____

10. Are you studying for a promotion? _____ How many hours a week? _____

11. Are you moonlighting (working part-time at another job)? _____
    If yes, what type of work? _____

12. Is your wife employed? _____ If yes, what type of work? _____
    _____

13. What was your occupation before you became a policeman? _____
    _____

14. What was your father's major occupation? _____

15. Have any members of your family or your wife's family ever been police officers? _____ If yes, which ones? _____

16. Your age _____ Your wife's age _____

17. Your ethnic background _____
    Your religion _____

18. Are you a high school graduate? _____

19. How many years of college have you completed? _____ Did you graduate? _____
    If yes, type of degree _____ Major _____

20. How many years of graduate work have you completed? _____
    Advanced degree _____ Major field _____

21. Is your wife a high school graduate? _____

22. How many years of college has she completed? _____
Did she graduate? _____ If yes, type of degree _____
Major _____

23. How many years of graduate work has she completed? _____
Advanced degree _____ Major field _____

24. Are you now going to school?_____ If yes, at what level?_____
_____

25. Is your wife now going to school? _____ If yes, at what level? _____
_____

26. Do you live in the city?_____ the suburbs? _____ or a rural area? _____

27. Do you live in a private house? _____ or an apartment house?_____

28. Do you own your home? _____ or rent your home or apartment? _____

29. How many years have you been married? _____

30. How many children do you have?_____ Their ages_____

31. How did you meet your wife? _____
_____
_____

Part 2

Instructions: Please place a check next to the choice that best expresses your answer to each of the questions in Part 2.

1. When you are at work, does your wife worry about your safety?
   a. A lot
   b. A little
   c. Not at all

2. How much do you tell your wife about the police job?
  a. Everything
  b. A lot
  c. A little
  d. Nothing

3. How often has your wife observed you while you were on duty?
  a. Frequently
  b. Sometimes
  c. Never

4. What do you consider the most important part of your police duty?
  a. Maintenance of order
  b. Prevention of crime
  c. Enforcement of law
  d. Service to the people in the community

5. Which of the following assignments would you prefer, if you had your choice?
  a. Foot patrol
  b. Radio car patrol
  c. Detective
  d. Plainclothes
  e. Clerical work
  f. Youth work
  g. Community relations

6. Which of the assignments listed in item 5 do you think your wife would prefer you to have? _____

7. What would your reaction be if you were assigned to radio car patrol with a policewoman as your steady partner?
  a. In favor of the assignment
  b. Neutral about the assignment
  c. Opposed to the assignment

8. Briefly state the reason or reasons for your answer to item 7 above.
  _____
  _____
  _____

9. How would you classify the action of a police officer who accepts a free meal or a Christmas present from a businessman on his post?

      a.   A serious violation of law

      b.   A minor violation of police regulations

      c.   No violation at all

10. How does your wife react to the fact that your police duty often brings you into close contact with women?

      a.   She is deeply concerned about it

      b.   She is somewhat concerned about it

      c.   She is not concerned at all about it

11. How would you classify the promotion system in your police agency?

      a.   Fair

      b.   Unfair

12. How would you classify the disciplinary system in your police agency?

      a.   Fair

      b.   Unfair

13. How would you classify the system of selecting and appointing new police officers in your police agency?

      a.   Fair

      b.   Unfair

14. How would you classify the salary scale in your police agency?

      a.   High

      b.   Adequate

      c.   Low

15. In your opinion how does the *general public* rate the police occupation in prestige?

      a.   High

      b.   Average

      c.   Low

16. How do *you personally* rate the police occupation in prestige?

      a.   High

      b.   Average

      c.   Low

17. In your opinion how does *your wife* rate the police occupation in prestige?

      a.   High

      b.   Average

      c.   Low

18. How do you feel about being a police officer?
    a. Happy
    b. Resigned to it
    c. Unhappy

19. In comparison with the average family, do you believe that a police family is forced to cope with
    a. More problems
    b. The same problems
    c. Fewer problems

20. Because you are a police officer, does your family behave
    a. More carefully than other types of families
    b. About the same as other types of families
    c. Less carefully than other types of families

21. If a police officer stopped your wife for a traffic violation while she was driving, would you expect him to
    a. Treat her like any other driver and give her a summons
    b. Extend professional courtesy and let her go with a warning after she identifies herself as the wife of a police officer

22. How do members of your community react when they become aware that you are a police officer?
    a. In a friendly fashion
    b. In a normal fashion
    c. In a hostile fashion

23. Do you and your wife socialize with other police couples?
    a. Frequently
    b. Seldom
    c. Never

24. At social gatherings do you identify yourself as a police officer?
    a. Always
    b. Frequently
    c. Seldom
    d. Never

25. What do you usually do when you and your wife go out for an evening?
    a. Go to a movie
    b. Go to a play
    c. Go to a concert

    d.   Go to visit friends
    e.   Go dancing
    f.   Watch a sports event
    g.   Go bowling, skating, etc.

26. When you become eligible for retirement, do you plan to
    a.   Remain in the police department
    b.   Retire completely and not work at all
    c.   Retire from the department and start work in a second career

27. Who makes most of the important decisions in your family?
    a.   You
    b.   Your wife
    c.   You and your wife jointly
    d.   Your children

28. How do you feel about the women's liberation movement?
    a.   Very much in favor of it
    b.   Somewhat in favor of it
    c.   Indifferent to it
    d.   Somewhat opposed to it
    e.   Very opposed to it

29. How do you think your wife feels about your being a police officer?
    a.   Happy
    b.   Resigned to it
    c.   Unhappy

30. How does your police work schedule affect your family life?
    a.   It strengthens it
    b.   It does not affect it much
    c.   It weakens it

31. How serious a problem is the necessity of safeguarding the police revolver at home?
    a.   It is a serious problem
    b.   It is a minor problem
    c.   It is no problem at all

182

Part 3

Instructions: Please indicate your answer by placing a check in the appropriate column to the right of each item listed in Part 3.

1. In your family who takes primary responsibility for each of the following tasks?

	Wife	Husband	Husband and Wife Jointly
a. Disciplining the children	_____	_____	_____
b. Important financial decisions	_____	_____	_____
c. Household chores	_____	_____	_____
d. Social life	_____	_____	_____
e. Marketing	_____	_____	_____
f. Gardening	_____	_____	_____
g. Chauffeuring	_____	_____	_____
h. Child care	_____	_____	_____
i. Preparation of meals	_____	_____	_____

2. In your home how often do these common family problems arise?

	Frequently	Sometimes	Never
a. Lack of communication between parents and children	_____	_____	_____
b. Lack of communication between husband and wife	_____	_____	_____
c. Financial difficulties	_____	_____	_____
d. Children's misbehavior	_____	_____	_____
e. Husband's school or promotion study takes too much time	_____	_____	_____
f. Police job interferes with family life	_____	_____	_____
g. Police schedule causes difficulties	_____	_____	_____
h. Wife feels frustrated, tied down	_____	_____	_____
i. Husband is unhappy with job	_____	_____	_____
j. Sexual incompatibility	_____	_____	_____

3. When you are off duty how do you cope with a bad day?

		Frequently	Sometimes	Never
a.	Do household chores	_____	_____	_____
b.	Watch TV	_____	_____	_____
c.	Read a book	_____	_____	_____
d.	Go shopping	_____	_____	_____
e.	Eat	_____	_____	_____
f.	Drink	_____	_____	_____
g.	Go to bed	_____	_____	_____
h.	Religious observance	_____	_____	_____
i.	See the doctor	_____	_____	_____
j.	Telephone friends	_____	_____	_____
k.	Visit friends	_____	_____	_____
l.	Take a pill	_____	_____	_____
m.	See a movie	_____	_____	_____
n.	Athletic activities	_____	_____	_____

4. How would you rate the mass media's portrayal of the police and police work?

		Favorable to Police	Objective about Police	Unfavorable to Police
a.	Television programs	_____	_____	_____
b.	Newspapers	_____	_____	_____
c.	Books	_____	_____	_____
d.	Movies	_____	_____	_____
e.	Magazines	_____	_____	_____
f.	Radio	_____	_____	_____

5. How important to you would it be for your children to possess the following qualities?

		Very Important	Moderately Important	Not Important
a.	Obedience to parents	_____	_____	_____
b.	Dependability	_____	_____	_____
c.	High achievement in school	_____	_____	_____
d.	Popularity	_____	_____	_____
e.	Perseverance	_____	_____	_____
f.	Independence	_____	_____	_____
g.	Respect for authority	_____	_____	_____
h.	Thrift	_____	_____	_____
i.	Honesty	_____	_____	_____

6. How often do your children participate in the following after-school activities?

		Regularly	Sometimes	Never
a.	Religious studies	_____	_____	_____
b.	Music lessons	_____	_____	_____
c.	Art lessons	_____	_____	_____
d.	Dancing lessons	_____	_____	_____
e.	Dramatics	_____	_____	_____
f.	Team sports	_____	_____	_____
g.	Skating, swimming, tennis lessons	_____	_____	_____

Part 4

Instructions: Please write in your answers to each of the questions in Part 4.

1. How would you classify your method of raising your children: Strict, flexible, or permissive?

   _____

2. What would your reaction be if your grown son wanted to become a police officer?

   _____
   _____
   _____
   _____

3. What career would you prefer for your son?

   _____

4. What would your reaction be if your grown daughter wanted to become a police officer? _____

   _____
   _____
   _____

5. What career would you prefer for your daughter?

   _____

6. Which TV program about the police is your favorite?

   _____

7. Does the police department provide any orientation, counseling, or other type of service for families of police officers?

8. If your answer to question 7 was "yes," briefly describe the type of service offered: _____

9. What type of services do you think the police department should provide for families of police officers?

10. Do you have any advice that might be of help to other police families?

We thank you for your assistance.

The Questionnaire for Police Officers' Children

Male _____ Female _____ Age _____ Grade _____ Religion _____

1. What would you like to be when you grow up?

2. Have you seen your father at work? Often _____ Sometimes _____ Never _____

3. Does your father talk to you about his work? A lot _____ A little _____ Not at all _____

4. Have you seen your father in uniform? Often _____ Sometimes _____ Never _____

5. Would you like to be a police officer when you grow up? Yes _____ No _____ Why? _____

6. What do you think is the most important thing policemen do? _____

7. What do you like to do most when you and your father are together?

   _____

8. Do you tell your friends that your father is a policeman? Yes _____ No

   _____

9. How do your friends react when they learn that your father is a police officer? _____

10. If you had your choice, what kind of work would you want your father to do? _____

11. Would you like your mother to be a policewoman? Yes _____ No

    _____

12. What do you think is the most important thing policewomen do? _____

13. Does your father have to work on holidays or your birthdays? Often _____ Sometimes _____ Never _____
    How do you feel when this happens? _____

14. Has the fact that your father is a policeman ever helped you? Yes _____ No _____
    How? _____

15. Has the fact that your father is a policeman ever hurt you? Yes _____ No

    _____
    How? _____

16. Would you say that your father is strict or easygoing with you? _____

17. What is your favorite TV program about policemen? _____

18. Because your father is a police officer, do you behave more carefully _____ less carefully _____ or the same as _____ other children?

19. Do you worry about your father's safety when he is at work? A lot _____
A little _____ Not at all _____

20. Can you tell something funny, sad, or interesting that happened to you because your father is a police officer? _____

The Questionnaire for Police Chaplains

Dear Chaplain:

I am a professor of sociology at John Jay College and a former police officer retired from the New York City Police Department. I have written several books on the police. Now my wife and I are writing a book about police families in which we hope to dispel some of the misapprehensions and instead, provide a realistic portrait of the police family. The one ingredient that would be most helpful would be the ideas of the chaplains who have had such a unique and vast experience counseling police families.

We would appreciate it greatly if you would take five minutes to respond to the questions below. No names are requested and all information will be treated as confidential. Thank you.

Your religion _____ Number of years as a police chaplain _____

1. In comparison to other families you have known, would you rate the average police family as

    A. Happier   B. About as happy   C. Less happy

2. In comparison to other marriages you have known, would you rate the average police marriage as

    A. More stable   B. About as stable   C. Less stable

3. In comparison with other children you have known, would you rate the average child of a police officer as

    A. Better adjusted   B. About the same as other children in adjustment   C. Less well adjusted

4. In comparison with other wives you have known, would you rate the average wife of a police officer as

    A. More content   B. About as content   C. Less content

5. In your experience what are the three problems that police families encounter most frequently?

    1. _____ 2. _____ 3. _____

6. In your experience what are the three most serious problems occurring in police marriages?

    1. _____ 2. _____ 3. _____

Appendix C
The Responses

Responses of Policemen: Part 1

Description of the Sample of American Police Officers
(N = 182)

Characteristic	Patrolmen and Detectives (N = 120)	Superior Officers (N = 62)	Total (N = 182)
Average age	32	41	35
Years married	8	16	11
Number of children	1.5	3	2
Number moonlighting	21	15	36
College graduates	12	23	35
Father a police officer	7	4	11
Time on job	7	17	10
Residence			
Own home	86	56	142
Suburbs	64	37	101
City	41	20	61
Rural	16	5	21
Religion			
Catholic	90	46	136
Protestant	13	8	21
Jewish	7	5	12
Ethnic background			
Irish	34	21	55
Italian	27	9	36
German	15	5	20
Black	5	1	6

Responses of Policemen: Part 2

	Patrolmen and Detectives (N = 120)	Superior Officers (N = 62)	English and Australian Policemen (N = 29)	Total (N = 211)
1. When you are at work, does your wife worry about your safety?				
a. A lot	39	13	4	56
b. A little	66	36	18	120
c. Not at all	13	12	6	31
2. How much do you tell your wife about the police job?				
a. Everything	7	1	0	8
b. A lot	28	14	5	47
c. A little	74	41	22	137
d. Nothing	11	7	2	20
3. How often has your wife observed you while you were on duty?				
a. Frequently	6	2	5	13
b. Sometimes	42	21	16	79
c. Never	72	39	8	119
4. What do you consider the most important part of your police duty?				
a. Maintenance of order	9	7	7	23
b. Prevention of crime	33	9	4	46
c. Enforcement of law	28	5	4	37
d. Service to the people in the community	57	41	15	113
5. Which of the following assignments would you prefer, if you had a choice?				
a. Foot patrol	2	6	6	14
b. Radio car patrol	23	11	6	40
c. Detective	62	26	10	98
d. Plainclothes	26	4	5	35
e. Clerical work	5	2	4	11
f. Youth work	9	0	1	10
g. Community relations	10	11	2	23
6. Which of the assignments listed in item 5 do you think your wife would prefer you to have?				
a. Foot patrol	3	1	3	7
b. Radio car patrol	15	1	3	19
c. Detective	50	19	6	75
d. Plainclothes	10	2	1	13
e. Clerical work	24	21	10	55
f. Youth work	8	0	2	10
g. Community relations	14	13	3	30

	Patrolmen and Detectives (N = 120)	Superior Officers (N = 62)	English and Australian Policemen (N = 29)	Total (N = 211)
7. What would your reaction be if you were assigned to radio car patrol with a police-woman as your steady partner?				
a. In favor of the assignment	8	2	2	12
b. Neutral about the assignment	35	26	21	82
c. Opposed to the assignment	58	34	5	97
8. Briefly state the reason or reasons for your answer to item 7 above.				
a. Increased danger	49	11	3	63
b. Jealousy of wife or sexual involvement	6	6	0	12
c. Inadequacy of policewomen	15	16	2	33
9. How would you classify the action of a police officer who accepts a free meal or Christmas present from a businessman on his post?				
a. A serious violation of law	8	15	3	26
b. A minor violation of police regulations	78	36	17	131
c. No violation at all	33	12	9	54
10. How does your wife react to the fact that your police duty often brings you into close contact with women?				
a. She is deeply concerned about it	5	3	1	9
b. She is somewhat concerned about it	40	13	4	57
c. She is not concerned about it at all	73	46	24	143
11. How would you classify the promotion system in your police agency?				
a. Fair	72	41	22	135
b. Unfair	48	20	7	75
12. How would you classify the disciplinary system in your police agency?				
a. Fair	34	41	23	98
b. Unfair	85	19	6	110

Responses of Policemen: Part 2 (cont.)

	Patrolmen and Detectives (N = 120)	Superior Officers (N = 62)	English and Australian Policemen (N = 29)	Total (N = 211)
13. How would you classify the system of selecting and appointing new police officers in your police agency?				
a. Fair	69	42	26	137
b. Unfair	49	19	3	71
14. How would you classify the salary scale in your police agency?				
a. High	9	12	1	22
b. Adequate	59	37	15	111
c. Low	51	13	13	77
15. In your opinion how does the general public rate the police occupation in prestige?				
a. High	18	4	11	33
b. Average	43	35	13	91
c. Low	59	23	5	87
16. How do you personally rate the police occupation in prestige?				
a. High	58	32	13	103
b. Average	47	23	13	83
c. Low	13	6	2	21
17. In your opinion how does your wife rate the police occupation in prestige?				
a. High	46	24	12	82
b. Average	60	31	14	105
c. Low	13	5	2	20
18. How do you feel about being a police officer?				
a. Happy	86	46	22	154
b. Resigned to it	29	14	6	49
c. Unhappy	2	2	0	4
19. In comparison with the average family do you believe that a police family is forced to cope with				
a. More problems	82	41	19	142
b. The same problems	35	18	8	61
c. Fewer problems	2	3	1	6
20. Because you are a police officer, does your family behave				
a. More carefully than other types of families	42	25	15	82
b. About the same as other types of families	76	36	13	125

	Patrolmen and Detectives (N = 120)	Superior Officers (N = 62)	English and Australian Policemen (N = 29)	Total (N = 211)
c. Less carefully than other types of families	1	0	0	1
21. If a police officer stopped your wife for a traffic violation while she was driving, would you expect him to				
a. Treat her like any other driver and give her a summons	22	9	19	50
b. Extend professional courtesy and let her go with a warning after she identified herself as the wife of a police officer	96	52	8	156
22. How do members of the community react when they become aware that you are a police officer?				
a. In a friendly fashion	28	19	9	56
b. In a normal fashion	80	43	18	141
c. In a hostile fashion	13	5	1	19
23. Do you and your wife socialize with other police couples?				
a. Frequently	44	15	10	69
b. Seldom	67	41	16	124
c. Never	7	6	2	15
24. At social gatherings do you identify yourself as a police officer?				
a. Always	4	1	1	6
b. Frequently	17	13	4	34
c. Seldom	58	27	15	100
d. Never	42	20	7	69
25. What do you usually do when you and your wife go out for an evening?				
a. Go to a movie	58	28	9	95
b. Go to a play	11	12	2	25
c. Go to a concert	4	7	2	13
d. Go to visit friends	78	40	24	142
e. Go dancing	15	12	4	31
f. Watch a sports event	5	8	2	15
g. Go bowling, skating, etc.	12	2	1	15

Responses of Policemen: Part 2 (cont.)

	Patrolmen and Detectives (N = 120)	Superior Officers (N = 62)	English and Australian Policemen (N = 29)	Total (N = 211)
26. When you become eligible for retirement, do you plan to				
a. Remain in the police department	18	17	1	36
b. Retire completely and not work at all	9	3	11	23
c. Retire from the department and start work in a second career	90	39	15	144
27. Who makes most of the important decisions in your family?				
a. You	23	15	7	45
b. Your wife	2	1	1	4
c. You and your wife jointly	91	47	20	158
d. Your children	0	0	0	0
28. How do you feel about the women's liberation movement?				
a. Very much in favor of it	2	2	1	5
b. Somewhat in favor of it	33	18	5	56
c. Indifferent to it	40	25	15	80
d. Somewhat opposed to it	34	15	5	54
e. Very opposed to it	10	2	2	14
29. How do you think your wife feels about your being a police officer?				
a. Happy	39	25	17	81
b. Resigned to it	74	34	10	118
c. Unhappy	7	4	0	11
30. How does your police work schedule affect your family life?				
a. It strengthens it	10	6	3	19
b. It does not affect it much	58	39	16	113
c. It weakens it	50	16	9	75
31. How serious a problem is the necessity of safeguarding the police revolver at home?				
a. It is a serious problem	28	13	2	43
b. It is a minor problem	40	16	3	59
c. It is no problem at all	52	33	9	94

Responses of Policemen: Part 3

	Patrolmen and Detectives (N=120)			Superior Officers (N=62)			English and Australian Policemen (N=29)			Total (N=211)		
	W	H	W and H	W	H	W and H	W	H	W and H	W	H	W and H
1. In your family who takes primary responsibility for each of the following tasks?												
a. Disciplining the children	9	10	79	3	7	45	3	5	17	15	22	141
b. Important financial decisions	3	27	89	3	16	40	1	11	17	7	54	146
c. Household chores	83	1	35	49	1	10	25	0	4	157	2	49
d. Social life	23	6	88	11	5	47	3	6	20	37	17	155
e. Marketing	84	5	26	46	3	10	21	2	6	151	10	42
f. Gardening	32	39	33	18	20	18	7	11	11	57	70	62
g. Chauffeuring	24	49	45	13	22	23	0	19	9	37	90	77
h. Child care	53	1	45	33	0	22	16	0	9	102	1	76
i. Preparation of meals	97	4	13	54	1	6	28	1	0	179	6	19
	F	S	N	F	S	N	F	S	N	F	S	N
2. In your home how often do these common problems arise?												
a. Lack of communication between parents and children	4	55	42	4	44	7	1	15	9	9	114	58
b. Lack of communication between husband and wife	8	92	19	6	47	7	1	16	12	15	155	38
c. Financial difficulties	18	80	15	6	30	23	1	17	11	25	127	49
d. Children's misbehavior	6	72	16	1	51	4	2	18	5	9	141	25

Note:
W = Wife
H = Husband
W and H = Wife and husband jointly

Responses of Policemen: Part 3 (cont.)

	Patrolmen and Detectives (N = 120)			Superior Officers (N = 62)			English and Australian Policemen (N = 29)			Total (N = 211)		
	F	S	N	F	S	N	F	S	N	F	S	N
e. Husband's school or promotion study takes too much time	15	49	53	10	30	19	2	8	19	27	87	91
f. Police job interferes with family life	28	72	18	8	36	15	10	15	4	46	123	37
g. Police schedule causes difficulties	25	74	18	7	39	14	8	17	4	40	130	46
h. Wife feels frustrated and tied down	19	68	26	7	35	15	1	17	7	27	120	48
i. Husband is unhappy with job	6	52	58	3	32	25	1	15	12	10	99	95
j. Sexual incompatibility	4	41	71	2	22	34	0	11	18	6	74	123

Note:
F = Frequently
S = Sometimes
N = Never

3. How do you cope with a bad day?	F	S	N	F	S	N	F	S	N	F	S	N
a. Do household chores	2	59	54	3	32	33	2	16	10	7	107	97
b. Watch TV	28	82	10	7	43	7	8	17	3	43	142	20
c. Read a book	11	81	23	8	38	6	6	14	5	25	143	34
d. Go shopping	4	47	63	0	32	26	1	8	16	5	87	105
e. Eat	12	77	29	4	33	17	0	19	7	16	129	53
f. Drink	6	64	41	1	30	23	3	12	11	10	106	75
g. Go to bed	6	60	45	0	32	25	1	15	10	7	107	80
h. Religious observance	4	34	76	0	30	29	2	7	18	6	71	123
i. See the doctor	0	21	95	0	5	53	0	3	23	0	29	171
j. Telephone friends	3	53	56	0	21	38	0	10	17	3	84	111
k. Visit friends	5	69	37	2	35	21	1	13	12	8	117	70

	F	S	N	F	S	N	F	S	N	F	S	N
l. Take a pill	0	7	104	0	5	52	0	3	21	0	15	177
m. See a movie	3	71	36	1	32	17	0	8	19	4	111	72
n. Athletic activities	17	64	29	2	42	13	5	14	7	24	120	49

Note:
F = Frequently
S = Sometimes
N = Never

4. How would you rate the mass media's portrayal of the police and police work?

	F	O	U	F	O	U	F	O	U	F	O	U
a. Television programs	45	39	35	20	13	23	6	13	6	71	65	64
b. Newspapers	6	31	81	1	20	38	3	11	11	10	62	130
c. Books	27	62	26	17	20	22	7	11	4	51	93	52
d. Movies	34	41	43	19	15	23	7	7	11	60	63	77
e. Magazines	14	63	43	8	27	23	4	10	8	26	100	74
f. Radio	11	57	50	5	30	20	11	13	2	27	100	72

Note:
F = Favorable to police
O = Objective about police
U = Unfavorable to police

5. How important to you would it be for your children to possess the following qualities?

	VI	MI	NI	VI	MI	NI	VI	MI	NI	VI	MI	NI
a. Obedience to parents	92	20	0	41	17	0	21	8	0	154	45	0
b. Dependability	88	27	1	38	18	2	28	1	0	154	46	3
c. High achievement in school	37	83	1	20	36	3	12	17	0	69	136	4
d. Popularity	15	85	13	6	44	8	4	19	6	25	148	27
e. Perseverance	69	47	1	39	18	1	20	8	0	128	73	2
f. Independence	66	50	1	34	23	0	17	12	0	117	85	1
g. Respect for authority	99	16	2	36	22	0	21	6	0	156	44	2

Responses of Policemen: Part 3 (cont.)

	Patrolmen and Detectives (N = 120)			Superior Officers (N = 62)			English and Australian Policemen (N = 29)			Total (N = 211)		
	R	S	N	R	S	N	R	S	N	R	S	N
h. Thrift	36	75	6	14	41	4	11	17	0	61	133	10
i. Honesty	110	7	0	52	4	0	27	2	0	189	13	0

Note:
VI = Very important
MI = Moderately important
NI = Not important

6. How often do your children participate in the following after-school activities?

	R	S	N	R	S	N	R	S	N	R	S	N
a. Religious studies	25	16	21	20	20	8	6	7	6	51	43	35
b. Music lessons	7	11	43	9	12	26	5	4	11	21	27	80
c. Art lessons	2	12	49	1	11	33	1	6	11	4	29	93
d. Dancing lessons	10	4	48	2	7	37	2	4	13	14	15	98
e. Dramatics	2	5	59	1	6	39	0	6	11	3	17	109
f. Team sports	23	15	24	17	18	11	8	7	3	48	40	38
g. Skating, swimming, tennis lessons	17	20	23	13	20	12	9	10	1	39	50	36

Note:
R = Regularly
S = Sometimes
N = Never

Responses of Policemen: Part 4

	Patrolmen and Detectives (N = 120)	Superior Officers (N = 62)	English and Australian Policemen (N = 29)	Total (N = 211)
1. How would you classify your method of raising your children?				
a. Strict	19	14	11	44
b. Flexible	84	40	15	139
c. Permissive	2	3	0	5
2. What would your reaction be if your son wanted to become a police officer?				
a. Positive	39	29	15	83
b. Uncertain or no answer	51	22	8	81
c. Negative	33	11	6	50
3. What career would you prefer for your son?				
a. Lawyer	36	7	8	51
b. Doctor	19	13	5	37
c. Whatever he desired	20	18	6	44
d. A profession	17	2	0	19
e. Law enforcement	3	4	2	9
f. Business	5	5	3	13
4. What would your reaction be if your daughter wanted to become a police officer?				
a. Positive	29	12	10	51
b. Uncertain or no answer	34	18	6	58
c. Negative	57	32	13	102
5. What career would you prefer for your daughter?				
a. Lawyer	9	5	1	15
b. Doctor	6	4	3	13
c. Whatever she desired	17	10	4	31
d. A profession	2	1	1	4
e. Office work	7	3	4	14
f. Nurse	19	7	5	31
g. Housewife	17	6	3	26
h. Teacher	17	17	4	38
6. Which TV program about the police is your favorite?				
a. Police Story	51	22	0	73
b. Kojak	36	17	0	53
c. Adam 12	17	3	0	20
d. Streets of San Francisco	3	1	0	4
e. Columbo	5	4	0	9
7. Does the police department provide any orientation, counseling, or other type of service for families of police officers?				
a. Yes	32	22	10	64
b. Don't know	10	5	0	15
c. No	72	30	19	121

200

Responses of the Wives: Part 1

Description of the Sample of Wives of American Police Officers (N = 184)

Characteristic	Wives of Patrolmen and Detectives (N = 127)	Wives of Superior Officers (N = 57)	Total (N = 184)
Average age	30	36	32
Years married	9	13	10
Number of children	2	3	2.3
Number working	42	23	65
College graduates	13	10	23
Father a police officer	8	5	13
Residence			
Own home	93	51	144
Suburbs	68	40	108
City	40	14	54
Rural	17	2	19
Religion			
Catholic	92	21	113
Protestant	15	8	23
Jewish	10	3	13
Ethnic background			
Irish	37	24	61
Italian	22	14	36
German	12	4	16
Black	3	1	4

Responses of the Wives: Part 2

	Wives of Patrolmen and Detectives (N = 127)	Wives of Superior Officers (N = 57)	Wives of English and Australian Policemen (N = 29)	Total (N = 213)
1. When your husband is at work, do you worry about his safety?				
a. A lot	43	15	5	63
b. A little	70	29	17	116
c. Not at all	12	12	7	31
2. How much does your husband tell you about the police job?				
a. Everything	11	0	0	11
b. A lot	43	15	9	67
c. A little	63	36	15	114
d. Nothing	9	5	4	18
3. How often have you observed your husband while he was on duty?				
a. Frequently	3	2	3	8
b. Sometimes	50	26	17	93
c. Never	73	29	9	111
4. What do you consider the most important part of your husband's job?				
a. Maintenance of order	9	7	3	19
b. Prevention of crime	29	14	6	49
c. Enforcement of law	44	15	6	65
d. Service to the people of the community	41	25	15	81
5. Which of the following assignments do you think your husband would prefer?				
a. Foot patrol	6	1	3	10
b. Radio car patrol	30	14	6	50
c. Detective	58	19	11	88
d. Plainclothes	19	4	1	24
e. Clerical work	2	9	5	16
f. Youth work	6	4	0	10
g. Community relations	8	14	3	25
6. Which of these assignments would you prefer for your husband?				
a. Foot patrol	3	0	2	5
b. Radio car patrol	20	7	5	32
c. Detective	36	12	8	56
d. Plainclothes	13	4	1	18
e. Clerical work	32	9	7	48
f. Youth work	8	6	1	15
g. Community relations	15	15	7	37
7. What would your reaction be if your husband were assigned to radio car patrol with a policewoman as his steady partner?				
a. In favor of the assignment	3	1	0	4

Responses of the Wives: Part 2 (cont.)

	Wives of Patrolmen and Detectives (N = 127)	Wives of Superior Officers (N = 57)	Wives of English and Australian Policemen (N = 29)	Total (N = 213)
b. Neutral about the assignment	33	25	23	81
c. Opposed to the assignment	90	29	3	122
8. Briefly state the reason or reasons for your answer to item 7 above.				
a. Increased danger	65	16	0	81
b. Jealousy of wife or sexual involvement	18	9	3	30
c. Inadequacy of policewomen	3	5	0	8
9. How would you classify the action of a police officer who accepts a free meal or a Christmas present from a businessman on his post?				
a. A serious violation of law	5	5	3	13
b. A minor violation of police regulations	46	22	15	83
c. No violation at all	74	27	11	112
10. How do you react to the fact that police duty often brings your husband into close contact with women?				
a. Deeply concerned about it	5	0	1	6
b. Somewhat concerned about it	26	14	1	41
c. Not at all concerned about it	74	41	27	142
11. How would you classify the promotion system in the police department?				
a. Fair	63	41	19	123
b. Unfair	58	12	9	79
12. How would you classify the disciplinary system in the police department?				
a. Fair	41	39	21	101
b. Unfair	76	13	4	93
13. How would you classify the system of selecting and appointing new police officers in the police department?				
a. Fair	62	40	22	124
b. Unfair	57	13	6	76
14. How would you classify the salary scale in the police department?				
a. High	5	4	1	10
b. Adequate	59	32	12	103
c. Low	61	18	15	94

	Wives of Patrolmen and Detectives	Wives of Superior Officers	Wives of English and Australian Policemen	Total
	(N = 127)	(N = 57)	(N = 29)	(N = 213)
15. In your opinion how does the general public rate the police occupation in prestige?				
a. High	10	2	6	18
b. Average	53	30	15	98
c. Low	62	25	8	95
16. How does your husband rate the police occupation in prestige?				
a. High	65	24	13	102
b. Average	42	27	13	82
c. Low	16	4	3	23
17. How do you personally rate the police occupation in prestige?				
a. High	62	20	12	94
b. Average	51	31	16	98
c. Low	9	4	1	14
18. In your opinion how does your husband feel about being a police officer?				
a. Happy	101	47	25	173
b. Resigned to it	20	8	4	32
c. Unhappy	3	0	0	3
19. In comparison with the average family, do you believe that a police family is forced to cope with				
a. More problems	78	38	20	136
b. The same problems	46	18	8	72
c. Fewer problems	0	0	1	1
20. Because your husband is a police officer, does your family behave				
a. More carefully than other types of families	34	17	13	64
b. About the same as other types of families	89	37	16	142
c. Less carefully than other types of families	0	0	0	0
21. If a police officer stopped you for a traffic violation while you were driving, would you expect him to				
a. Treat you like any other driver and give you a summons	65	32	24	121
b. Extend professional courtesy and let you go with a warning after you identified yourself as the wife of a police officer	58	23	4	85

Responses of Wives: Part 2 (cont.)

	Wives of Patrolmen and Detectives (N = 127)	Wives of Superior Officers (N = 57)	Wives of English and Australian Policemen (N = 29)	Total (N = 213)
22. How do members of your community react when they become aware that your husband is a police officer?				
a. In a friendly fashion	25	13	8	46
b. In a normal fashion	86	42	23	151
c. In a hostile fashion	13	2	1	16
23. Do you and your husband socialize with other police couples?				
a. Frequently	54	20	12	86
b. Seldom	60	31	15	106
c. Never	8	5	2	15
24. At social gatherings do you let people know that you are the wife of a police officer?				
a. Always	11	4	1	16
b. Frequently	31	14	7	52
c. Seldom	60	33	15	108
d. Never	22	5	7	34
25. What do you usually do when you and your husband go out for an evening?				
a. Go to a movie	57	28	5	90
b. Go to a play	5	8	3	16
c. Go to a concert	2	0	2	4
d. Go to visit friends	84	36	24	144
e. Go dancing	9	8	5	22
f. Watch a sports event	5	5	1	11
g. Go bowling, skating, etc.	6	3	0	9
26. When your husband becomes eligible for retirement, what would you like him to do?				
a. Remain in the police department	19	12	7	38
b. Retire completely and not work at all	26	6	9	41
c. Retire from the department and start work in a second field	76	35	13	124
27. Who makes most of the important decisions in your family?				
a. Your husband	26	13	7	46
b. You	0	2	1	3
c. You and your husband jointly	99	42	21	162
d. Your children	1	0	0	1

	Wives of Patrolmen and Detectives (N = 127)	Wives of Superior Officers (N = 57)	Wives of English and Australian Policemen (N = 29)	Total (N = 213)
28. How do you feel about the women's liberation movement?				
a. Very much in favor of it	5	5	1	11
b. Somewhat in favor of it	53	22	4	79
c. Indifferent to it	27	14	14	55
d. Somewhat opposed to it	27	12	5	44
e. Very opposed to it	13	4	6	23
29. How do you feel about your husband's occupation as a police officer?				
a. Happy	51	28	14	93
b. Resigned to it	69	28	13	110
c. Unhappy	5	0	2	7
30. How does your husband's police work schedule affect your family life?				
a. It strengthens it	25	9	4	38
b. It does not affect it much	66	36	19	121
c. It weakens it	33	9	7	49
31. How serious a problem is the necessity of safeguarding the police revolver at home?				
a. It is a serious problem	18	12	3	33
b. It is a minor problem	31	16	1	48
c. It is no problem at all	75	28	10	113

Responses of the Wives: Part 3

	Wives of Patrolmen and Detectives (N = 127)			Wives of Superior Officers (N = 57)			Wives of English and Australian Policemen (N = 29)			Total (N = 213)		
	W	H	W and H	W	H	W and H	W	H	W and H	W	H	W and H
1. In your family who takes primary responsibility for each of the following tasks?												
a. Disciplining the children	25	7	73	10	8	37	6	1	20	41	16	130
b. Important financial decisions	4	24	100	2	10	50	2	6	21	8	40	171
c. Household chores	104	1	29	47	1	9	24	0	5	175	2	43
d. Social life	43	8	79	9	4	43	2	5	22	54	17	144
e. Marketing	78	7	23	41	2	12	20	3	6	139	12	41
f. Gardening	48	45	30	15	18	18	7	11	11	70	74	59
g. Chauffeuring	48	33	36	18	13	25	3	14	10	69	60	71
h. Child care	72	1	35	34	0	16	15	2	12	121	3	63
i. Preparation of meals	114	3	12	49	0	6	27	1	1	190	4	19

Note:
W = Wife
H = Husband
W and H = Wife and husband jointly

	F	S	N	F	S	N	F	S	N	F	S	N
2. In your home how often do these common family problems arise?												
a. Lack of communication between parents and children	6	58	38	4	43	8	1	16	11	11	117	57
b. Lack of communication between husband and wife	21	84	24	9	38	11	0	17	12	30	139	47

	F	S	N	F	S	N	F	S	N	F	S	N
c. Financial difficulties	25	81	19	2	42	17	1	19	9	28	142	45
d. Children's misbehavior	6	86	9	3	44	6	0	20	7	9	150	22
e. Husband's school or promotion study takes too much time	15	41	66	5	28	25	2	13	13	22	82	104
f. Police job interferes with family life	27	64	30	5	32	21	10	14	5	42	110	56
g. Police schedule causes difficulties	27	72	28	5	29	19	10	12	7	42	113	54
h. Wife feels frustrated and tied down	20	65	36	6	34	14	2	14	13	28	113	63
i. Husband is unhappy with job	7	64	56	1	30	24	1	14	14	9	108	94
j. Sexual incompatibility	6	41	74	1	18	37	0	11	18	7	70	129

Note:
F = Frequently
S = Sometimes
N = Never

3. How do you cope with a bad day?

	F	S	N	F	S	N	F	S	N	F	S	N
a. Do household chores	42	68	17	16	24	13	15	11	2	73	103	32
b. Watch TV	28	80	19	12	24	15	2	21	6	42	125	40
c. Read a book	28	81	18	13	30	8	5	18	5	46	129	31
d. Go shopping	20	84	21	11	33	7	3	17	6	34	134	34
e. Eat	25	63	37	6	26	19	5	13	9	36	102	65
f. Drink	1	32	88	2	10	37	2	7	13	5	49	138
g. Go to bed	8	46	71	3	20	27	0	9	20	11	75	118

Responses of the Wives: Part 3 (cont.)

	Wives of Patrolmen and Detectives (N=127)			Wives of Superior Officers (N=57)			Wives of English and Australian Policemen (N=29)			Total (N=213)		
	F	S	N	F	S	N	F	S	N	F	S	N
h. Religious observance	11	53	60	4	22	27	3	4	22	18	79	109
i. See the doctor	3	27	96	2	9	40	0	4	23	5	40	159
j. Telephone friends	23	73	31	10	27	12	1	16	10	34	116	53
k. Visit friends	18	70	33	5	33	10	2	20	5	25	123	48
l. Take a pill	0	17	101	1	3	46	0	4	25	1	24	172
m. See a movie	2	36	87	1	14	37	0	4	24	3	54	148
n. Athletic activities	4	35	84	3	17	28	1	6	22	8	58	134

Note:
F = Frequently
S = Sometimes
N = Never

	Wives of Patrolmen and Detectives (N=127)			Wives of Superior Officers (N=57)			Wives of English and Australian Policemen (N=29)			Total (N=213)		
	F	O	U	F	O	U	F	O	U	F	O	U
4. How would you rate the mass media's portrayal of the police and police work?												
a. Television programs	50	34	37	18	21	12	8	14	7	76	69	56
b. Newspapers	4	39	75	1	22	26	0	16	13	5	77	114
c. Books	24	57	36	9	28	9	3	17	8	36	102	53
d. Movies	26	34	52	12	22	14	2	14	10	40	70	76
e. Magazines	11	61	42	4	31	11	1	16	10	16	108	63
f. Radio	9	67	37	5	37	10	10	14	1	24	118	48

Note:
F = Favorable to police
O = Objective about police
U = Unfavorable to police

5. How would it be for your children to possess the following qualities?

a. Obedience to	VI	MI	NI	VI	MI	NI	VI	MI	NI	VI	MI	NI
parents	98	23	0	44	9	0	26	3	0	168	36	0
b. Dependability	81	29	3	45	11	0	24	4	0	150	44	3
c. High achievement in school	47	65	8	16	39	0	10	19	0	73	123	8
d. Popularity	15	86	16	4	41	9	8	19	2	27	146	27
e. Perseverance	59	45	0	34	17	0	25	2	2	118	64	2
f. Independence	58	38	1	38	12	0	25	4	0	121	54	1
g. Respect for authority	82	13	0	48	4	1	26	3	0	156	20	1
h. Thrift	38	53	2	12	39	4	13	14	1	63	106	7
i. Honesty	69	13	2	54	1	0	29	0	0	152	14	2

Note:
VI = Very Important
MI = Moderately Important
NI = Not Important

6. How often do your children participate in the following after-school activities?

	R	S	N	R	S	N	R	S	N	R	S	N
a. Religious studies	34	16	17	14	6	12	7	7	7	55	29	36
b. Music lessons	10	12	44	7	8	23	5	5	11	22	25	78
c. Art lessons	2	15	46	2	5	33	4	3	12	8	23	91
d. Dancing lessons	12	13	42	3	5	29	1	4	15	16	22	86
e. Dramatics	2	11	52	0	4	34	1	4	13	3	19	99
f. Team sports	22	15	26	14	8	11	10	8	4	46	31	41
g. Skating, swimming, tennis lessons	15	29	24	6	12	15	11	8	0	32	49	39

Note:
R = Regularly
S = Sometimes
N = Never

210

Responses of the Wives: Part 4

	Wives of Patrolmen and Detectives (N = 127)	Wives of Superior Officers (N = 57)	Wives of English and Australian Policemen (N = 29)	Total (N = 213)
1. How would you classify your method of raising your children?				
a. Strict	29	11	7	47
b. Flexible	79	39	19	137
c. Permissive	2	3	0	5
2. What would your reaction be if your son wanted to become a police officer?				
a. Positive	57	22	12	91
b. Uncertain or no answer	31	19	10	60
c. Negative	39	16	7	62
3. What career would you prefer for your son?				
a. Lawyer	27	12	2	41
b. Doctor	28	7	0	35
c. Whatever he desired	39	21	10	70
d. A profession	5	4	6	15
e. Law enforcement	4	1	1	6
f. Business	7	4	1	12
4. What would your reaction be if your daughter wanted to become a police officer?				
a. Positive	29	16	10	55
b. Uncertain or no answer	21	16	11	48
c. Negative	77	25	8	110
5. What career would you prefer for your daughter?				
a. Lawyer	8	2	0	10
b. Doctor	8	3	0	11
c. Whatever she desired	30	15	9	54
d. A profession	1	6	0	7
e. Office work	8	4	3	15
f. Nurse	25	11	3	39
g. Housewife	10	5	0	15
h. Teacher	12	13	7	32
6. Which TV program about the police is your favorite?				
a. Police Story	32	11	0	43
b. Kojak	42	18	2	62
c. Adam 12	9	3	0	12
d. Streets of San Francisco	11	2	0	13
e. Columbo	6	7	3	16
f. Toma	8	0	0	8
g. Rookies	10	3	0	13
h. Policewoman	3	1	0	4

Responses of the Wives: Part 4 (cont.)

	Wives of Patrolmen and Detectives (N = 127)	Wives of Superior Officers (N = 57)	Wives of English and Australian Policemen (N = 29)	Total (N = 213)
7. Does the police department provide any orientation, counseling, or other type of service for families of police officers?				
a. Yes	22	12	4	38
b. Don't know	15	14	0	29
c. No	91	24	24	139

Responses of the Children

Children's Questionnaire

Question	Boys (N = 31)		Girls (N = 31)	
Religion	Catholic	25	Catholic	18
	Protestant	2	Protestant	9
	Jewish	1		
1. What would you like to be when you grow up?	Policeman	11	Teacher	9
	Architect	3	Secretary	5
	Baseball player	2	Veterinarian	3
	Doctor	2	Policewoman	2
2. Have you seen your father at work?	Often	1	Often	2
	Sometimes	18	Sometimes	14
	Never	7	Never	13
3. Does your father talk to you about his work?	A lot	8	A lot	3
	A little	17	A little	21
	Not at all	4	Not at all	2
5. Would you like to be a police officer when you grow up?	Yes	13	Yes	5
	No	18	No	26
8. Do you tell your friends that your father is a police officer?	Yes	27	Yes	25
	No	3	No	5

Children's Questionnaire (cont.)

Question	Boys (N=31)		Girls (N=31)	
10. If you had your choice, what kind of work would you want your father to do?	Policeman	6	Policeman	9
	Whatever he wants	5	Whatever he wants	5
	Doctor	4	Doctor	4
	Fireman	3	Fireman	3
11. Would you like your mother to be a policewoman?	Yes	8	Yes	6
	No	22	No	23
13. Does your father have to work on holidays or your birthdays?	Often	1	Often	2
	Sometimes	23	Sometimes	21
	Never	2	Never	2
14. Has the fact that your father is a policeman ever helped you?	Yes	9	Yes	13
	No	17	No	17
15. Has the fact that your father is a policeman ever hurt you?	Yes	4	Yes	2
	No	24	No	23
16. Would you say that your father is strict or easygoing with you?	Strict	3	Strict	6
	Easygoing	18	Easygoing	18
17. What is your favorite TV program about policemen?	Adam 12	9	Adam 12	6
	Rookies	9	Swat	6
	Swat	9	Policewoman	5
			Starsky and Hutch	4
18. Because your father is a police officer, do you behave	More carefully	8	More carefully	7
	Less carefully	0	Less carefully	0
	About the same as other children	18	About the same as other children	18
19. Do you worry about your father's safety when he is at work?	A lot	10	A lot	8
	A little	12	A little	13
	Not at all	4	Not at all	3

Responses of the Police Chaplains

(N = 33)

Question	Response	
1. In comparison to other families you have known, would you rate the average police family as A. Happier; B. About as happy; C. Less happy?	A. Happier	0
	B. About as happy	28
	C. Less happy	5
2. In comparison to other families you have known, would you rate the average police marriage as A. More stable; B. About as stable; C. Less stable?	A. More stable	0
	B. About as stable	16
	C. Less stable	17
3. In comparison with other children you have known, would you rate the average child of a police officer as A. Better adjusted; B. About the same as other children in adjustment; C. Less well adjusted?	A. Better adjusted	1
	B. The same in adjustment	31
	C. Less well adjusted	1
4. In comparison with other wives you have known, would you rate the average wife of a police officer as A. More content; B. About as content; C. Less content?	A. More content	1
	B. About as content	16
	C. Less content	16

Question	Rank	Frequent Problems	Number of Choices
5. In your experience what are the three problems that police families encounter most frequently?	1.	Work schedule and time	25
	2.	Money-finances	16
	3.	Lack of communication	8
	4.	Alcohol	7
	5.	Infidelity	5
	6.	Children	4

Question	Rank	Most Serious Problems	Number of Choices
6. In your experience what are the three most serious problems occurring in police marriages?	1.	Lack of communication	12
		Infidelity	12
	2.	Work schedule and time	10
	3.	Money-finances	8
	4.	Alcohol	7
	5.	Lack of understanding of the police job by the wife	5
	6.	Job stress	4

Index

Index

Adams, Thomas F., 112
Affair Next Door (Green), 19
Anna Karenina (Tolstoy), 1
Arts, appreciation of the, 81
Australia, 45, 62, 64, 84, 112, 116
Authoritarian role, 42, 48, 102-103, 149
Autobiography of a London Detective (Russell), 14-15

Baltimore, Md., 159
Balzac, Honoré de, 10-11
Battered wives, 66
Bayley, David H., and Harold Mendelsohn, 161
Benchley, Peter, 35
Bennett-Sandler, Georgette, and Earl Ubell, 60
Big Bow Mystery (Zangwill), 21
Biological rhythms, 72, 88, 155-156
Bleak House (Dickens), 12-13
Blue Knight (Wambaugh), 35, 38-39
Bodkin, M. McDonnel, 22-23

Cain, Maureen E., 128
Carter, Jimmy, 84
Carter, John, 13-14, 22
Charteris, Leslie, 25
Chesterton, G.K., 25
Chicago, 159
Child-rearing practices, 80-83, 145-153
Children, 45, 80, 81, 139-153; career choice, 81-82, 104-105, 148, 149; father image, 82, 139-142; lawbreakers, 151-152; teenage, 82-83, 142-145, 153
Christie, Agatha, 25, 36
Civil Rights Act of 1964, 117
Clarice Dyke, the Female Detective (Rockwood), 22, 23n
Clurman, Richard, 19
College education, 81, 84
Collins, Wilkie, 15
Commissioner (Dougherty), 34

Complementary needs, theory of, 102-103
Confessions, criminal, 43
Congdon, Tom, 35
Conrad, Joseph, 24
COP (Cops' Other Partners), 119
Cop! (Whittemore), 50n
Cops and Robbers (Westlake), 34
Corruption, 73-75
Coryell, John, 19
Courts, leniency of, 69
Crime and Punishment (Dostoevsky), 17
Cynicism, 41, 71, 113

Daley, Robert, 38, 108-109
Danger factor, 75-76, 79, 90-95
Danto, Bruce, 94-95
Dead Letter: An American Romance (Regester), 18
Denver, Colo., 161
Dey, Frederick, 19
Dickens, Charles, 12-13
Dictionary of Occupational Titles, 68-69
Divorce, 49-51, 155-170
Doll's House (Ibsen), 164
Dominant-submissive personalities, 102-103
Dostoevsky, Fëodor, 17
Dougherty, Richard, 34-35
Doyle, A. Conan, 19
Droge, Edward, 74, 75, 80
Dunne, Joseph A., 168
Durner, James A., 159

Economic factors, 126-127, 168
Eisdorfer, Simon, 105-106
Eliot, T.S., 15
Equal opportunity employers, 117-118, 127
Ethnic background, 5-6, 101-102
Experiences of a Lady Detective (Anonyma), 21-22

About the Authors

Arthur Niederhoffer joined the New York City Police Department in June of 1940. He was a policeman for twenty-one years until his retirement as a lieutenant. He earned the Ph.D. in sociology from New York University and the J.D. from Brooklyn Law School. In his second career as a professor of sociology at John Jay College of Criminal Justice, Niederhoffer has broadened his experience in police work through his contact with the thousands of police officers he has taught and advised. He is the author of four books on law enforcement.

Elaine Niederhoffer became a police wife in 1943. While raising the family she earned the M.A. in education and English from Brooklyn College. She has taught in the New York City public schools and has been editor-in-residence for Arthur's numerous publications.